N. C. S. D.

D1474237

Acquiring
conversational
competence

Language, Education and Society

General Editor
Michael Stubbs
Department of Linguistics
University of Nottingham

Acquiring conversational competence

Elinor Ochs and *Bambi B. Schieffelin*

Routledge & Kegan Paul
London, Boston, Melbourne and Henley

First published in 1983
by Routledge & Kegan Paul plc
39 Store Street, London WC1E 7DD,
9 Park Street, Boston, Mass. 02108, USA,
296 Beaconsfield Parade, Middle Park,
Melbourne, 3206, Australia, and
Broadway House, Newtown Road,
Henley-on-Thames, Oxon RG9 1EN
Typeset by Hope Services, Abingdon, Oxon
and printed in Great Britain by
T. J. Press, Padstow

Library of Congress Cataloging in Publication Data

Ochs, Elinor.

Acquiring conversational competence.
(Language, education, and society)
Bibliography: p.
Includes index.
1. Conversation – Addresses, essays, lectures.
2. Language acquisition – Addresses, essays, lectures.
3. Communicative competence – Addresses, essays,
lectures.   4. Discourse analysis – Addresses, essays,
lectures.   I. Schieffelin, Bambi B.   II. Title.
III. Series.
P95.45.03 1983   401'.9   83-3344

ISBN 0-7100-9459-0

Contents

General Editor's preface

Simply a list of some of the questions implied by the series title 'Language, Education and Society' gives an immediate idea of the complexity, and also the fascination, of the area.

How is language related to learning? Or to intelligence? How should a teacher react to non-standard dialect in the classroom? Do regional and social accents and dialects matter? What is meant by standard English? Does it make sense to talk of 'declining standards' in language or in education? Or to talk of some children's language as 'restricted'? Do immigrant children require special language provision? How can their native languages be used as a valuable resource in schools? Can 'literacy' be equated with 'education'? Why are there so many adult illiterates in Britain and the USA? What effect has growing up with no easy access to language: for example, because a child is profoundly deaf? Why is there so much prejudice against people whose language background is odd in some way: because they are handicapped, or speak a non-standard dialect or foreign language? Why do linguistic differences lead to political violence, in Belgium, India, Wales and other parts of the world?

These are all real questions, of the kind which worry parents, teachers and policy makers, and the answer to them is complex and not at all obvious. It is such questions that authors in this series will discuss.

Language plays a central part in education. This is probably generally agreed, but there is considerable debate and confusion about the exact relationship between language and learning. Even though the importance of language is generally recognized, we still have a lot to learn about how language is related to either educational success or to intelligence and thinking. Language is also a central fact in everyone's social life. People's attitudes and most deeply held beliefs are at stake, for it is through language that personal and social identities are maintained and recognized. People are judged, whether justly or not, by the language they speak.

'Language, education and society' is therefore an area where scholars have a responsibility to write clearly and persuasively, in order to communicate the best in recent research to as wide an audience as possible. This means not only other researchers, but also all those who are involved in educational, social and political policy-making, from individual teachers to government. It is an area where value judgments cannot be avoided. Any action that we take — or, of course, avoidance of action — has moral, social and political consequences. It is vital, therefore, that practice is informed by the best knowledge available, and that decisions affecting the futures of individual children or whole social groups are not taken merely on the basis of the all too widespread folk myths about language in society.

Linguistics, psychology and sociology are often rejected by non-specialists as jargon-ridden; or regarded as fascinating, but of no relevance to educational or social practice. But this is superficial and short-sighted: we are dealing with complex issues, which require an understanding of the general principles involved. It is bad theory to make statements about language in use which cannot be related to educational and social reality. But it is equally unsound to base beliefs and action on anecdote, received myths and unsystematic or idiosyncratic observations.

All knowledge is value-laden: it suggests action and changes our beliefs. Change is difficult and slow, but possible nevertheless. When language in education and society is seriously and systematically studied, it becomes clear how awesomely complex is the linguistic and social knowledge of all children and adults. And with such an understanding, it becomes impossible to maintain a position of linguistic prejudice and intolerance. This may be the most important implication of a serious study of language, in our linguistically diverse modern world.

This collection of papers is by two American researchers of international renown: Elinor Ochs and Bambi Schieffelin. Some of the articles are well-known, others originally appeared in relatively obscure places and deserve a wider audience. Together they present a substantial body of detailed research on children's language and communication, and more generally on the nature of interactive spoken discourse. As research work, the papers stand on their own and their implications for methodology, description and theory, especially in linguistics and psychology, are spelled out clearly in several places in the book. I will simply point out here that they show with great clarity what is to be gained from the meticulous study of naturally occurring language recorded in real social contexts — as opposed to the invented, introspective data or experimental studies which have characterized much recent linguistics and psychology.

However, what is only mentioned in a couple of papers, and not spelled out in any detail, is the interest of this work for educationalists, and I will make a few comments on this. The papers are clear and readable. Nevertheless, some are on fairly technical linguistic topics, and others present data from what readers may regard as 'exotic' cultures. Should educationalists be required to struggle with such material?

The short answer is that language is complex, and any satisfactory analysis is a complex and technical matter. We have seen all too often, in the educational literature, the dangers of superficial, facile and misinformed commentary on children's language. Educationalists deserve access to the best descriptions available, such as those presented here. They have also the responsibility to make an effort to come to grips with detailed and accurate analysis of language, just as linguists have the responsibility to present their analyses as clearly as possible to different audiences, including those who need their findings for practical purposes.

Beyond this general point, there are several themes in the book which are of direct interest to educationalists.

A first theme is the impressive and often underestimated complexity of very young children's communicative competence. It is obvious that infants communicate before they can produce comprehensible words. Any parent knows this and can often infer an infant's needs and wants before there is language. (Although, as the authors also show, such beliefs about children's communicative abilities differ in different cultures.) It has also been shown more precisely that infants learn, as it were, to engage in conversation before they learn language. That is, they engage in interactive, dialogue-like routines with mothers and other caretakers, from a very early age. Ochs and Schieffelin provide some of the most detailed analyses available on children's early inter-active discourse. Such analyses are of immediate interest to teachers of young children, and others such as speech therapists, who need as much information as possible on the language and communication of young children. In addition, such analyses must be taken into account in any debate on the concepts of language 'deficit' or 'deprivation'. In fact, they throw immediate doubt on any superficial use of such concepts. Ochs and Schieffelin show the impressive social and communi-cative skills of very young children, who are able to sustain coherent discourse by the age of 3 years. If children do not display such behaviour in schools, it may be the fault of the schools and not of the children.

A second theme is the nature of spoken language. Education used to be (and sometimes still is) equated with literacy. And highly standarized written English clearly has a special place in the education systems in Britain, America and other countries. More recently, however, the importance of oral skills has been increasingly emphasized. An understanding of the relationships between spoken and written language is therefore crucial for teachers. The authors provide substantial new insights into the differences between spontaneous, casual, spoken language on the one hand, and planned, formal, written language on the other.

A third theme is that the authors discuss not only the acquisition of language in a decontextualized way (as has been the case in many studies, especially from the early 1960s). They show how children acquire the communicative competence which makes them members of a culture: how children become adults (and also how adults' language remains child-like in some contexts and for some purposes). This is a central, general topic for any work on language in society. But the same theme can be reformulated with specific reference to schools. Schools reflect the values of the wider society, and generate their own cultures. Children become members of the school culture, by learning particular patterns of teacher–pupil discourse, by learning the appropriate use of particular styles of planned, formal, standard English, and so on. As another book in this series (by Mary Willes) expresses it, children are turned into pupils.

Fourth, the value of the cross-cultural data which the authors present is to show that what is often taken for granted by us as somehow 'normal' or 'natural' is relative, cultural knowledge. 'Us' may be White versus Black, middle class versus working class, British versus American, Western/Anglo-American versus 'other', and so on. Work on language in education has long been dogged by superficial assumptions and folk myths about what is 'normal', and scant attention and respect have often been paid to the linguistic and cultural values of minority ethnic and social groups. This is the value of the perspectives which Ochs and Schieffelin present from other cultures.

The book is of obvious interest to researchers in linguistics, psychology, sociology and anthropology. It deserves also to be more widely read by educationalists and others who are professionally concerned with children's language.

Michael Stubbs

Acknowledgements

The authors and publishers would like to thank the following for permission to reprint material: Academic Press, New York, for Chapter 2, 'Making it last: repetition in children's discourse', which first appeared in S. Ervin-Tripp and C. Mitchell-Kernan (eds), *Child discourse* (1977); for Chapter 5, 'Topic as a discourse notion; a study of topic in the conversations of children and adults', which first appeared in C. Li (ed.), *Subject and topic* (1976); for Chapter 7, 'Planned and unplanned discourse', which first appeared in T. Givon (ed.), *Discourse and syntax* (1979); Berkeley Linguistics Society for Chapter 8, 'Foregrounding referents: a reconsideration of left dislocation in discourse', which first appeared in the *Proceedings of the Berkeley Linguistics Society* (1976), pp. 240-57; Cambridge University Press for Chapter 1, 'Conversational competence in children', which first appeared in the *Journal of child language* (1974), 1 (2), pp. 163-83; for Chapter 6, 'Questions of immediate concern', which first appeared in E. Goody (ed.), *Questions and politeness: strategies in social interaction* (1978); Leisure Press, New York, for Chapter 9, 'Talking like birds: sound play in a cultural perspective', which first appeared in J. Loy (ed.), *The paradoxes of play* (1982); the Editor of *Papers and Reports in Child Language Development* for Chapter 3, 'Evolving discourse — the next step', which appeared in *PRCLD* (1975), 10, pp. 80-8.

Foreword

Talk comprises more than conversation, but it is conversation that seems to concern us most these days; to quote Kenneth Burke, 'we huddle, nervously loquacious, on the edge of an abyss.'

Old-fashioned school text-books still betray the belief of educators from a few generations ago, that the important kind of talk was rhetoric or elocution: which often meant the effective public recitation of a poem. This is what *public speaking* meant then, and no town was without someone to call on for important public occasions. Today, *public speaking* has different connotations. It might be thought of as what the sociologist Erving Goffman has called *relations in public*: sustaining a state of talk in a personal, everyday, social encounter. So, although the concept of *public* may have lost dignity, it has gained scientific relevance.

Within the study of language, scholars have become convinced that the locus of study is not one person, but two. Linguistics has been extended beyond the sentence into discourse – but it need not leave the individual speaker behind. Discourse studies can still focus on aspects of a single person's verbal production: memory, for example. Those academics who have done most to focus attention on discourse between persons are sociologists – and pioneering anthropologists, such as the authors of this book.

Anthropologists are accustomed to seeing durable patterns and norms. It is tempting, thereby, simply to record lovingly and faithfully the discourses of a community, its ritual narratives and the like. On the one hand, such a perspective is inadequate if it ignores the fact that social order is achieved as a contingent accomplishment: constructed anew on every individual social occasion. On the other hand, such a perspective is necessary, for if durable norms are ignored, they remain invisible and therefore closed to change.

We greatly need systematic studies of the ways in which different societies use and elaborate talk, for it is still an amazing fact that social science has developed cross-cultural typologies for almost everything in life except speech. Kinship, kingdoms, technologies, child rearing and dietary practices, or whatever: they are all described and analysed. But it is still not so with speech. Ethnographers in different communities have presumably heard much more talk than they have seen sex, but it is sex that is more adequately classified and theorized about.

At the root is the process analysed by the authors of this book: how children come to use certain kinds of language and not others. This is the heart of cultural reproduction through speech: the process by which children find order in the speech around them, and the process by which a social order is renewed.

In articles published in the late 1950s and early 1960s, I attempted to show the importance of language acquisition studies for an understanding of social life. Since that time, studies of language acquisition have grown dramatically, but the main growth up until now has not been concerned with social order and cultural values. This book by Elinor Ochs and Bambi Schieffelin encourages one to think, however, that the root dynamic may at last be given the attention that it merits. The authors clearly grasp the dialectic involved: on the one hand, children become a part of the whole culture; on the other, talk projects the culture, and through talk the roles and capacities of children are perceived.

The term *ethnography of speaking*, which I first used twenty years ago, has become a familiar expression, but not a familiar practice in the sense in which it was intended. It has too easily become a label for any study of language use which has an anthropological tinge. This book encourages the belief that the original intention may yet result in cumulative scholarship, which is flexible and responsive to different cultures, yet which also tries to discover what different peoples make of the universal resource of speech.

Dell Hymes
University of Pennsylvania

Preface

To establish and maintain a conversation demands a variety of skills and areas of knowledge. Minimally, a speaker must know how to secure the listener's attention, introduce novel topics, make topically relevant propositions, assume and relinquish the floor at socially appropriate times. These dimensions of conversational competence are fundamental to making sense. Along with knowledge of grammatical structure, knowledge of conversational norms is necessary for successful communication to take place. A speaker who cannot capture an intended listener's attention, for example, nor signal that his remarks are on or off the topic, cannot function in most verbal interactions.

The knowledge and skills we are considering here are part of a broader range of competence that has been referred to as 'communicative competence' (Hymes, 1967). Communicative competence covers all areas of competence in language use expected within a speech community, including both formal and informal speech situations and single-party as well as multi-party discourse. The chapters in this volume focus primarily on norms underlying relatively informal verbal interaction, hence the use of the term 'conversational competence' in the volume title. Two exceptions to this orientation are the comparison of planned and unplanned discourse in Chapter 7 and the discussions of sound play in Chapters 1 and 9. Sound play is in many ways a special way of speaking, with distinct norms and cultural interpretations. The conditions under which it is used (who, where, to whom, how, etc.) are considered for two very different sets of children — American white middle class and Kaluli (Papua New Guinea).

As the reader skims through the chapters in this volume it will quickly be apparent that the authors are examining both adult and child speech behaviour. Further, the reader will see that our consideration of adult speech goes beyond adult-child conversation to a range of adult-adult communicative contexts. This book is about adult conversational competence as much as it is about children's conversational competence. Our modus operandi in carrying out research has been to document adult speech patterns through recording and transcription so that they may be compared with children's speech that has been similarly documented. As has been the case with other researchers, the areas of competence examined in young children's speech have very often not been described for adults, making a concurrent adult study necessary. The employment of such a methodology has led to exciting insights concerning not only the character of adult conversational competence but the process of acquiring such competence as well. In this volume we set forth strategies for conversing at different stages of life, but we also relate these strategies and formulate hypotheses concerning the dynamics of language variation and change.

The chapters in this volume have been organized into three major sections. In Part I, 'Constructing conversation', the basic structures and strategies for opening and maintaining a verbal interaction are presented. The focus of this section is on differences between children's and adults' conversational strategies. Chapter 1 ('Conversational competence in children') establishes that young children do indeed carry out conversations with one another and have conventions for carrying out this type of discourse. Along with Chapters 2 ('Making it last: repetition in children's discourse') and 3 ('Evolving discourse – the next step'), Chapter 1 explores ways in which coherent and sustained discourse is produced by twin boys around the age of 3 years. The use of repetition is a predominant strategy in these early conversations. Chapter 2 shows how young children use repetition to carry out a variety of speech acts, including agreement, disagreement, querying, greeting, imitation and insulting/accusing. This chapter suggests that a distinction should be made between repetition and the speech act it performs, a distinction not captured in previous literature, where imitation and repetition are coterminous.

Chapter 4 ('Looking and talking: the functions of gaze direction in the conversations of a young child and her mother') reviews adult studies of the function of eye contact in conversational turn-taking and documents the developmental changes in gazing patterns as language is acquired. In particular, gazing patterns are examined with regard to both the type of speech act performed in an utterance and the type of speech event (chained or holistic, cf Bloom, 1973) of which an utterance is a part.

In Chapter 5 ('Topic as a discourse notion: a study of topic in the conversations of children and adults') and 6 ('Questions of immediate concern'), we lay out the steps necessary to communicate a proposition. We show that, in contrast to adult–adult conversation where a proposition is usually conveyed in the course of a single utterance, in adult–child and child–child conversation a proposition is often conveyed over a sequence of utterances. As such, there is a functional relation between discourse structure (in particular, conversational discourse structure) and sentence structure, i.e. syntax. These chapters spell out the work involved in getting a proposition attended to and understood by a very small child. Of particular interest is the work of getting a young child to attend to the topic of some utterance. It is quite common for white middle-class English-speaking caregivers to introduce the topic in one (or more) utterance(s) and only when the topic is recognized by the child for the predication or point to be made in subsequent utterances. In these interactions, the interrogative is a common modality for introducing topics. Indeed we feel that the notion of topic is best expressed by the phrase 'question of immediate concern'.

Part II, 'Using discourse and syntax to express propositions', examines adult speech behaviour from the point of view of children's communicative strategies. Chapter 7 ('Planned and unplanned discourse') suggests that various verbal strategies of children are also employed by adults under certain conditions. When talk is relatively unplanned (spontaneous and casual), adults will express propositions through discourse just as children do, rather than exclusively through syntactic means, for example. In relatively planned talk (or relatively planned writing), syntactic strategies appear more frequently. The major point here is that the relation between discourse and syntactic structure is not simply an ontogenetic one but a sociolinguistic or pragmatic one as well, the two strategies varying according to social context. Chapter 8 ('Foregrounding referents: a reconsideration of left dislocation in discourse') discusses in depth one particular construction that seems a blend of syntax and discourse, a construction referred to as left dislocation (Ross, 1967). This construction is found frequently in relatively casual (or relatively unplanned) adult discourse in English.

The final section of this volume ('Cross-cultural perspectives on caregiver–child communication') represents the emerging research of the authors in acquiring language in non-Western societies. The two chapters in this section emphasize that as young children are acquiring their language, they are acquiring their culture as well. This very important point has been missed by most in the field of child language. Partly because the researchers, the readers and the subjects of study typically participate in the same culture, the cultural values and beliefs underlying caregiver–child communication have not been noticed. Our experiences in a Papua New Guinea (Kaluli) and Samoan society have led us to see that there are different communicative patterns and different interpretations of what caregivers and children are doing with words from one society to another. Chapter 9 ('Talking like birds: sound play in a cultural perspective') shows us the interface of language acquisition and culture in Kaluli society.

Chapter 9 focuses on Kaluli children's sound play. The cultural beliefs that underlie this prohibited verbal interaction are presented as part of a larger Kaluli theory of language acquisition and language use. The turn-taking structure, formal features and content of sound play are analysed and suggest that children as young as 30 months are capable of complex verbal and social interactions.

Chapter 10 ('Cultural dimensions of language acquisition') introduces the reader briefly to the social and cultural environment of a child growing up and acquiring language in a traditional Samoan community. One outstanding difference from white middle-class society is the fact that most social interactions involve more than two persons. Young children must learn appropriate norms for participating in multi-party conversations at a very early age. A second important difference concerns beliefs and expectations about what children can say and do at different stages of life. For a number of reasons, explained in this chapter, Samoan caregivers place greater responsibility on the child for making intentions clear. The type of clarification procedures and proposition-building across discourse discussed in Chapters 5 and 6 of this volume do not characterize caregiver–child communication in Samoan society. Indeed, it appears to us at this point that the discourse patterns we have so carefully documented for English-speaking children are linked in complex and profound ways to our own cultural preferences and practices (Ochs and Schieffelin, in press).

Note from the authors: the following convention has been adopted to represent ages – (a) 2;9 means 2 years, 9 months; (b) 16,3 means 16 months, 3 weeks.

Part I
Constructing conversation

1

Conversational competence in children[1]

E. Ochs Keenan

1.1 Introduction

This paper examines the development of communication skills in young
children. It focuses, in particular, on the emergence of skills that underlie the exchange of talk. Any child who learns to speak has interacted
with other members of the society. Before he utters a single word of
the adult language, he is able to respond to the social overtures of others
(Bruner, 1975; Escalona, 1973; Richards, 1971). Escalona finds that
even in the first month of life, a child responds to the presence of
another by gazing, smiling and/or vocalizing. As a child matures, he is
able to engage in reciprocal games, such as peek-boo (after five months),
to comply with requests and/or answer questions (eleventh month)
and independently initiate interactions by expressing a wish or demand,
by showing or giving things to people. The emergence of speech in a
child must be seen in the context of these social skills.

How, then, do children use language in interacting with others?
In what sense are they able to produce and respond appropriately to
requests, invitations, greetings, summons, insults, narratives, comments?
In what sense are they able to maintain a sustained and coherent
dialogue? Questions such as these have been posed by Bloom (1970),
Ervin-Tripp (1973), Halliday (1973), Hymes (1972b) and Ryan (1972,
1974) among others. Discussion of these questions draws primarily
from observations of adult (usually the mother)–child interactions.
This paper hopes to broaden the scope of these observations to include
child–child interaction.

1.2 Method

Since September 1973, observations of the speech of two children have been made. The children are my own twin boys, Toby and David, age 2; 9 at onset of research. Initially, the conversations of the children were recorded on an audio recorder. From 22 October, a video recorder was used. This equipment was then used once a month over a period of a year.

The bulk of our observations of the children's conversations take place in the children's bedroom in the early morning hours. This setting was selected as it provided a locus where the children speak to one another outside the presence of any adult. One of the focal interests of this research is to examine how children maintain a dialogue on their own. Twins, in general, are particularly interesting in this respect as neither is linguistically more sophisticated than the other. In terms of their communicative competence, both share roughly the same level of development. The children have also been recorded interacting with adults (nanny, parent) and with another child approximately the same age (2;10).

1.3 The problem defined

We now turn to the conversations held by Toby and David when on their own. Our primary interest is in investigating the ways in which these children co-operate in talk. This focus presupposes that young children do engage in meaningful, sustained talk-exchanges. It opposes the Piagetian view (1926) that children tend not to address or adapt their speech to a co-present listener. The high percentage of egocentric language (47 per cent for one child, 43 per cent for a second child) observed by Piaget is not characteristic of early morning dialogue between Toby and David. For example, in the conversation of 15 September 1973, of 257 conversational turns (one or more utterances bounded by long pauses or by the utterances of another speaker), only 17 or 6.6 per cent appear to be unequivocally not addressed or adapted particularly to the co-present interlocutor. Of these turns, seven involve the construction of a narrative, three involve speech addressed to a toy animal, and seven involve songs and sound play. The narratives appear to be addressed to some imaginary interlocutor or to some audience, which may include the co-present child but not him exclusively. This shift in audience is signalled by a shift in voice quality by the speaker. Generally, narratives are marked by greater loudness in contrast to the immediately preceding utterances. The speaker appears to be talking to an interlocutor who stands some distance away.

The division of speech into egocentric and social, private and public, and the like, is riddled with difficulties. What one investigator may call egocentric or private another may call social or public. For example, Piaget considers utterances which repeat an immediately previous utterance as non-adaptive and egocentric, whereas I consider repetitions as highly social in intent! (The argument for this classification is to be discussed below.) I would like to discard this dichotomy in favour of an approach that considers talk-exchanges in terms of a speaker's expectations and a hearer's obligations (Schegloff, 1968; Goffman, 1971).

Two interlocutors who wish to communicate with one another are faced with what Lewis (1969) calls a co-ordination problem. To interact effectively, they need to share not only a linguistic code, but also a code of conduct. That is to say, interlocutors need to establish a loose set of conversational conventions. These conventions establish certain expectations on the part of speaker and hearer. For example, speaker-hearers may establish speech conventions concerning turn-taking, points of interruption, audibility. These expectations cut across all types of dialogue. Other expectations may be tied to particular utterance types. A speaker producing utterance X may expect a particular sort of verbal/non-verbal response from a hearer. That is, the speaker expects the hearer to recognize the speaker's utterance as a certain kind of talk and expects the hearer to respond in a manner appropriate to that talk. Generally, if the hearer recognizes the category of talk offered by the speaker and if he responds in the manner appropriate to that talk, then we can say that the hearer has satisfied the speaker and that the talk-exchange is a 'happy' one.

Let us illustrate this principle of the happy exchange. One category of utterance which occurs frequently in the dialogues between Toby and David is the comment. Comment is a term used by Bloom (1970) to refer to utterances that describe some ongoing activity or some activity about to be performed in the immediate future. Comments also name or point out co-present objects. Applied to the dialogue at hand, comments also include descriptions of the state or condition of objects and persons.

1.3.1 *Examples of comments*[2]

1. Descriptions of on-going activity:	*I got feathers/* *I got/ I got big one/* *I rip it now/*

2. Descriptions of immediately subsequent activity:	*goin'* [æ] *scratch/* (= 'Going to scratch') [gʌ] *go scratch it/* (= 'Gonna go scratch it')
3. Descriptions of state/condition of objects/persons:	*oh/ house broken/ oh dear/* *very quiet/* *all very quiet/*
4. Naming, pointing out of objects: (looking at letters in book)	*ABC in 'er/* = 'ABC in there') *that ₍A/ ₍B/ that ₍A/* [i:]³ *moth/* (3 times) (= 'There's a moth') *some over in 'er/ David/ some over in 'er/* (= 'Some in there David; some in there') *some in there/ lots in 'er/* (= Some in there. Lots in there')

Bloom states as well that comments contrast with directions in that the former 'do not attempt to influence the behaviour of the receiver' (1970, p. 22). One interpretation of this generalization is that, in uttering a comment, a speaker has the primary intention of expressing a certain belief about the world to a hearer; the primary intention of the speaker is not that the hearer should carry out some course of action. Grice (1975) discusses the distinction between these two types of utterances. For him, the distinction is not between comments and directions, but between indicatives and imperatives. In Grice's analysis, indicatives and imperatives can be distinguished in terms of their 'meaning-intended effect'. The meaning-intended effect of an indicative utterance is that the hearer should think that the utterer believes something. The meaning-intended effect of imperative-type utterances is that the hearer should intend to do something.

Clearly we want to distinguish between the conventionalized use of these two types of utterances — comments and directions. It could be a mistake to infer, however, that the uttering of a comment incurred no behavioural obligations on the part of a co-present hearer. In the dialogues between Toby and David, for example, a speaker uttering a comment expects the hearer to *acknowledge* that comment. That is, once a comment has been produced by a speaker, the co-present interlocutor is normally obligated to respond verbally to that comment. If the hearer recognizes the utterance as a comment, and if he responds appropriately with some form of acknowledgement, we can say that the talk-exchange is a happy one.

Let us look at the data that support this generalization. How can we justify the assertion that the speaker expects some form of acknowledgement from the co-present hearer? One basis for this assertion is simply the observation that comments are almost always followed by some utterance that addresses itself to that comment. For example, out of the first 76 conversational turns containing comments three received no verbal acknowledgement. This absence of response cannot always be explained, but often it may be due to its place in a topic-related conversational episode. If the comment has occurred after a number of exchanges it may not receive a response. That is, the topic has been exhausted, and a new topic is taken up.

(1) (Toby and David are looking through an alphabet book).
   – ﹨*ABC in 'er* (= 'ABC in there').
   – *that* ﹨*A*/ ﹨*B*/ *that* ﹨*A*/
   – ﹨*A*/
   – *that* ﹨*A*/ ﹨*C*/
   – ﹨*X*/
   – ﹨*tickles*/

(2) – *you*/ *pillow*/ *you rip it*/ *ee*/ *I find feather*/ *I find feather*/
   – *yes*/ *I find* (?)/ *I get one*/ *now I get good one*/ *I get good one*/ *a big one*/
   – *oh yes*/ *got one*/
   – *I got big one*/ *I got big one*/ *I got big one*/ *I got big one*/
   – *oh dear*/ *oh dear dear dear*/ *piggy fall down*/

Generally, comments do receive acknowledgements. Acknowledgement is expressed by any one or a combination of the following forms:

I. Positive particle: *yes, yeah*, etc.
   (3) – *got feathers*/ *got feathers*/ *baby one one*/ *feathers one*/ *big one*/ *big one*/
      – *oh yes*/
      – *big one*/
      – *yes*/

II. Negative particle: *no, not*, etc.
   (4) – ﹨*Sockerbopper*/ (Sockerbopper is the name of a toy)
      – ﹨*No*/ *Sockerbopper*/

III. Expletive: *oh, oh dear, oopsee*, etc.
   (5) – *My lost it*/ (= 'I lost it')
      – *Oopsee*/

IV. Indicatives

(*a*) Indicatives that carry no new information: exact repetitions of comment, partial repetitions of comment (deletions).

(6) – *big one/ no/ big one/*
   – *big one/*
(7) – *Mommy's silly/*
   – *Mommy's silly/*

(*b*) Indicatives that carry new information:

(i) Extended repetitions

(8) – *big one/ yes/ big one/*
   – *I got/ I got big one/*
(9) – *flower broken/ flower/ its flower broken/* [ɛ]/ *oh/ end/*
   – *many flowers broken/*

(ii) Negative repetitions:

(10)– *you silly/*
   – *no you silly/*
(11)– *cradle will rock/ cradle fall/ cradle will rock/*
   – *no cradle will rock/*

(iii) Other extensions (predicates that do not repeat comment):

(12)– *many moths/*
   – [i: gɔ:d]/ *on the ceiling/* (= 'He go-ed on the ceiling')
(13)– *fall down now* (2)/
   – *no/ I not fall down/ I* ALRIGHT[4]/ *I not fall down/*

A second body of evidence in support of the assertion that one who comments expects a response comes from exchanges in which acknowledgement is not immediately provided. In many such cases, the comment is repeated until it is acknowledged.

(14)– [i:] *moth* (2)/
   – *goosey goosey gander/ where shall I wander/*
   – [i:] *moth* (4)/
   – *up downstairs lady's chamber/*
   – [i:] *moth* (3)/
   – [i:] [le:] *moth/*

In this example, the speaker solicits the attention of the hearer by uttering the comment over and over (a total of nine occurrences). In other cases, the speaker may accompany the comment with an explicit directive (request, command) to acknowledge the comment:

(15) – `see it/ ´ABC/ `see it/ ˏsee/ ´ABC/ `look/
     – `oh yes/
(16) – `tree (2)/ see got `grass/
     – yes I `see it/ I `see it/

These examples show that most comments are directed to the co-present hearer. Acknowledgement by the hearer is expected by the speaker, and when no such acknowledgement is forthcoming, the speaker solicits it. Comments, then, do not fit into Piaget's notion of egocentric speech: 'The child talks either for himself or for the pleasure of associating any-one who happens to be there with the activity of the moment . . . He feels no desire to influence his hearer nor to tell him anything' (Piaget, 1926, p. 9). I point this out particularly because included in the category of egocentric speech are repetitions. 'The part played by this [repetition] is simply that of a game; the child enjoys repeating the words for their own sake, for the pleasure they give him, without any external adaptation and without an audience' (ibid.).

It is clear from the examples provided above that a child may repeat utterances not for himself but for the benefit of his co-conversationalist. This is true for the two types of repetition seen in these examples. First, there is repetition in which a child repeats an utterance he himself has previously produced. As seen in (14), this kind of repetition may serve as an attention-getting device. The speaker solicits some form of acknowledgement from his co-conversationalist. Second, there is repetition in which a child repeats an utterance previously produced by his conversational partner. As seen in (6) and (7), repetition of an antecedent utterance serves to acknowledge that utterance. Given that acknowledgement is expected by the initial speaker, repetitions here are sociocentric rather than egocentric. The hearer has honoured his obligations with respect to the speaker.

1.4 Categories of talk

We have discussed in some detail the handling of comments by Toby and David. Let us consider several other categories of speech behaviour found in the bedroom dialogues. In addition to comments, there are:

1.4.1 Questions

I use this term as defined by Bloom (1970) to refer to utterances used by the child to seek information or confirmation. Whereas comments are expressed by utterances in the indicative mood, questions are expressed by utterances in the interrogative mood. (I include here declarative sentences uttered with a question intonation.)

(17)– ‚*oh what's that*/
 – ‚*house broken* (2)/ ⅃*rip it* (2)/ ‚*see*/
(18)– ⌁*you do this*/
 – ‚*yes*/

1.4.2 Mands

Mands are one category of interpersonal directive in which the primary intention of the speaker is to direct the hearer to carry out some course of action. I use the term mand rather than directive, as the utterances tend to be in the speaker's interests (requests, demands) rather than in the hearer's interests (directions, warnings) (Ross, 1968). Mands are expressed in a number of ways. The majority are expressed by utterances in the imperative mood. The subject of the imperative may be the addressee or a third party:

(19)– *I do this*/ ⌁*look*/
 – *oh yes*/ ⌁*you do that*/
(20)– `*Toby* `*kiss it* (3)/
 – *No* ⌁[zæt]/
 – `*kiss it*/
 – *no* `[zit]/
 – `*kiss it* (2)/
 – *no* ⌁[zit]/
 – `*kiss it*/
 – *no kiss*⌁ *it*/
 – ⌁*kiss it*/ (2)
 – ⌁*Joanie*[5] *kiss it*/

Mands may also be formed from utterances which express a wish or need or which specify the object of that wish or need (Halliday, 1973):

(21)– *Jack Jill*/ *I want Jack and Jill*/
 – *Jack and Jill*/
 – *yes*/

A third form of mand includes the use of a performative verb. The verb specifies what social act is being performed by the speaker in uttering that mand.

(22) – *tell*[6] *David to do this/ do this* (3)/ *do this in 'er/ do make eye/*
    – *oh yes/*
(23) – *make*[6] *you wake up/ you you wake up/*
    – *no* (?)/ *no/*

1.4.3 Narratives

Narratives are closely related to comments in that they tend to be formed from indicative utterances. They differ in that they describe a sequence of two or more events which the child imagines take place. Furthermore, unlike comments, narratives are not addressed specifically to the co-present interlocutor (see the above discussion). The speaker does not expect a topic-related response from the co-present interlocutor and is not upset when one is not forthcoming.

(24) – *I see ribbon/ get shop/ I* [gɛ]/ *get house/* (?) *ask lady/*
    – *I go shop/byebye* (4)/ *I goin' shop/ big bend/ I get shop/*
      byebye (4)/
(25) – *I go bye bye now/ gone/ I go mommy/*

1.4.4 Songs, Rhymes

Songs and rhymes occur often throughout the dialogue between Toby and David. In the dialogue of 15 September, of 257 conversational turns, 21.5 turns involved songs and rhymes.

(26) – *Jack and Jill* (2) *fetchapail water/*
    – *Jack fall down and broke crown/*
    – *and* (?) *after/* (?) *caper/*
    – *went to bed/ broke his head/*
    – [gʌg ʌgʌgʌgʌpi] *paper/*

1.4.5 Sound play

This category of utterance is one of the most frequently occurring types of talk between the children.

Sound play refers to exchanges in which speaker and hearer focus primarily on the sounds of words. That is, a basic motivation for uttering the word(s) is to manipulate, to play with possible sound combinations. Sound play is an example of what Jakobson (1960) calls the poetic function of language (see also Weir, 1962). It enters into most of the children's utterances to varying degrees. For example, the performing of songs is strongly motivated by the enjoyment experienced in articulating the words in a rhythmic manner. In this analysis, however, I have restricted the category primarily to those cases which are unambiguously sound play. That is, I have restricted the notion of sound play to utterances which cannot be referentially interpreted by an adult native speaker. Of course, one could assume that the children have constructed a code in which these utterances do assume conventional meaning. However, I argue against this position. First, *paralinguistic cues* indicate that the children themselves realize they are using language in some manner out of the ordinary. Sound play is often engaged in on a relatively high pitch level. Further, it is generally accompanied by laughter. An utterance is produced. A burst of laughter follows. The utterance is repeated or modified by the co-present interlocutor and so on.

(27)— [zaeki su]
  — (laughing) [zæki su] (2) (both laugh) [æ:] (laughing)
  — [api:]
  — [olp] [olt] [olt]
  — [opi:] (2)
  — [api:] (2) (laughing) [api] (3)
  — [ai] [ju]
  — (laughing) [ai] [ju] [api] (repeats over and over) (laughs) [kaki] (repeats over and over)
  — [ai] [i:] [o:]
  — [ai] [i:] [o] [o:]

Secondly, the *direction* of the dialogue seems to be motivated by the phonological properties of the utterance rather than by any semantic considerations. Particular words which do have referential meaning are produced in the course of this play, but the motivation is purely formal. The word happens to fit the sound pattern being explored in the dialogue. In fact, the realization that a 'real' word fits the paradigm is greeted with enormous hilarity:

(28)— [ʃa] [batʃ]

　　－ [batʃi:] [bi:tʃi:] [badi:] [bi:di] [babi]
　　－ [badi:] (laughing)

Focus on the shape of the utterance is seen as well in the frequency of *repetitions* of particular utterances. It is characteristic of sound play that particular lexical items be repeated over and over, as many as 15 times. These repetitions may be uttered by one speaker or by both interlocutors simultaneously.

(29)－ [ga:] [ba:] [ba:] [blæk] [ʃip] [hæveg] [ʌl:] (yawns)
　　　[bægz] [lejʌl] [baki:] (repeats over and over)
　　－ [baki:]
　　－ [baki:] (repeats over and over) (laughs)
　　－ [baki:] (repeats over and over)
　　－ [tapu:ts] (repeats over and over)
　　－ [tapu:] [tapu:ts]
　　－ [tapu:t] (laughs)
　　－ [o:]

In sound play, the speakers attend not only to different points of articulation, but to prosodic features of the code as well. Thus, the focus of a particular exchange may be intonation contours or stress patterns or tempo.

(30)－ [ˋæpl] (2) [o:wo:wo:] [o]
　　－ [ˊæpl] [ˋæpl] [ˌæpl] [ˋæpl]
　　－ [æpl ˋki:nz] [æpl ˋki:z] [æpl ˋki:nz] ⎱
　　－ [ˋæpl] (repeats over and over)　　　　⎰ (simultaneous)

It is difficult to say whether or not this type of dialogue is a twin phenomenon. Conversations of this sort have not been reported in the literature. However, it may be more characteristic of children's discourse than acknowledged. For example, an illustration of a collective monologue cited by Kohlberg, Yaeger and Hjertholm (1968, p. 693) resembles the sound-play exchanges reported here:

　　Brian: *I'm playing with this.*
　　David: *A what's, a what's.*
　　Brian: *Oh nuts, oh nuts.*

Furthermore, sound play by a solitary child has often been described (Bloom, 1970; Chao, 1951; Jespersen, 1922; Jakobson, 1968; Weir, 1962).

　　Comments, questions, mands, narratives, songs and sound play represent the major categories of talk used by Toby and David on their own. They can be distinguished in terms of mood (indicative, imperative, interrogative), in terms of presence or absence of propositional content (sound play vs comments, questions, etc.), in terms of hearer addressed (narrative vs comment, for example). They can also be distinguished in terms of the type of response expected by the speaker from the hearer. That is, we can consider each of these uses of language in terms of the obligations each imposes on the hearer. Very roughly, we can divide the set into two groups. In the first group fall comments, questions and mands. All categories of talk in this group impose some form of obligation on the co-present hearer. Minimally, this obligation consists of the hearer acknowledging that the speaker has addressed some utterance to the hearer. Songs, sound play and narratives fall into the second group. None of these categories of talk obligates the co-present hearer to respond. Many times the co-present hearer does respond but he is under no obligation to do so. Speakers initiating a song or sound play, for example, do not necessarily expect that the hearer will attend to the utterance. They are content to play with sound or sing or narrate for long stretches. In fact, when used in this way, these three categories fit Piaget's definition of egocentric speech (i.e. speech which is not addressed or adapted to a listener).

(31) – (begins to sing, yawning) *twinkle twinkle little star/ how I wonder/* (yawns)/ *up so high like a diamond dum/ rockababy on treetop/ when wind blows cradle rock/ bow breaks/ cradle fall/*

In looking at the data, I have the impression that these passages would go on for longer if they were not interrupted by the other child. That is, rather than the speaker expecting some attention from the hearer, the hearer expects some attention from the speaker. Rather than the speaker becoming irritated because the hearer has failed to attend (as happens, for example, with mands and comments), the hearer becomes irritated because the speaker has failed to attend to the hearer. Often the co-present child does not like the fact that the speaker has withdrawn from the dialogue. If the speaker appears to be drifting off into an exclusive universe of talk, the co-present child will try to solicit his attention, to bring him back into conversational play. This may be done by contributing to the speaker's utterance. That is, the co-present child may interrupt the speaker's talk with the next line of a song he is singing or with sound play appropriate to the speaker's paradigm.

(32) – *goosey goosey gander, where shall I wander/ upstairs downstairs/*

la lady's chamber/ [m:] [ma] *met it old man/* [a:] / *say*
prayers/ fall down stairs/ [la] *lady's chamber/* [m:] [ma]
met it old man/ rockababy on the tree top/ and the windows/
– big rock/ biggy will fall/
– and cradle all/
– and all/

Another strategy is to interrupt the monologue with a comment, mand
or question. The motivation behind using these categories of talk is
obvious. In addressing any one of those speech acts to the co-present
child, the speaker obligates the latter to evidence his attention. Thus
the excluded child insures that he will be excluded no longer. In order
to attend to the comment, mand or question of the other, the speaker
must discontinue his own talk. The speaker is not always willing to do
this, and often the co-present child may find it necessary to repeat his
comment, question, etc., several times before it is acknowledged.

(33)– (yawns) *goosey goosey gander/*
  – (sings a song to toy pig)
  – (whispers) *goosey goosey gander/*
  – [i:] *moth/* [i:] *moth/*
  – *goosey goosey gander where shall I wander/*
  – [i:] *moth/* [i:] *moth/* [i:] *moth/* [i:] *moth/* [i:] *moth/*
  – *up downstairs lady's chamber/*
  – [i:] *moth/* [i:] *moth/* [i:] *moth/*
  – [i:] [le:] *moth/*
(34)– *I see ribbon get shop/ I get house/* (?)/ *ask lady/*
    byebye/ byebye/ I go shop/ byebye/ byebye/ byebye/ byebye/
    I goin' shop big bend/ I get shop/ byebye/ byebye/ byebye/
    byebye/ (?) *toys/ byebye/ byebye/ byebye/ byebye/*
  – (interrupting) (?) [i:]/ *what's 'at/* [i:]/ *what's 'at/* [i:]/
    what's 'at/ [i:]/ *what's 'at/*
  – *hello/ hello/ hello/ hello/* (?) [i:] *god/*
  – [i:] *god/* [i:] [da:]/

This behaviour of the co-present child indicates once again the highly
social nature of these dialogues. Egocentric speech on the part of one
child is not tolerated by the other child. This description again contrasts
with that provided by Piaget. Piaget's observations showed co-present
children using egocentric speech for extended stretches of discourse.
One explanation for this contrast may be that the interlocutors are
twins, and perhaps they cannot be considered representative examples

of interacting children. Only further research can substantiate this claim. Another explanation may be that the setting and social activity of Piaget's subjects and the subjects of this study differed radically. Piaget observed children as they interacted in a nursery school classroom. The exchange of talk between children was accompanied by a variety of non-verbal activity. The dialogues between Toby and David took place in the familiar surroundings of their bedroom. Furthermore, they conversed in semi-darkness (early morning). During most of the talk, the children remained in their beds. The point I wish to stress is that in the nursery school setting there existed a variety of stimuli (visual, tactile) to interest the child; the child need not depend on talk alone to interest him. In the bedroom setting, these stimuli are not present to the same extent: the major activity in this setting is the exchange of talk, and when one child fails to participate in the exchange, the other child rapidly becomes bored; his only alternatives are to fall asleep, to talk to himself, or to re-engage the other in conversational play. If this hypothesis is correct, it suggests that the talk of children (like that of adults) is sensitive to context. The commitments of speaker to hearer and hearer to speaker differ according to range and kind of activities they are engaged in. Collective monologues (Piaget, 1926) may be tolerated by interlocutors in a nursery school setting, where other forms of play absorb the child. In a less provocative environment, however, speakers and hearers may be obliged to attend more closely to each other's talk.

1.5 Recipes for a dialogue

In his lectures on logic and conversation, Grice (1975) has suggested a number of conversational maxims to which speakers generally adhere. One of these maxims concerns the relation of the speaker's utterance to the 'accepted purpose or direction of the talk-exchange'. This maxim is simply: *be relevant*. Of course, speakers do not conform to this principle in every instance. But generally interlocutors expect each other's utterances to relate to some mutually accepted orientation. One of the communication skills which a child must learn is, then, this maxim.

The notion of relevance implies that the utterances at hand can be assigned a meaning. When we say that an utterance is relevant to some previous talk, we mean that the utterance is referentially or sociologically (as a kind of speech act) tied to the topic or direction of the talk. Before we can discuss to what extent children's utterances are relevant, we must clarify the extent to which their dialogues are meaningful (i.e. have meaning).

At 2;9 Toby and David entertain conversations of two sorts. First, they have conversations in which the verbal contributions are referentially interpretable. That is, they use utterances which have a referential meaning. Second, they have conversations in which the verbal contributions cannot be assigned a referential meaning. These conversations are exchanges of nonsense, what we have previously discussed as 'sound play'. These dialogues are coherent in the sense that both interlocutors co-operate in the same social act. And they are coherent in the sense that the interlocutors attend to the phonological shape of one another's utterances. A nonsense syllable from an initial conversational turn is repeated or modified slightly:

(35)– [apʃi:] [autʃi:] (2) [o:tʃi:] [o:ʃabatʃ]
  – [ʃa:ʃabatʃ:]
  – [ʃo:babatʃ]
  – [ʃo:babat] [ʃobabatʃ] (laughs)
  – [ʃo:bababatʃ]
  – [ʃo:batʃ] (laughs)
  – [ʃo:batʃ]
  – [baptʃ]
  – [ʃo:batʃ]
  – [batʃi] [bitʃi] [badi] [bidi] [babi]
  – [badi] (laughing)
  – (?) [dænju]
  – [atla:ju]
  – [latodu] [latlogu]
  – [latlodo]
  – [bau:] (laughing) [gali gu:du]
  – [i:ja] [gi:ja]
  – [gi:ja] (both laugh) [dabu:t] (15)
  – [daˋbu:t] [ˋda:but]
  – [daˋbu:t] (repeats over and over)
  – [gal] [gʌl]

This particular sequence of talk was interrupted by a comment by one of the children. After a brief exchange, however, it was resumed for another ten conversational turns. Interrupted once again by a song sung by one child, it was continued for a further ten lines.

This example is no exception. The conversational discourse of these children is laced with sound-play exchanges of this sort. The frequency

and length of these exchanges make it clear that it is perfectly acceptable
for interlocutors to address their utterances to the form of an immediately preceding utterance. This applies not only to utterances which are
clearly instances of sound play. It applies as well to utterances which
can be referentially interpreted. That is, it is often acceptable to reply
to a comment, mand, question or song with an utterance which attends
only to the form of that talk.

(36) – *wake up/ wake up/*
   – [he:kʌt] (laughing)
   – [he:kʌt]
   – [be:kʌp]
   – [bre:kʌt] [bre:kʌp]
   – *wake up/* [wi:kʌp] (laughing) [wi:kʌp]

(37) – *black sheep (4)/*
   – *black/* [bakʃi] (?)
   – [badijotʃ] (2)
   – [badzots]
   – [batʃi] [batʃiotʃ]

For these children, the maxim *be relevant* can be interpreted as 'Tie
utterance to phonological form of previous utterance'. This interpretation
is not, however, shared by adult interlocutors in western society (at
least not to the same extent). Normally,[7] it is not acceptable for adult
interlocutors to attend solely to the form of one another's utterances.
An adult who responded to the command */wake up/ wake up/* with the
utterance [he:kʌp] would be regarded as very strange indeed. This
difference in interpretation of relevancy may be an important criterion
in distinguishing the conversations of adults and young children.

   Let us now consider dialogues which have referentially interpretable
turns. Some of these dialogues are dominated by genres such as songs
or nursery rhymes. The song or rhyme provides a more or less fixed
routine in which the children can co-operate in talk.

(38) – (unclear sound play)/ *fetch a pail of water/ Jack fall down/*
   – *Jack/ Jill/ Jack Jill/*
   – *broke crown/* (?)
   – *Jack/*
   – *Jack fall down/ broke/*
   – *Jack fall down/ broke crown/ after/*
   – *Jack and Jill fetch a pail of water/* ⎫
   – *broke crown/*   ⎬ *simultaneous*
   – (?) *paper/*   ⎭

In other instances, however, these dialogues may consist of comments, acknowledgements, questions and/or mands centering on one or more topics. As the interlocutors rely on no ready-made routine (song, rhyme), it is reasonable to assume that in these cases a coherent dialogue is more difficult to achieve. A close examination of these conversations shows that to a large extent the interlocutors achieve coherency by applying a few formal operations to one another's utterances. An initial utterance offered by one speaker is modified in some way by the second speaker and offered as a response or part of a response. We refer to these modifications as functions. The nature of the modification defines the function that relates the utterances.

The bulk of the conversations between Toby and David at 2;9 can be accounted for in terms of two major functions. The first is what the author calls the *focus* function. Focus functions take an initial conversational turn, focus on a constituent of it, and repeat it in a subsequent turn. The constituent focused on may be a whole utterance within a turn.

Focus functions can be broken down into a number of specific types:

I. The *basic focus* function focuses on a constituent of an antecedent turn and repeats it exactly as it appeared originally (including intonation). The constituent most often repeated is the predicate or some part of the predicate (e.g. direct object) of a preceding utterance.

(39)(Toby and David are looking at letters in book)
    – *that* ⟍*A*/ ⟍*B*/ *that* ⟍*A*/
    – ⟍*A*/

Other constituents repeated in the data are subject, subject + predicate, and subject + partial predicate.

(40)– *Mommy to do*/ *Daddy to do*/
    – *Daddy to do*/
(41)– *Mommy's silly*/
    – *Mommy's silly*/

II. In addition to the *basic focus* function, there are a number of *complex focus* functions. These functions are complex in the sense that basic focus is accompanied by some further formal modification.
(*a*) *Focus + prosodic shift* repeats a constituent within an antecedent turn but alters the intonation or voice quality assigned to the constituent.

(42)– ⟍*flower broked*/ ⟍*flower broken*/
    – ⟋*flower*/

(*b*) *Focus + constituent expansion* focuses on a constituent within an antecedent turn and expands it syntactically. This expansion does not alter the grammatical status of the focused constituent.

(43) – *flower broken/ flower/ its flower broken/ eh/ oh/ end/*
　　　 – *many many flowers broken/*

(*c*) *Focus + constituent embedding* focuses on a constituent within an antecedent turn and embeds it in a larger construction.

(44) – *big one/ yes/ big one/*
　　　 – *I got/ I got big one/*

Both (*b*) and (*c*) may be accompanied by prosodic shift as well.

These focus operations also relate utterances within a conversational turn. For example, the turn 1 *and teddy bear/* 2 *teddy bear have ribbon/* 3 *teddy bear have ribbon/* 4 *teddy bear have/* 5 *teddy bear have ribbon/* includes utterances related by basic focus (e.g. 2 and 3) and focus + embedding functions (e.g. 1 and 2, 4 and 5). Focus functions can be applied to many such utterance sequences mentioned in the literature on child language. Bloom's 'expansions' (1970), Braine's 'replacement sequences' (1965), and Weir's 'build-ups' and 'break-downs' (1962) can all be characterized in terms of these operations. For example, Weir's 'break-downs' (*Anthony jump out again/ Anthony jump/*) are related by the basic focus function. Weir's 'build-ups' (*block/yellow block/ look at all the yellow block/*) can be explained by complex focus functions, for example, focus + constituent embedding, focus + constituent expansion.

What the present study contributes to this literature is the fact that these syntactic modifications can be applied by a young child to utterances of another child (or adult). The current literature tends to focus on sequences produced by one child to show the level of syntactic complexity achieved by the child. The present study indicates that the production of such sequences can be a co-operative enterprise and a means by which young children achieve a dialogue.

Let us now consider the second major function that relates utterances in the dialogues of Toby and David. In addition to focus functions, there are *substitution* functions. Substitution functions take an utterance within a conversational turn and replace a constituent within it with a constituent of the same grammatical category. (An entire utterance may not be replaced.)

(45) – *two moths/*
　　　 – *many moths/*

Again these functions can apply to utterances within a turn as well as to utterances between turns. For example, in the sequence by one child: *Mommy to do/ Daddy to do/* the utterances are related by a substitution function. (The subject Mommy is replaced by the subject Daddy.) Again such a function can apply to many sequences reported in the psycholinguistic literature. For example, in the sequence reported by Bloom for Kathryn at stage II: 1 *make ə block/* 2 *make ə house/* 3 *blocks/* 4 *make ə house/* utterances 1 and 2 are related by a substitution function. In fact, the entire sequence can be described in terms of both the focus and substitution functions. Utterances 1 and 3 are related by focus + expansion, 2 and 4 by basic focus.

The bulk of the utterances between conversational turns are linked formally through these functions. The child uses all or part of an initial utterance in the formulation of a subsequent utterance. However, every utterance in the corpus cannot be explained in terms of these formal modifications. Some utterances appear which have no formal relation whatsoever to previous discourse. We have categorized these utterances into two groups:

I. *Response constants.* The bulk of the formally unrelated utterances are drawn from a small set of particles. The set includes the affirmative particles *yes, yeah, oh yes;* the negative particles *no, not;* and the expressive particles *oh, oh dear, oopsee, ouch, eegod, ee.* These particles may appear alone in a conversational turn or may accompany another utterance. They usually serve to acknowledge an utterance offered by the other speaker. (See discussion of comment-acknowledgement exchanges above.)

II. *Novel utterances.* A novel utterance is any utterance which is not related to an antecedent turn by some function and is not a response constant. Most novel utterances appear in a conversational turn after some utterance that is functionally related to previous discourse.

(46)– *I gets some ribbon/* (?) *too/*
    – *I see ribbon/ get shop/ I* [gɛ] *get house/* (?) *ask lady/ byebye (2)/ I go shop/ byebye* (4) . . . (continuation)

In some cases, an entire turn may contain novel utterances relative to the immediately preceding turn.

(47)– *no silly/*
    – *big one/ piggy one/ pig it/* (?) *it piggy/*

Although it is difficult to make any definitive judgment about the semantic relationship between turns related in this way, I feel that such exchanges are usually collective monologues (Piaget, 1926) rather than semantically coherent dialogues. Semantically coherent dialogues are achieved largely by means of focus and substitution functions and response constants, as the following example illustrates:

(48)	*Turns tied by*
– *you ˎsilly/ you ˎsilly/*	
– *ˎno Toby's silly/*	focus + constituent embedding
– *you ˎsilly (2)/*	focus + prosodic shift (2)
– *ˎno/ ˎyou silly/ no not ˎyou silly/*	response constant & focus + prosodic shift (2)
– *ˎyou silly/*	basic focus
– *ˎno/ ˎnot/ ˎno silly (2)/*	response constant (2) & focus + embedding
– *ˎno silly (2)*	basic focus (2)
– *ˎno/ ˎno you silly (2)/ ˎyou silly/*	response constant & focus + embedding & focus + embedding
– *ˎyou silly*	basic focus
– *ˎno you silly/ ˋoh/*	focus + embedding + prosodic shift & response constant
– *you ˎsilly*	focus + prosodic shift
– *ˎno/ ˎyou silly/*	response constant & focus + prosodic shift
– (unclear mumbling)	(unclear)
– *no ˎyou silly/ you ˎsil'ly/*	
– *you ˎsilly (5)* ⎫	focus + prosodic shift
– *you ˎyou silly/* ⎬ simultaneous	focus + prosodic shift (3)
ˎyou silly (2) ⎭	
– *ˎno you silly*	focus + embedding + prosodic shift
– *ˎyou silly (3)*	focus + prosodic shift (3)
– *ˋno silly (3)*	focus + embedding
– *you ˎsilly* (repeats over and over) ⎫	focus + prosodic shift
– *no ˎno silly/* ⎬ simultaneous	focus + embedding + prosodic shift (3)
ˎno silly (2)/ ⎭	
– *ˎno* (repeated)/ ⎫	response constant & focus + prosodic shift & (?)
ˎsilly/ ˋno/ ˋsilly/ ⎬	
(?) ˋsilly ⎬ simultaneous	
– *ˎno* (repeated)/ ⎭	focus & focus + embedding + prosodic shift (2)
no ˎsil'ly/	

– ⌐*silly* (3)/	focus + prosodic shift (3)
– ⌐*no sil ly*/	focus + embedding + prosodic shift
– '*silly*/ ⌐*sil″ly*/	focus + prosodic shift (2)
– ⌐*no silly*/	focus + embedding + prosodic shift
– ⌐*silly*/	focus + prosodic shift
– ⌐*no*/	response constant

(This dialogue continues in this fashion for a further 16 conversational turns.)

We are now in a position to suggest a partial formalization of discourse procedure (for young children). It is possible to represent the options available for responding to a conversational turn in terms of a set of phrase structure rules:

1.5.1 Notation

X = a particular antecedent turn
Resp to X = response to X
f(X) = a function applied to X (any one of those in phrase structure rules)
F = focus function
F_b = basic focus function
F_c = complex focus function
Pros. Shft = prosodic shift
Expansion = constituent expansion
Embed = constituent embedding
Sub = substitution function
RC = response constant
NU = novel utterance
(Resp to X)^n = response to X repeated n times
$f_1(f_2(X))$ = function$_1$ applied to function$_2$ which is applied to X

1.5.2 Phrase structure rules

$$\text{Resp to X} \longrightarrow \begin{cases} F(X) \\ \text{Sub}(X) \\ \text{RC} \\ \text{NU} \end{cases}$$

$$F(X) \longrightarrow \begin{Bmatrix} F_b(X) \\ F_c(X) \end{Bmatrix}$$

$$F_b(X) \longrightarrow \begin{Bmatrix} \text{subj }(X) \\ \text{pred }(X) \\ \text{partial pred }(X) \\ \text{subj + pred }(X) \\ \text{subj + partial pred }(X) \end{Bmatrix}$$

$$F_c(X) \longrightarrow \begin{Bmatrix} \text{Pros. Shft }(F(X)) \\ \text{Expansion }(F(X)) \\ \text{Embed }(F_b(X)) \end{Bmatrix}$$

Resp to X $\longrightarrow$ (Resp to X)^n

Resp to X $\longrightarrow$ Resp to X + Resp to X

These rules apply only to referentially interpretable responses. To cover all possible responses, the set of response options would have to be expanded to include sound play as well. A first examination of sound-play dialogue shows that not just any phonological sequence is offered as a response. Turns containing sound play are closely related in form. In fact, with some modifications, the relations between sound-play turns can be analysed in terms of focus and substitution functions. For example, we can replace the notion 'constituent' with the notions 'syllable' and 'sound' in our definition of focus functions. This function can be represented as F_{syl} and defined as follows: F_{syl} functions take an utterance, focus on one or more syllables or one or more sounds within a syllable and repeat it (them) in a subsequent turn.

(49)   *Turns tied by*

   – [i:] [ga:b] [i:] [golb]

   + [i:] [golb] F_{syl}

   – [golb] F_{syl}

Just as in referential discourse the focus functions may be basic or complex, so in sound play this distinction is readily applicable. The basic focus function takes a syllable or sound within it and repeats it exactly as it appeared in the antecedent turn. Complex focus functions modify the intonation or voice quality (F_{syl} + prosodic shift), expand a syllable to include other sounds (F_{syl} + expansion), or add new syllables to a focus syllable (F_{syl} + add).

(50)– [du:] (3)   *Turns tied by*

   – (laughing) [dutʃ] F_{syl} + expansion

   – [du] (repeats over and F_{syl}
     over) (pause)

   – [fʌpi] [du:] F_{syl} + add

Similarly, substitution functions can be applied to sound play. Substitution functions (Sub_{syl}) replace one or more sounds within a syllable (but not all the sounds) with another sound (or sounds) occupying the same linear position within the syllable;

(51)   *Turns tied by*
  − [giːnɔg] (3)
  − [giːnan] (repeats over and Sub_{syl}
    over)
  − (laughs)
  − [kiːtan] (2) Sub_{syl}

The systematic nature of sound-play discourse brings out the degree to which young children attend to the formal features of one another's utterances. Extended stretches of co-operative talk are achieved by reproducing exactly or modifying slightly each other's utterances. This is true for referential as well as for non-referential (sound-play) discourse. Novel utterances may appear as topically relevant comments on an antecedent utterance. But normally such exchanges are short-lived. Extended sequences of novel utterances in adjacent turns are either part of a routine (e.g. lines of a rhyme or song), or they are non-attentive or egocentric speech (e.g. narratives).

Notes

1. This research is supported by the Social Science Research Council, grant no. HR 2941/1. I am grateful to Ewan Klein of the Unit for Research in Medical Applications of Psychology, University of Cambridge, for his considerable help in analysing the data.
2. The notation used throughout the paper is to be interpreted as follows: / = terminates breath group; − = turn by single speaker; + = turn by both speakers; (?) = unclear utterance. Intonation notation follows Kingdon (1958): ＼ = low fall, ＼ = emphatic low fall, ′ = high fall, ″ = emphatic high fall, ⁄ = low rise, etc.
3. [iː] is a general deictic particle. It could be glossed as 'there', 'here', 'he', etc.
4. Small capitals indicate the utterance that belongs to this category of acknowledgement.
5. Personal referent not present.
6. Performatives.
7. I am grateful to David Crystal for pointing out to me that sound-play-like exchanges may appear in adult conversations as 'jocular chidings'. In informal conversation, one adult may brush off the worries or complaints of another by converting his utterance to sound play: e.g. A: *My hair's falling out. I'm worried.*/ B: *Hair shmair, who cares?* This kind of sound play is short-lived, however, in contrast to the extended exchanges sustained by the children.

2

Making it last: repetition in children's discourse

E. Ochs Keenan

The counterfeit is poorly imitated after you

(Shakespeare) *Sonnets* liii

2.1 Introduction

One of the most commonplace observations in the psycholinguistic
literature is that many young children often repeat utterances addressed
to them. Just as commonplace are generalizations concerning the
importance of this behaviour to the development of language in the
child. We have, on the one extreme, those who consider all linguistic
knowledge to be obtained through this vehicle, and on the other
extreme, we have those who place no importance whatsoever to the
repetitions of young children.

Throughout the 1960s and into the 1970s the literature is dominated
by studies which purport to show that language does not develop
through repetition. Typically, the class of repeated utterances of the
child is compared to the class of spontaneous or free utterances. Over
and over these studies show that, with the exception of the child's
repetition of adult expansions (Slobin, 1968; Brown and Bellugi, 1964),
repeated utterances are no longer nor transformationally more complex
than spontaneous utterances (Ervin, 1964; Menyuk, 1963; Bloom, 1970).

If repetition is irrelevant to language development, we are left with
the question: Why *do* young children repeat the utterances of others
with such frequency? This question has not been seriously addressed.
At this point in time, we still do not understand what children are
doing when they repeat a given utterance. This state of affairs exists
because, until quite recently, psycholinguists have been insensitive to
the status of utterances as social acts. With some exception (Bloom,
1970; Weir, 1962; Scollon, 1976; Slobin, 1968), they have focused on

the form of repeated utterances to the exclusion of their function in real communicative situations. An expressed intention of this chapter is to remedy this state of affairs. I present here an analysis of repetition in child language from a pragmatic perspective. By pragmatic perspective, I mean simply one that relates an utterance to its context of use. Context, of course, is an infinitely extendable notion, but can include such things as the speaker's communicative intention, the speaker-hearer relationship, the extralinguistic setting of the utterance, the linguistic setting of the utterance (e.g. prior discourse, topic at hand, etc.), and other areas of background knowledge, such as knowledge of conversational norms and conventions.

Data used to substantiate this presentation are drawn from a number of existing sources. However, I will rely primarily on observations carried out by myself on the spontaneous conversations of twin boys (2;9 at the outset). Their conversations were recorded (video and audio) on a monthly basis over a period of a year.

2.2 Children as communicators

It is no accident that the positive function of repetition in children's speech has not been investigated. For one thing, perspectives adopted in developmental psycholinguistics are heavily influenced by current paradigms in linguistics. It is only in the past 5 years that pragmatics have been seriously considered within the field. Secondly, within developmental psycholinguistics, there has persisted a stereotype of the child as a noncommunicator. Over and over, we find attempts to set children apart from adults in their verbal activity. We are told that children are egocentric in their speech; that is, they are not interested in directing their talk to an addressee. Co-present individuals are merely used as sounding boards for the child, as the child has no interest in obtaining a response to his utterance. Furthermore, when others talk, the child experiences difficulty in attending and evaluating their communicative intentions. In short, we are told that, unlike adults, children typically do not engage in dialogue. More characteristic of their speech are collective monologues (Piaget, 1926).

With this prejudice in hand, the psycholinguist quite naturally believed that the primary motive of the child in interacting with adults was mastery of the adult code. In line with this, it was quite natural for researchers to associate repetition with this goal. Why did children repeat? Behaviourists claimed that young children repeated utterances as an attempt to produce the same utterance themselves. That is, they repeated because they wished to imitate the adult form of an utterance. Repetition in the speech of young children became strongly associated with imitation. In fact, throughout the rationalist counter-argument, the association of repetition with imitation was never challenged. It was tacitly accepted that children repeated as an attempt to copy a prior utterance; what was denied was that the attempt was successful, or a means by which mastery was obtained.

Notice here that contextual grounds have subtly entered into the psycholinguist's categorization of repetitions as imitation. The psycholinguist perceives these repetitions as imitations because the repeater is a young child and the initial speaker is an adult. Constrained by the current paradigm, the relationship is translated into that between master of the code and learner of the code. This is important to note as most psycholinguists try to define imitation in terms of repetition alone. That is, they try to treat imitation as a formal relation between two utterances and not as a social act.

I have argued in an earlier paper (Keenan, 1974b) that attempts to define imitation on formal grounds alone have been unsuccessful and inconsistent. The constraints on what counts as a repetition vary enormously from investigator to investigator. Rodd and Braine (1971), Freedle et al. (1970), and Ervin (1964), for example, consider only immediate responses to an utterance as possible imitations. Bloom et al. (1974), on the other hand, are willing to look to the next five to ten utterances for a candidate imitation. Then there is the problem of cross-utterance similarity. Just how much of the initial utterance must be repeated in order for it to count as an imitation? For many investigators, the repeated utterance could omit but not substitute items of the initial utterance. Further, the repeated utterance had to be a more or less telegraphic version of the adult string, omitting the function words but retaining some or all of the content words. For other investigators (Rodd and Braine, 1971), it was sufficient that the child repeat a particular construction under investigation for the utterance to count as an imitation.

On top of these practical difficulties is the fact that repetition alone is neither necessary nor sufficient to characterize imitation. It is not a necessary criterion in that attempts to copy may not, in fact, repeat the prior utterance. Hence there may be innumerable unsuccessful imitations — e.g., inarticulate mutterings, wild stabs, false starts, and the like — which are not repetitions in any accepted sense of the word. Note here, then, that when psycholinguists address themselves to the role of imitation in language development, they are considering only successful imitations in their data base. We have no idea whatsoever of the character of these unsuccessful imitations. We don't know what type of adult utterance is responded to in such a way, and we do not know the nature of the distortion. It is evident that even on its own terms, the imitation literature stands on shaky ground.

Repetition is not a sufficient criterion for imitation in that it is possible to find repeated utterances that are not attempts to copy. Slobin illustrated this beautifully in his 1968 article on imitation. He provides the following dialogue between Adam (2;6) and his mother:

MOTHER: *It fits in the puzzle someplace.*
ADAM: *Puzzle? Puzzle someplace?*
MOTHER: *Turn it around.*
ADAM: *Turn it around?*
MOTHER: *No, the other way.*
ADAM: *Other way?*
MOTHER: *I guess you have to turn it around.*
ADAM: *Guess turn it round. Turn round.*

In this dialogue, Adam appears first to be using repetition as a vehicle for querying a prior utterance, and then as a vehicle for informing himself and/or agreeing with the mother's comment.

It is clear that all repetitions are not imitations and all imitations are not repetitions. In order to establish a given utterance as an imitation, contextual criteria must be provided as well. Further, it is not sufficient to define the context as simply that of a child interacting with an adult. We have seen that this relationship may be held constant through a variety of social uses of repetition (imitation, query, self-informing). In order to establish that an imitation has taken place, the investigator must somehow contend with the communicative intentions of the child. This is not to say that for an imitation to have taken place the child must have the conscious intention to reproduce a prior utterance. There may be degrees to which the child is aware of his own behaviour. It is only to say that the presence or absence of the intention to imitate must be reckoned with. In particular, we can not accept that a repetition overtly elicited in an experimental situation can be equated in all cases with a repetition uttered in spontaneous conversation between caretaker and child. The overtly elicited repetition counts as an imitation because the child has been asked to copy the experimenter's utterance. While this sometimes may be the case in spontaneous conversation, we can not assume all repeats to be of this character. Claims made about the nature of repetition in the laboratory situation, then, should not automatically extend to ordinary verbal interactions between caretaker and child.

Once we address ourselves to the communicative intentions of the child, we can begin investigating a variety of interesting questions. For example, we know that children who repeat utterances increase this activity until about 2;6 and then it begins to decline. It would be interesting to follow a repeater through this cycle, indicating the ways in which the repetition was used in discourse. We could begin asking in what order the different communicative uses of repetition emerge. It may be the case that the child first uses repetition to imitate and later comes to use it to perform other communicative tasks. It may be the case that, as Slobin (1973b) has suggested for syntax, the child uses an old form for new functions. That is, some children may latch onto repetition quite early as a device for participating in discourse, and use this device to perform novel communicative tasks. Further, it may be the case that repetition is more appropriate or more efficient for some tasks than others. For example, if you want to copy the utterance of another speaker, then repetition is a good device to employ. Similarly, if the child wishes to let his caretaker know that he has understood ('communication check') the caretaker's utterance, then repetition is appropriate. On the other hand, there are only a few types of questions one can ask by repeating all or part of a prior utterance. It may be the case that as the child becomes competent in a greater number of speech acts, he finds repetition a less and less satisfying device.

A second area of inquiry opened up concerns the differences and similarities between children who rely heavily on repetition and those who rarely repeat (Bloom et al., 1974). The distinction has been posed in the literature between those children who are imitators and those children who are non-imitators. Addressing ourselves to the communicative intentions of children, we may discover that this dichotomy misses the mark. It may be the case that 'imitators' are not, in fact, imitating, and that all of these children do similar communicative work; they simply differ in the formal devices used to carry out this work.

2.3 Repetition and prior discourse

I would like now to examine in some detail the varied uses of repetition in conversational discourse. In investigating these uses, I look for clues in prior discourse and in subsequent discourse. Here I consider the relation of repetition to prior discourse.

One of the characteristics of the literature on imitation is that it generally ignores the illocutionary force of the utterance that the child is responding to. The utterance repeated by the child is not described as a request for information, request for services, an assertion, a greeting, a rhyme, or song. All utterances are lumped together under the cover term 'model sentence'. The use of this term, of course, reflects the general assumption that all repetitions are imitations. Furthermore, in comparing an utterance with its repetition, the investigator judges only the extent to which the repetition succeeds as an imitation. It is typical of repetitions, in fact, not to succeed completely. Ervin (1964), for example, mentions that only a small percentage of the spontaneous 'imitations' in her data were exact requirements. As imitations, then, the repetitions of young children are inferior reproductions.

If, on the other hand, children are repeating not to imitate but to satisfy some other communicative obligation, then inexact repetition might be the intended, not unintended, desire of the child. The fact that the child, particularly the child from 2–3 years, fails to copy in entirety a previous utterance in conversation, may reflect the child's *competence* and not his *incompetence*. Consider, for example, the model sentences used by Rodd and Braine (1971) in their study of imitation. In this study, the investigator directed to a child of 2;1 years the sentence *Is the baby sitting down?* The child's response was *Uhhuh, baby down.* Here, it is perfectly appropriate for the child not to repeat the previous utterance. In fact, it would be inappropriate for the child to produce an exact copy. Clearly, the child has grasped the communicative intentions of the investigator. The child's response shows that the child treats the investigator's utterance not as a model to be imitated, but as a question to be answered. The repetition is far more successful as an answer than as an imitation.

Repetition with omissions are appropriate in response to utterances other than information questions as well. For both adult and child alike, it is appropriate to repeat just one or two words from the utterance of a conversational partner to comment attitudinally:

(1) (Toby and David at 2;9 conversing with their nanny, Jill)
JILL: *And we're going to have hot dogs.*
TOBY: *Hot dogs!* (excitedly)
JILL: *And soup.*
DAVID: *Mmm soup!*

To agree with:

(2) (Toby and David at 2;9 with their nanny, Jill)
JILL: *And we're gonna build a fire.*
DAVID: *Mmm.*
TOBY: *Oh yeah/ build fire.*

To self-inform:

(3) (Toby and David at 2;9 with their nanny, Jill)
JILL: *And we're going to cook sausages.*
TOBY: *Cook sausages.*
JILL: *And bacon.*
TOBY and DAVID: *Bacon.*
JILL: *And eggs.*
TOBY and DAVID: *Eggs.*

To query:

(4) (Toby and David at 2;10. Toby engaged in sound play)
TOBY: */diɔt/tziju/ i/ u/ bɔ/ ɔt/*
DAVID: *ˇbɔt*
(5) (Toby and David at 2;11)
DAVID: *ˋMy hands are cold.*
TOBY: *ʹCold.*

To imitate:

(6) (Toby and David at 2;9 with their nanny, Jill)
JILL: *Aren't I a good cook? Say 'Yes, the greatest!'*
TOBY: *Yes the greatest.* (softly)
JILL: *That's right.*
DAVID: *The greatest!* (loudly)

Even in the case of explicit imitation, the child repeats selectively. For example, the child does not repeat the performative verb 'say' in the previous utterance. The child has shaped the repetition to satisfy his obligations as a conversational partner. In each case the shaping reflects the child's orientation to the expectations of the prior speaker.

We have established, then, that children are sensitive to the illocutionary force of prior utterances in discourse. They repeat as an attempt to respond appropriately to particular types of utterances. I have mentioned some of these types in the previous discussion, but this mention by no means exhausts the list. In addition to its usefulness in answering questions, commenting, affirming, self-informing, querying, and imitating, repetition may be used to make counterclaims of the following sort:

(7) (Toby and David at 2;9)

DAVID: *You ⌄silly/ you ⌄silly/ you ⌄silly/ you ⌄silly/ you ⌄silly/*

TOBY: *⌄You/ ⌄you silly/ ⌄you silly/ ⌄you silly/ ⌄no you silly/*

Further, repetition may be used to match a claim made by a previous speaker (Keenan and Klein, 1975). That is, the second speaker may claim what was predicted by the first speaker holds for the second speaker as well:

(8) (Toby and David at 2;9 with their nanny, Jill)

DAVID: *Doggie bib.* (I have) *doggie bib.* (see).

   I have doggie bib (2x). (?) *bib.*

JILL: *David's got brown flowers in his.*

DAVID: *Yeah.*

TOBY: (I) *have doggie bib.*

JILL: (You've got a) *doggie bib.*

(9)

DAVID: *I get them off.*

TOBY: *I get them off.*

In counterclaims and matching claims, we see that an utterance that replicates another in form does not replicate it in meaning. The utterances differ in meaning precisely because they differ in context. In each case, the meaning of the deictic item (*I, you*) depends on who the speaker is and who the addressee is. Such examples indicate the difficulty involved in earlier claims that imitations must preserve the meaning of the model utterance (Ervin, 1964). Preservation of meaning must surely be the exception rather than the norm in repeated utterances. Even if the repeated utterance contains no deictic items, the position of the utterance as a response (i.e. second pair part, cf. Schegloff and Sacks (1973)) makes it pragmatically distinct from the initial utterance.

In addition to the above-mentioned uses of repetition, there are examples in the data of repeating to greet back, to reverse the direction of an order, to reverse the direction of an information question, and to request clarification of an utterance:

(10) (Toby and David at 2;11)

DAVID: *(fae:b)*

TOBY: *(fae:b). You mean that/*

In short, there appears to be no end to the ways in which cross-utterance repetition is employed in conversational discourse. Repetition is probably one of the most misunderstood phenomena in psycholinguistics. It is associated with the language of children, who, in turn, are underrated as communicators. It is obvious, however, that with some exceptions, the kind of repetition described here is quite characteristic of adult speakers as well. Any of the following exchanges could appear in adult discourse:

(11) Greeting
A: *Hello.*
B: *Hello.*
(12) Self-informing and/or displaying knowledge
A: *That's Halley's comet.*
B: *Ah, that's Halley's comet.*
(13) Agreeing
A: *That's dreadful.*
B: *Dreadful.*
(14) Matching claim
A: *I'm fat.*
B: *I'm fat.*
(15) Counterclaim
A: *You're thinner than I am.*
B: *You're thinner than I am.*
(16) Querying
A: *Yes.*
B: *Yes?*
(17) Answering
A: *Yes?*
B: *Yes.*
(18) Reversing direction of question
A: *Well?*
B: *Well?*
(19) Imitating
A: *Say 'cheese'.*
B: *Cheese.*
(20) Commenting
A: *But my diet.*
B: *Diet schmiet. Let's eat.*

What then is going on when a child repeats the utterance of a co-present speaker? Is the child learning anything about his language? Is there any way in which repetition is developmentally progressive with respect to language? We can say that in repeating, the child is learning to communicate. He is learning not to construct sentences at random, but to construct them to meet specific communicative needs. He is learning to query, comment, confirm, match a claim and counterclaim, answer a question, respond to a demand, and so on. In short, he is learning the human uses of language, what Dell Hymes has called 'communicative competence' (1972a).

2.4 Repetition and subsequent discourse

I would like to turn now to the relation between repetition and discourse subsequent to a repetition. It has been often noted in the literature (Slobin, 1968; Brown and Bellugi, 1964) that when caretakers repeat and expand the utterances of children, they often do so as a kind of 'communication check'. The caretaker presents his or her interpretation of the child's utterance to the child for verification.

(21) (Toby and David at 2;9 with their nanny, Jill)
TOBY: *Gramma Ochs/*
JILL: *Gramma Ochs?*
TOBY: *Yeah/*
(22) (Toby and David at 2;9 with their nanny, Jill)
TOBY: *Airplane/*
JILL: *Oh. She went on an airplane, did she?*
TOBY: *Yeah/*

It is similarly the case that children repeat the utterances of adults to let them know they have understood their utterances at some basic level. (Examples (1-3) illustrate this point.) It is characteristic of some adults that they in fact wait for such repetitions by the child before proceeding with the discourse. These communication checks are not unique to adult-child interaction, however. They are also prevalent in child–child conversational discourse as well:

(23) (Toby and David at 2;11)
DAVID: (putting head on Toby's bed) . . . *Help me/ David's falling/ help me/ David's falling/ help me/ help me/ help me/ Its got me/ help me/ help me/ oooo/.*
TOBY: *Help me/. you saying help me/.* (See also Example (10))

Children often experience enormous difficulty in getting their message across (Ryan, 1974), and many of them come to expect verification of their message through repetition. In the case of Toby and David, when verification was not expressed by a co-conversationalist, the child would solicit it (see Chapter 1 and Keenan and Klein, 1975). The child would repeat his utterance over and over until it was acknowledged:

(24) (Toby and David at 2;10 with their nanny Jill, in the process
of making a picture)

TOBY: *Put it Toby's room/*
JILL: *Toby's got a worm?*
TOBY: *No/ Put it Toby's room/*
JILL: *Toby's what?*
DAVID: *Room/* ⎫
TOBY: *Toby's room/* ⎬ (simultaneously)
JILL: *Toby's room?*
TOBY: *Yeah/*
DAVID: (?)
JILL: *Oh. Put it in Toby's room.*
TOBY: *Yeah/* (See Example 23 for child–child interaction)

The child might accompany his utterance with an explicit request to
attend and acknowledge:

(25) (Toby and David at 3;0)
TOBY: *My big tractors coming/*
DAVID: *No/* (?)
TOBY: *Its coming/* **look** *its coming/ its coming/*
DAVID: *Now its coming/ Its coming/ Its coming/* **look** *its coming/*
TOBY: *I see/*

In short, the children observed in this study established a convention,
whereby given an utterance by one partner, some evidence of attentiveness or base comprehension from the other was expected to follow. It is
certainly the case that adults in our society depend on communication
checks (nods of the head, eye contact, mutterings of 'umhum', etc.)
in talking with one another. However, the dependence does not appear
to be as extreme or as frequent as is the case for young children. For
example, when one adult native speaker converses with another such
speaker, he or she usually assumes that the message has been successfully
decoded by the addressee. Adult speakers usually take it for granted
that conversational partners 'know' in some sense (e.g. are aware of)
the messages previously exchanged in the course of a particular conversation. In the absence of a challenge from the addressee, a speaker can
treat these utterances as shared knowledge (Givon, 1975a), and in
subsequent discourse, he or she can consider these utterances to be
known, or old information.

Children, on the other hand, cannot make these assumptions.

Because of the production difficulties they experience on all levels (phonological, syntactic, semantic), they cannot assume that their utterances have been decoded. Simply uttering a proposition does not assure that it is 'shared knowledge' between speaker and addressee. *Hence, what communication checks do is to precisely turn an utterance into shared knowledge.* That is, when an addressee repeats (expands) an antecedent utterance, he evidences his knowledge of that utterance. Henceforth, both interlocutors can treat the propositions contained in the utterance as given or old information.

It is often the case in adult discourse that known or old information emerges as the topic of a subsequent utterance. The topic is the unchallengeable or presupposed element about which some new predication ('comment') is made. Similarly, in the discourse of young children, information made known through repetition may serve as future topics in subsequent discourse. It is often the case that an utterance is produced by one speaker, part or all of it is repeated by the addressee, and the repeated information becomes the topic of a next utterance. For example:

(26) (Toby and David at 2;10, eating lunch)
TOBY: *Piece bread then/*
DAVID: *No piece bread/ piece bread/ Its gone/*
(27) (Toby and David at 2;11 in bedroom. An alarm clock rings.)
DAVID: *Bell/*
TOBY: *Bell/*
DAVID: *Bell/ its mommy's/*
TOBY: *(?) It/*
DAVID: *Was mommy's alarm clock/*
TOBY: *'Larm clock/ yeah/ goes ding dong ding dong/*
DAVID: *No/ no/ goes fip fip/ fip fip/*

These two examples bring out a number of points. Example (26) illustrates the way in which the repeated information may become the topic of a subsequent utterance in the form of a pronoun. Pronouns normally refer to an established or already known referent. In this case, it is perfectly appropriate for the speaker to use a pronoun, because repetition has given the referent this status. In Example (27), we see that the initial utterance *bell* is repeated and treated as the topic of the following utterance *Its mommy's*. Again the known information is represented in the form of a pronoun. On the other hand, the repetition of *alarm clock* later in the dialogue is incorporated directly as topic of *goes ding dong ding dong* without the mediation of a pronoun. Further, Example (27) illustrates nicely the recursive nature of topic-comment sequences in conversational discourse. We see that the new information *bell* serves as old information topic for the comment *was mommy's alarm clock*. However, part of this predicate *alarm clock* becomes old information through repetition by the other child. Having achieved this status, it then becomes the topic of the subsequent utterances *goes ding dong ding dong* and *goes fip fip/ fip fip/*. Whole stretches of discourse are linked in this way: New information is transformed into old information through repetition, yielding topics for subsequent discourse. One positive role of repetition in discourse is, then, to establish topic candidates (see Chapter 1). The topic candidates can be utilized in the discourse of either conversational partner. In Example (26), the child who repeats the utterance exploits it as a topic. In Example (27), we have a case in which the child who introduces the new information is the one who topicalizes it in later discourse. (David first points out the existence of a *bell* and later makes a claim about it: *its mommy's*, etc.)

Two additional points need to be made with respect to the role of repetition in establishing topic candidates. The first is that such sequences are characteristic of many adult–child interactions as well as child–child interactions. It is often the case that an adult will present new information, the child will repeat some or all of it, and will use it as the topic of utterances:

(28) (Toby and David at 2;9 with their nanny, Jill)
JILL: *Jiji's going camping this afternoon.*
TOBY: *Oh yeah/*
DAVID: *Camping/ oh exciting/* } (simultaneously)

Or the child will initiate an assertion, the adult will repeat it and use it subsequently as a topic:

(29) (Toby and David at 2;9 with their nanny, Jill)
TOBY: *Jiji's wonderful/*
JILL: *Wonderful. I know it.*

With respect to the earlier mentioned topic of children who are imitators and those who are not, it may be worth investigating if the so-called non-imitators engage in conversations primarily like Example (29), whereas the so-called imitators engage in conversations primarily like Example (28). That is, it may be characteristic of some caretaker–child interactions that the caretaker takes an utterance of a child and makes it old information through repetition, using it as a topic in further discourse. This kind of discourse would give a 'non-imitative' look to the child's utterances. In other caretaker–child interactions, however, the child himself or herself may transform the utterance of another into old information through repetition ('imitating'), providing either the caretaker or the child with a topic candidate.

Second, now that we understand some of the work that is being carried out through discourse, we can understand more clearly the meaning of any single utterance of an interlocutor (child or adult). For example, we can retrace the history of the discourse to isolate the communicative work of an utterance. In many cases (though by no means in all cases), the first mention of a referent by a child or by an adult talking to a child is simultaneously a claim and a request to be ratified as a topic candidate. The second mention of the referent (the repetition) ratifies the information as known, and subsequent mentions take for granted that it is established, old information.

Furthermore, without discourse history, it would be difficult to separate what is new information from what is old information in any single utterance. That is, it would be difficult to isolate what is being asserted from what is already taken for granted or presupposed. The linguist cannot, for example, rely on the range of syntactic cues expressing old information in adult speech. The use of pronouns to express old information is a relatively late development in child language (Bloom et al., 1975). Further, even if pronouns are available for this purpose, as in the speech of Toby and David, there still is an absence of definite articles, relative clause nominalizations, and other syntactic means for codifying taken-for-granted information. For many children, taken-for-granted information is marked through discourse and not through syntax. Ratification of a word, phrase, etc., in discourse is sufficient in itself to establish these items as presupposed in subsequent utterances. This is the case in Example (27), where *alarm clock* is the old information, or topic addressed by the next two utterances *goes ding dong ding dong* and *no/ no/ goes fip fip/ fip fip/*. We end this chapter with the hypothesis that cross-utterance repetition anticipates the syntactic marking of old information, and that heavy reliance on repetition gives way once syntactic devices for topicalization emerge in the child's speech corpus.

3

Evolving discourse – the next step[1]

E. Ochs Keenan

3.1 Introduction

In this paper I examine the transition in young children from highly repetitious conversational discourse to formally and semantically more diverse discourse. In previous papers (see Chapter 1 and Chapter 2) I have suggested that the decline of X-utterance repetition was linked in part to the child's developing use of old information markers, such as anaphoric pronouns, definite articles and so on. For example, whereas at an earlier stage a child might respond to the utterance 'Tractor's comin'' by repeating 'Tractor's comin'', at a later stage the child might respond 'It's comin''. Both responses are performing the same pragmatic work; for example, they both acknowledge the previous speaker's utterance, but the latter looks considerably more like adult discourse. Here I wish to focus on related dimensions of this critical transition. I would like to claim that the transition is marked by two developments: first, a development in the formal relation obtaining across utterances; second, a development in the semantic links obtaining between lexical items across utterances.

3.2 Data base

The present analysis is based on audio and video taped conversation of twin boys, Toby and David. The children, 2 years 9 months at the outset of the observations, were recorded on three successive days each month for a year. The primary setting for the conversations was the children's bedroom in the early morning hours. However, conversations accompanying meals, baths and organized games were also recorded.

3.3 Formal relations across utterances

In this section, I examine 'repetition' as a formal operation. Not all instances of X-utterance repetition are the same. The data show that when a child repeats a previous utterance, he utilizes two formal strategies (one or both). One strategy is to take an antecedent utterance and repeat all or part of it without interrupting it in any way:

(1) (Toby and David at 2;11, bedroom)
(David picks up stuffed rabbit and truck. Toby begins to whistle)
DAVID: *rabbit* (2X)/ *I find truck/ rabbit/* (?) *as like rabbit/ truck/ rabbit/ truck/ rabbit/ truck truck rabbit/ truck/ rabbit/ truck/ rabbit/ truck/ rabbit/* (David shows truck and rabbit to Toby)
TOBY: *truck/ rabbit/*

This relation across utterances I have called the focus operation (Chapter 1): one or more lexical items in an antecedent utterance is 'focused' on and repeated without disruption in subsequent utterances. Focus operations were characteristic not only of referential discourse; they also appeared in nonsense discourse or sound play:

(2) (Toby and David at 2;9, bedroom)
TOBY: *i:ja/ gi:ja/*
DAVID: *gi:ja/* Both Toby and David laugh)/ *dabut* (15X)
TOBY: *da:but* (2X)/

A second strategy is to repeat part of an antecedent utterance but replace a lexical item appearing in the antecedent string with a different lexical item. Both the lexical item and its replacement perform the same semantic role in the utterances, e.g. both function as agents, vocatives, existential nominals, and so on:

(3) (Toby and David at 2;9, bedroom)
TOBY: *hello* (3X)/ *hello gramma* (2X)/
DAVID: *hello grampa/*

I have called such an operation a substitution operation (Chapter 1). Substitution operations also appeared in sound play: a single phone or phone sequence in an antecedent string is replaced in a subsequent string:

(4) (Toby and David at 2;9, bedroom)
DAVID: *i:bi:/ i:ji:/*
TOBY: *iji:/ i:ji:/ i:gɔd/*

DAVID: (laughs) /š/ /š/ /i:ji:/ /i:kaki/
TOBY: /i:/ɛ :/ /i:gɔl/

Although both focus and substitution operations appear in the earliest discourse examined (2;9), substitution was utilized far less frequently than focus. Examining a sample of 500 utterances at 2;9, I found 235 tokens of focus as opposed to 72 tokens of substitution. I would like to argue that substitution operations are more complex than focus operations. In substitution operations, the child not only repeats, he attends to the constraints of a particular environment within an antecedent utterance and substitutes items appropriate to that environment.

Table 3.1 Occurrences of focus and substitution operations,
from 2;9 to 3.0 (sample: 500 utterances)

	2;9	3;0
Focus (total)	235	161
Sound play	98	1
Referential	137	160
Substitution (total)	72	77
Sound play	49	7
Referential	23	70
Anaphora (total)	8	45

That substitution is a more complex operation than focusing is supported by the data:

1. Although at 2;9, both operations appear in sound play and referential discourse, focus operations figure prominently in both contexts whereas substitution operations are confined largely to sound plays (see Table 3.1). For example, of the 72 tokens of substitution found in the 500 utterance sample, 49 (68 per cent) appear in sound play. If we agree that sound play is an inherently simpler form of speech behaviour than referential discourse,[2] then it appears that substitution is limited primarily to 'easy' discourse.

2. If we follow the use of these operations in conversational discourse from 2;9 to 3;0, we see that the ratio of substitution to focus increases. Whereas at 2;9 the ratio of substitution to focus was 1:3.26, at 3;0 the ratio was 1:2.09. In terms of gross number of occurrences, the number of focus operations decreases (235 to 161), whereas the number of substitution operations increases (72 to 77).

3. Although the increase in occurrences of sound play from 2;9 to 3;0 appears to be minimal, the gross total is deceptive. Breaking substitution into sound play and referential, substitution operations increases sharply (23 to 70) and the number of sound play substitutions decreases sharply (40 to 7). The dramatic increase in referential substitution (over 200 per cent) is not matched in referential focus (16 per cent) during this time.

To summarize, at 2;9 focus operations are used more widely and more frequently than substitution operations. However, over time, substitution operations come to be used more and more. The children begin to rely on substitution in contexts where previously focus operations predominated.

3.4 The role of sound play in discourse operations

The findings in Table 3.1 suggest that sound play plays an important role in the development of more sophisticated discourse operations. In particular, sound play appears to function as a testing ground for the use of substitution operations. That this is the case is strongly supported by Table 3.1. For example, we see that substitution operations figure more prominently in sound play than referential discourse at 2;9. Further, as substitution operations begin to be regularly employed in referential discourse, sound play as a discourse mode begins to die out. By 3;0, sound play is nearly extinct. On the other hand, at 3;0, substitution is an unmarked mode for achieving coherency in discourse.

Further evidence for the instrumental role of sound play in developing complex discourse operations comes from examining particular expressions of these operations. If we examine examples of substitution, we see that two dimensions at least may vary: the number of items replaced in a single utterance and the number of successive utterances linked by substitution operations.

Considering the first of these, we see that, at 2;9, substitution operations apply to only one item in referential discourse. There are no cases of multiple substitution. In sound play at 2;9, however, we find the discourse laced with simultaneous substitution of phone sequences:

(5) (Toby and David at 2;9, bedroom)
DAVID: *latlaju:/*
TOBY: *latlodu:/ latlogu:/*
DAVID: *latlodo/*

(6) (Toby and David at 2;9, bedroom)
DAVID: *hekʌt/*
TOBY: *bekʌp/*
DAVID: *brekʌt/ brekʌp/*

Multiple substitutions appear in referential discourse at 2;10 and continue throughout the following months:

(7) (Toby and David at 2;10, afternoon nap)
    (toy breaks)
DAVID: *mend it/*
TOBY: *I might mend it now/*
DAVID: *ah/* (shrieks)/
TOBY: *I maybe fix it now/*
(8) (Toby and David at 2;11, bedroom)
    (David drawing on window with finger)
DAVID: *this is two/ thats one/*
(9) (Toby and David at 3;0, bedroom)
    (Toby relating narrative)
TOBY: *one day/ was little rabbit/ . . ./ one day was big farmer left/*

In terms of the number of successive utterances linked through substitution operations, sound play again anticipates referential usage. Longer substitution sequences emerge in sound play before they emerge in referential discourse. This is particularly true in the case of substitutions involving other speakers' utterances. In sound play at 2;9, substitution across three or more turns occurs (see Examples (4), (5) and (6) above). On the other hand, the substitution of lexical items is limited to a single exchange in referential discourse at this time (see Example (3) above). Longer stretches of discourse linked through substitution appear at 2;10:

(10) (Toby and David at 2;10, kitchen)
DAVID: *what's this/*
TOBY: *kamon:ni:z^3/*
DAVID: *no macaronis/ skɛti:z^4/*
TOBY: *sʌbatiskɛti^4/*

By 3;0, sequences such as the following are routine:

(11) (Toby and David at 3;0, bedroom)
TOBY: *tractors coming/*
DAVID: *my truck is coming/*
TOBY: *cars coming so fast/*

DAVID: *its going fast now/*
TOBY: *cars coming/*
DAVID: *cars coming now/ my cars coming now/*
TOBY: *my big tractors coming/*

The suggestion has been in the air for some time that sound play may be instrumental in developing morphemic and syntactic structure (Jakobson, 1968; Weir, 1962). I would like to suggest that this sort of play is instrumental in developing discourse structure as well. This study supports earlier research carried out by Garvey (1974) and by Keenan (1974b; Keenan and Klein, 1975) that finds conversational skills in themselves a resource for co-operative play.

3.5 Substitution and semantic domains

Much attention has been directed to the development of substitution operations because these operations appear critical to the transition away from highly repetitious discourse. When a child uses substitution operations, he sets up contextual frames in which particular lexical items are contrasted:

(12) (Toby and David at 2;9, bedroom)
     (both see moth)
DAVID: *two moths/*
TOBY: *many moths/*
(13) (Toby and David at 2;11, bedroom)
DAVID: *i:^{5} raining down/*
TOBY: *i: raining some up there/*
DAVID: *i: raining again/*
TOBY: *i: raining cold/*
(14) (Toby and David at 3;0, bedroom)
DAVID: *`I drive it/*
TOBY: *`you could drive/ `you drive it/ `my drive it too/*

The lexical items appearing in these frames have at least that environment in common. From the child's point of view, the items undergoing substitution share some features, and hence members of some semantic domain: items that refer to quantity (Examples (8), (12)), agents (or drivers, as in Example (14)), things that move (Example (11)), things to eat (Example (10)), and so on. It is of course extremely difficult to assess the exact nature of the domain. It is difficult to judge whether, for example, in (11) the child thinks of cars, trucks and tractors as vehicles or things that move or things with wheels, and so on. However, it is the domain-creating process itself which is significant.

I would like to claim that the creation of lexical sets through substitution operations is instrumental in developing discourse that is not bound by the here-and-now. As discussed in Keenan and Klein (1975), before substitution operations are prominent, the child relies heavily on items that are acoustically or visually salient in the immediate context in creating coherent discourse. That is, the child would make use of things he heard (e.g. repeating prior utterances) or things he saw in producing relevant responses. In substituting, however, the child goes beyond replicating what he hears or sees. Like the adult, the child draws on his background knowledge to respond relevantly to some prior utterance. The initial speaker also draws on his background knowledge in accepting the response as relevant to his contribution.

In examining the conversations between Toby and David from 2;9 to 3;0, I find that relevant next responses draw more and more from knowledge of semantic domains and depend less and less on the form of the previous speaker's utterance. The child stops relying primarily on repetition as a means of acknowledging a previous conversational contribution. Substitution operations create discourse that is intermediate to these stages. It is a form of repetition, and it is based on background knowledge.

In many cases, it looks as if the children's discourse is motivated by their interest in semantic paradigms. Conversations may at first focus on semantic set and then drift on to other sets, leaving unresolved an initial discussion:

(15) (Toby and David at 3;0, bedroom)
TOBY: *my told you/ called shoes/*
DAVID: *I told you/ its slippers/ I told you/ its not shoes/ I told*
         you not shoes/ it slippers/
TOBY: *Its one slipper/*
DAVID: *two slippers/ two slippers/ I told you/*
TOBY: *one slipper/*
DAVID: *its one slipper/ I smack your ear/*

In this discourse, the children are first concerned with things you put on your feet, and then move on to the quantity of these things present.

Monologues as well often move in and out of several domains as (16) illustrates:

(16) (Toby and David at 3;0)
    (David looking at book)
DAVID: *Peter Rabbit was// bunny/*
TOBY: *// Mr MacGregor/*
DAVID: *was a tiny rabbit/ go hippity hop hippity hop/ two little*
            rabbits/ called Lucy/ One day was big farmer left/ and
            left cow/ . . .

In this narrative, the child replaces 'bunny' with 'tiny rabbit' and then goes on to discuss the quantity of rabbits ('two little', 'lot of') and so on.

Notice in (16) that some of the utterances appear to play on what constitute binary contrasts in the adult lexicon. The child talks about something small ('little rabbit') and then goes on to refer to something big ('big farmer'). This type of contrast is extremely common in the conversational data.[6] An item is referred to in an initial utterance, and in subsequent utterances an item that contrasts with it is incorporated:

(17) (Toby and David at 2;11, bedroom)
    (Toby and David standing by window)
DAVID: *my hands are cold* (2X)/ *I go sit down there/*
TOBY: (opening curtains) *curtains up* (2X)/ *I so hot/ curtains up/*

3.6 Emerging discourse skills

The development of semantic domains in conversational discourse has far-reaching effects. One effect is that the child is able to use paraphrase to correct or 'repair' (Schegloff, personal communication) his own utterance.

(18) (Toby and David at 3;0, bedroom)
    (Toby relating narrative)
TOBY: *. . . I saw/ no/ Toby saw/ I saw one on road/*
DAVID: *did you?/*
TOBY: *yeah/*

The child may paraphrase in anticipation of another's misunderstanding or in response to a request for clarification from another speaker.

A second manifestation of the emergence of semantic domains in discourse is the emergence of anaphoric pronouns. The use of a pronoun as a replacement for a noun form involves all the formal and semantic skills discussed in this paper. It requires that the child has competence in the formal operation of substitution. And it requires that the child has a sense of semantic appropriateness — that two or more lexical items are appropriate descriptions for some referent. As indicated in Table 3.1, the use of anaphoric pronouns increases dramatically from 2;9 to 3;0 and in many ways parallels the emergence of substitution operations. Anaphora itself, however, was not necessarily manifest through the substitution operation. Normally anaphora was part of some formally novel utterance.

(19) (Toby and David at 2;11, bedroom)
     (David shows battery to Toby)
DAVID: *see battery/*
TOBY: *I see it/*
DAVID: *you see it?/*

In the discourse observed, anaphora began to be employed regularly after substitution operations were commonplace. Its appearance marks the move away from highly repetitious discourse.

3.7 Conclusion

This paper has documented ways in which young children construct coherent discourse at different stages in their development. It has indicated that young children are sensitive to Grice's (1975) maxim 'Be Relevant' and are able to produce utterances that relate to prior utterances at a fairly early point in time. The paper has addressed the relation between emergence of discourse skills, namely competence in producing coherent discourse, and emergence of knowledge of semantic domains. On a methodological level, the paper indicates that that the study of children's discourse can reveal their knowledge of semantic domains. As such, children's discourse is an excellent source for research on acquisition of meaning.

Notes

1. This research was supported by the Social Science Research Council, Grant no. HR 2941/1.
2. The child in sound play is constrained only by the phonological and morphological structure of his language without regard to meaning. In referential discourse, the child must contend with both.
3. Macaroni.
4. Spaghetti.

5. Deictic particle.
6. The type of phenomenon apparent in (15)–(17) has been discussed by sociologists (Jefferson, 1974; Sacks, 1968; Schegloff, personal communication) for adult conversation.

4

Looking and talking: the functions of gaze direction in the conversations of a young child and her mother[1]

Bambi B. Schieffelin

4.1 Introduction

Everyone acknowledges that very small children can communicate before they put words together. Using very little language they are able to express their wants and needs as well as to sustain interactions. One of the resources available to them before they have developed sophisticated verbal skills is the use of non-verbal behaviours, such as gazing. This case study documents how one child (age 16,3–22 months) used gaze in relation to talk while interacting with her mother. Following a brief review of the literature on the relationship between talking and looking, the results of this naturalistic study will be presented. The significance of looking at the mother will be discussed in terms of how it functions for the language-learning child, for the mother, and the insights it can provide for the researcher interested in the development of communicative competence.

4.2 Previous research

The relationship between gaze and speech in interaction is part of a large body of research on non-verbal behaviour and communication (Weiner et al., 1972). Visual behaviour has been discussed in terms of three main functions in dyadic interaction. Social psychologists have investigated gaze for what it can tell us about the personalities and attributes of individuals (Ellsworth and Ludwig, 1972).

Looking has also been examined for its monitoring function and as a regulator of the pacing and sequencing of talk. The majority of research on adults has been carried out in clinical and experimental settings. The following researchers represent some of the major research in this area: Exline, 1963; Exline and Winters, 1966; Kendon and Cook, 1969; Nielsen, 1962; Argyle and Cook, 1976.

Kendon, working in non-clinical settings, has emphasized the monitoring function of gaze, where the looker can control the degree to which he monitors the other's behaviour. He has also described how gaze acts in its regulatory and expressive function, in that by looking or not looking one can seek to control the behaviour of others. These functions of gaze are seen to have a role in the management of conversation in that gaze direction can signal speaker turn-taking. Kendon suggests that during fluent speech the speaker looks more and during hesitant speech the speaker looks less, needing the time to plan speech as well as hold the turn until he can finish, since only when the speaker is looking at the listener can the listener then take his turn. When the listener takes his turn, he looks away before beginning to speak.

In addition to the literature on gaze during adult interaction, the study of infants' looking has, in recent years, been part of the general interest in the development of social behaviour. Visual contact and facing position between mother and infant have been considered to be cardinal attachment behaviours thought to play an important role in forming early mother–infant ties (Coates et al., 1972; Maccoby and Feldman, 1972; Robson, 1967).

Stern (1971) analysed the visual behaviour of a mother and her infant twins. He found that by the third month of life the visual system can perform subtle instant-by-instant regulation of social contact, giving the infant control over the amount of visual contact he makes. In a second paper Stern (1974) investigated the gaze patterns of mothers and infants at play. Here he suggests that gaze has a signal function in that the onset of gaze signals the readiness and intention to engage in interaction. Gaze aversion is seen as a signal of termination or of reduction in the intensity of interaction. Stern reported great variation in gaze patterns for the same infant on different days as well as across infants. He pointed out that it is the infant, not the mother, who makes and breaks mutual gaze. At this early age infants rely mainly on control by visual attention and only later will rely on vocal and facial behaviours to hold maternal visual attention.

Stern et al. (1975) reported on the high incidence of simultaneous vocalization between 3–4-month-old infants and their mothers. In this study they suggest that this 'coactional' vocalizing pattern conforms closely to the dyadic mutual gazing pattern observed between mother and infant. Furthermore, coactional vocalizing occurs almost invariably during mutual gaze. Unfortunately there is a large gap in the research on infants' vocalizing and looking, and therefore developmental findings are not yet available.

For the purpose of this study, the most relevant research is that of Schaffer et al. (1977) reporting on the vocal behaviours (all utterances both verbal/vocal) and looking patterns of two groups of children. Schaffer et al. examined 10-minute videotaped samples of sixteen mother–child pairs from two age groups. The first group was preverbal and ranged from 12–15 months of age. The second group was verbal and ranged from 23–27 months of age. Schaffer et al. reported that in the videotape samples mothers spent 90 per cent (mean) of the time looking at their child, which is in violation of the gazing patterns described for adults.

There were some clear differences between the two groups. For one, the children in the older group looked at their mothers considerably more often than the younger children. In fact, the mean number of looks more than doubled. Schaffer et al. offered the following explanation for this: 'Impressionistically, it appeared that the older children found it much easier to play *with* the mother, that they were able to include her in their ongoing concerns with toys and that their looking patterns thus reflected this increasing flexibility' (p. 311). However, mean length of looks did not differentiate the groups. These findings were based on cross-sectional data and there was variation within each group. No attempt was made to examine the nature of the vocalizations.

Schaffer et al. also reported that looks for the two-year-olds were not distributed in a random fashion throughout the discourse. Instead, they showed a definite association with the *child's* vocal activity. Looks at the mother tended to begin either during or immediately following the child's utterances. They conclude that it is unlikely that the child's looks play any important part in vocal turn-taking. Furthermore, looks are not used to regulate the exchange of speaker/listener roles. Schaffer et al. see looking in association with talking as fulfilling a monitoring function for the child. It may have signal value for the mother in emphasizing the other-directed nature of the child's vocal behaviour. They conclude that whatever precise functions looks play within the vocal interchange emerges only *after* the onset of language: 'It is also likely that intentional signalling is not an all-or-none ability that develops at the same rate in all behaviour systems' (p. 322). What previous research establishes is that visual behaviour has a number of important functions for the infant–mother relationship. It also changes as the child matures and begins to use language to communicate. Gazing and vocalization patterns of infants and their mothers are radically different from those described in the adult–adult literature. But as in adult patterns, there is individual variation in the amount of looking and in the patterns of looking. Contextual variation has not yet been investigated. One major question that emerges from this previous research is how does the system of looking and talking develop? In particular, are there patterns of gaze that develop as the child develops more complex linguistic structures and a greater variety of communicative acts? What can looking at the language tell us about the functions of gazing patterns?

4.3 The present study

This study differs from the previous research in several ways. It is a longitudinal case study of a single child (age 16,3-22 months) playing with her mother. It builds on research done on language acquisition and examines in detail the language used in naturalistic interaction. The four half-hour videotapes of Lois and Allison Bloom which form the data base of *One Word at a Time* (Bloom, 1973) were used for this analysis. These tapes recorded a variety of naturalistic and spontaneous activities between mother/investigator and her child for a study of language development. These activities took place in a studio 'play space' and the same activities were repeated across sessions, thus making it possible to examine changes in specific events (snack time, doll play) over time. While it would have been preferable to examine the relationships between gaze and talk for both participants, the camera tended to focus on the child's face and the mother's gaze direction could not always be determined. However, when the mother's face is in view, she is gazing almost continuously at her child and engaged in focused interaction with her.

The videotape transcripts included in *One Word at a Time* were coded for all instances of eye contact made by the child with the mother. Using slow-motion video playback, the initiation of Allison's eye contact was noted with a ↑ and the termination of Allison's eye contact was noted with ↓ placed with regard to their temporal relationship to either the ongoing verbal or nonverbal context. It was not difficult to tell when Allison was looking at her mother's face since (because of her size) she had to look up to see her mother, and raised her eyebrows when doing so. It is the case that:

> In real life interaction we tend to either give a direct eye gaze or to look away from the face of another person. This being the case, then observer judgement can be expected to be fairly accurate in studies where eye gaze/non-gaze is monitored (Vine, 1971, p. 326).

4.4 Results

4.4.1 Frequency of eye contact for Allison

To date no norms for frequency of eye contact have been established for individuals at different ages in various situations. As mentioned earlier, research on both children and adults report extensive variation in the amount of time spent in gazing. Rather than computing the amount of time spent in gazing, this researcher counted the number of times Allison made eye contact in each sample. (Recall that the participants and situation were the same for each sample except for the fact of Allison's increasing maturity.)

Table 4.1 Frequency of eye contact, age and language development

Sample	Age (months, weeks)	Language	Number of looks
I	16,3	single words	50
II	19,2	single words	74
III	20,3	MLU* 1.13	78
IV	22	MLU* 1.73	101

* MLU stands for Mean Length of Utterance and is measured in morphemes. (See Brown, 1973.)

Table 4.1 presents the number of looks at mother in each sample and includes information on the increasing complexity of Allison's language. As one can see, over the four samples the number of times Allison made eye contact with her mother doubled. I suggest that this increase is directly related to Allison's increasing ability to mark socially intended interaction and to an increase in socially directed speech.

4.4.2 Types of eye contact

Two patterns of eye contact occur in these data. I have defined them as those occurring within-speaker turn (WST) and across-speaker turn (AST). Within-speaker turn eye contact is made and terminated within a child or adult speaker's turn and has the possibility of four temporal relationships to the speaker's utterance. WST eye contact can occur:

(1) immediately before an utterance (↑↓u/);
(2) after an utterance (u/↑↓) of a speaker (child or mother);
(3) around an utterance (↑u/↓); and
(4) during an utterance (u/$\overset{\uparrow\downarrow}{}$).

WST eye contact may occur with or without an utterance from the child. For example:[2]

WST with child utterance:

↑*mommy open*/↓;

WST without child utterance:
M: *Well, let's have a snack,* ↑*and*
   then we'll put the coat back on. ↓

In the first sample Allison made many WST eye contacts before, during and around her own speech. However, in the II–IV samples she established a pattern of using WST eye contact with speech by looking at her mother immediately before or during her own speech, and looking away from her mother immediately after speaking. This change in Allison's gaze patterns is displayed below:

Sample I   ↑↓u/
              ↑↓
              u/
              ↑u/↓
Sample II–IV ↑u/↓
              ↑
              u/↓

Thus a greater degree of regularity in gazing in relation to speech was established in the II–IV samples.

WST eye contact was used by Allison in a number of patterned ways in the four samples. One of the most frequent occurrences of eye contact was in the context of answering a question. For example:[3]

I:44(16,3)
Is that the lamb?

↑*no*/↓

II:29(19,2)
What't the baby say?

↑ɛ*h*/↓

III:69(20,3)
More? What? More what?

↑*puppet*/↓↑*hair*/↓

IV:46(22)
Are you peeking at the lady?

↑*peeking lady*/↓

In these situations Allison initiates WST eye contact before she begins her answer and terminates eye contact after completing her speech. She does not elicit further talk about the topic by maintaining eye contact into the next speaker's turn.

Another situation in which Allison frequently used WST eye contact was when making a counterclaim to something said by her mother. For example:

> I:79(16,3)
> *Let's put the cows on the chair.*   ↑
>   *no/↓*
>
> III:25(20,3)
> *You have to take your coat off.*
>   *↑on/↓*

In situations such as these eye contact may be used to add emphasis and finality to Allison's responses. She does not watch for what her mother will say next.

A third situation of WST eye contact occurs during Allison's self-repetitions. For example:

> II:3(16,3)
> (Allison sitting on floor)   *man/ man/*
> (Allison pointing to photographer)   *↑man/ man/↓*
> III:32(20,3)
> (Allison holding a zipper)   *zip/↑zip/↓*
> IV:48(22)
> (Allison pointing to a horse that has
> fallen down)   *horse tumble/↑horse tumble/↓*
> (Allison pointing again)   *horse tumble/*
> *Horse tumble. Yes, the horse fell down.*

It appears that two tasks are being accomplished — the production of the utterance and the marking of that utterance as social through the use of eye contact. These self-repetitions were said in rapid succession. Thus it is highly unlikely that self-repetition in these cases was due to lack of listener response.

The second major pattern of Allison's looking is across (at least one) speaker turn. For example:

> IV:20(22)
> *What are you doing?*
> (Allison wiping her chin with her dress) *baby lap// wiping baby↑ chin/*
> *Wiping baby chin? How bout wiping*
> *your chin with your napkin?↓*

Like WST, AST eye contacts occurred with Allison's responses to her mother's questions.

IV:5(22)
What were we gonna do?

eat/ ↑cookies/

Shall we eat cookies?

ah/

Shall we?

mm/

Mmm hm. That's a good idea. ↓

However, unlike the situations in which WST eye contact is used, Allison used AST contact to elicit a response from her mother. Allison did not terminate eye contact until she received a confirmation of her suggestion ('eat cookies'), in this sequence taking five speaker turns. Additionally, in yes/no questions (which occurred in sample IV) Allison used AST looks when she was adding new information and was monitoring her mother, waiting to have a confirmation of what she has said.

IV:49(22)
Is this the big cow?

no/ ↑tiny/

Tiny. ↓

AST eye contacts also occurred with Allison's self-repetitions.

III:11(20,3)
(Allison sits on the floor)   *mommy/ floor/*
(Mother standing)   *↑mommy/ floor/*
Mommy floor?

down/ ↓sit down/
↑sit down/↓

These two patterns of gaze, WST and AST, differ in that WST eye contact does not elicit a listener response. It often has the effect of terminating the topic of conversation. AST eye contact, in contrast, does elicit more from the adult listener, and gives the next turn to that person. Other researchers have not discussed these two types of gazing so one cannot know if they reflect an individual pattern, a developmental stage or a pattern that is found in other white middle-class speakers of English. In any case, the use of both patterns of eye contact supports the communication that occurs in these speech events.

The general trend over the four samples was a decrease proportionally in WST eye contact (70–55 per cent) and an increase proportionally in AST eye contact (30–45 per cent). This is in keeping with the general increase in conversation and socially directed speech.

4.4.3 Patterns of eye contact and the structure of speech events

The videotape transcripts in *One Word at a Time* are divided into speech events 'primarily for the purpose of reference. The criterion used for the division was essentially a shift in topic' (p. 148). Eye contact does not occur randomly throughout all speech events. In some speech events there are no instances of eye contact. For example:

II:51(19,3)
(Allison pushes truck past Mother off
rug; stands up)   *uh!/*
(Allison pulling truck back on to rug)   *back/*
Back.
(Allison struggling to pull truck onto
rug)   *up/*
Off?
(Allison getting truck onto rug)   *there/ up/*
On?
(Allison pulling truck closer)   *on/*
(Allison standing up)   *there!/*
IV:36(22)
(Allison going to truck with horse
in hand)   *dump truck/* X/
(Allison trying to put horse in truck)   *dump truck/* 3X
(Allison finally gets horse in truck)   *dump truck/*

In these speech events Allison is concentrating on her own actions or goals and apparently not intending to communicate them to her mother.

In other speech events there are numbers of or clusters of eye contacts made by Allison. As Allison gets older, eye contacts (which increase in number) also tend to cluster within speech events and topics. One might ask what there is in certain speech events which might account for these marked differences in visual behaviour.

After careful examination of the patterns of clusters of eye contacts (both WST and AST) I found that these patterns are related to and support Bloom's proposed two types of event structures in early language.

As a first type Bloom describes events with chained successive utterances which occur with successive movements and shifting goals (Bloom, 1973, p. 47). An example of this, II:51, is cited above; in this example the child's utterances are tied to particular movements or shifts in context. Her speech is not directed to her mother as she comments on her own actions. Eye contact does not occur in speech events such as these.

The second type of structure Bloom describes is one with holistic successive utterances in which the entire situation appears to be defined to begin with, and utterances are not tied to particular movements (ibid.).

II:80 (19,3)
(Allison picking up blanket; handing
blanket to Mother)   *blanket/ ↑cover/*
Blanket? Cover?↓
(Allison touches doll's head)   *head/*
(Allison touching doll's head in
front of her)   *↑head/ head/*↓
Head?

                                                ↑cover/↓

Cover her head?

In this example Allison's utterances are not tied to specific movements, nor is her speech a comment on her own actions. She clearly has a goal in mind, to have her mother cover the doll's head. Her speech is supported by her visual behaviour which adds social force to her request.

Although both kinds of event structures existed in each video sample, there is a developmental progression from predominantly chained successive utterances to holistic successive utterances in the period from 16,3–22 months (Bloom, 1973, p. 50). The increase in both the number of eye contacts, use of eye contact across speaker turns (AST), and the clustering pattern of both rapid and sustained eye contacts within speech events directly corresponds to the two types of event structures described by Bloom.

All events in samples II–IV that had clusterings of eye contact were holistic in structure. As Bloom describes the holistic structure, successive utterances are related to each other in that they refer to a mental representation of a set of intersecting relations in an immediately anticipated event. When Allison had the whole event in mind she did not need as much contextual support from her immediate physical surroundings. That is, in terms of her visual behaviour, she was not looking for objects that would aid in the unfolding of an as yet unformed

event as she was with the chained structure. She did not need to draw
upon the objects that were around her to help get her ideas about the
objects across. In addition, she could use language in ways that were
less tied to the immediate context. In fact, in events where Allison
had the whole idea or goal in mind, she could direct her gaze to the
person to whom she was speaking, with whom she was exchanging
information. When utterances were planned (holistic) Allison could
mark her utterances as social since the very act of looking at someone
marks the exchange as socially directed, socially intended, and not
self-directed.

Not all holistic events in these data occur with clusters of eye
contact. The reason for this is that although the child may have the
'idea in mind', she may not be directing the speech to another person.
For example, in pretence situations when Allison is directing her speech
to a doll or animal she does not make eye contact with her mother
unless she wishes to include her mother in the interaction. We can say,
then, when the child has the 'idea in mind' (holistic) and intends to
share it with someone else, we find clusters of eye contact in the
speech event.

4.4.4 *Patterns of eye contact and the pragmatics of speech events*

One of the defining characteristics of a holistic speech event is that
the child has the whole schema in mind at the outset. Several types of
speech acts (within speech events) require this in order for there to be
successful communication. One of these speech acts is requests; others
include conversational exchanges and narratives. In the data examined
for this paper there are a large number of requests and conversational
exchanges which are accompanied by clusters of eye contact.

Before a request can be responded to effectively, the speaker must
secure the attention of the listener (see Chapter 5). Use of the vocative,
body positioning, pointing and eye contact are all important attention-
getting devices, signalling to the addressee an intention to share information. In her discussion of holistic event structures (Bloom, 1973,
p. 51) Bloom says, 'from her speech and behavior and the context,
it was clear that Allison wanted me to wipe the doll's bottom (III:90),
and zip up her coat (III:3)'. These requests are marked by a number
of non-verbal social behaviours, i.e. giving the doll to be wiped and
making eye contact. For example:

III:61(20,3)
(Allison holding doll out to Mother)   *Mommy/ ↑help/*
Mommy help?↓

Requests that are adequately marked as socially directed (as well as being verbally informative) are responded to by the mother throughout. However, there are other occurrences of verbal requests that do not get responded to. For example:

IV:19(22)
(Allison looking down at unopened
can on floor)   *Mommy open/*

In this situation Allison has not marked her utterance as socially directed and it gets lost. However, one may also imagine that Allison was not really interested in the opening of the can and that her own level of involvement was in fact quite low.

As Allison matures she increasingly has conversations with her mother that are both related and unrelated to the immediate context. These speech events, which may involve retelling an event from the past (either recent or relatively distant) or negotiating a solution to a problem, co-occur with clusters of eye contact. In these speech events Allison is drawing on her mental representations of events and engaging in communicating them with her mother. For example:

III:21(20,3)
(Allison wants to put a diaper on
her doll)
We don't have any pins.

                                         buy↑ store/

Buy store?

                                         pin/

Buy pins at store?↓

                                         mm/

*Okay, maybe we will buy pins
at the store.*
(Allison pointing to doll)   *baby doll/ pin/ baby/ doll/
                                         ↑baby doll/*

Baby doll?↓

                                         sharp/ ↑hand/

Sharp? Hands?↓ What's sharp?

                                         ↑pin/

Oh, a pin is sharp, isn't it?↓

In this event Allison uses a series of AST eye contacts to elicit response and feedback from her mother. She manages to control the topic of conversation by indicating her interest and waiting to hear what her mother says in response to her talk.

IV:58(22)
(Allison puts pig in truck as she squats over truck)
(Allison starts to sit on truck, sharp corner hits her bottom; Allison pushes truck away)
(Allison touching sharp corner of truck with her finger)   *bang/*
(Allison pointing to her back)   *baby↑ back/*
Bang baby back?↓
(Allison pointing to sharp corner)   *sharp/*
Oh it's sharp?↑ Oh, I see. Yes, it is sharp.↓

                                              baby ride truck!/↑
Baby ride truck? Can you ride that truck?

                                              sharp/
It's sharp.↓ So you have to be careful.↑
(Allison putting hand on back)   *back/↓*
What's on your back?
(Allison putting pig to sharp corner of truck)   *pig/ pig/*
(Pulling pig back to her)   *↑sharp!/↓*
Oh, it's sharp.
(Allison showing pig to Mother 'twisting' at its tail)   *↑pig/ pig/ ↓↑pig/ pig/↓*
What — What's that? What is that? That's the pig's —
(Allison pointing to pig's tail)   *hurt knee/*
Oh, he hurt his knee?
(Allison pointing to truck)   *hurt/ ↑hurt truck/↓*
Hurt truck?↑ Did he hurt his knee?↓ Or did he hurt the —
(Allison looking at pig)   *be careful/*
Be —

(Allison pointing to truck)   ↑*sharp*/
Be careful! It's sharp! Yes, please
be careful.

                                               hmm/↓

In this speech event Allison is truly concerned with including her mother in her activities and telling her what is on her mind. She manages to maintain the topic of conversation by including her mother and using objects when she needs them. Throughout this speech event Allison is very excited and maintains her mother's involvement by constantly looking at her for an acknowledgement of her understanding. Allison terminates the interaction by turning away her gaze when she is convinced that her mother has understood her. By examining the use of eye contact one can see when she is intending to communicate with her mother and when she is 'talking to the pig'.

Over the four samples there is an increase in the social marking of requests as well as an increase in conversation. Allison is learning not only how to formulate her ideas verbally but she is also learning the concomitant nonverbal skills required to support the type of communication she wishes to have. The appropriate use of gaze direction is part of the communicative competence that Allison is learning at this time.

4.4.5 Patterns of eye contact and affect

On another level altogether is the use of eye contact and affect. This included laughing, teasing and acknowledging pretence. Eye contact co-occurs with these behaviours as a communicative act with increasing frequency in the second through to the fourth samples.

IV:15(22)
(Allison is eating Mother's cookie and
showing it to Mother)   ↑*eat Mommy* ↓↑*cookie*/
Eat Mommy's cookie? Are you
eating Mommy's cookie?↓
(Allison and Mother laugh)   ↑*mm*/↓
Oh. Funny.
(Allison looking at her own cookie
in her hand)   *Allison cookie*/↑↓
Allison's cookie, mm.
(Allison looking at Mother's cookie
in Allison's hand)   ↑*eating Mommy cookie*/

Eating Mommy cookie.
(Allison gives cookie to Mother)
Thank you, darling. ↓

Using eye contact while teasing and laughing indicates to the mother that Allison knows that she is playfully teasing. It communicates the message of 'play' and that Allison is not seriously intending to eat the cookie, but to tease her mother. In situations such as these eye contact marks intimacy and the sharing of a mutually understood pretence or tease. Particularly in the second through to the fourth tapes when a lot of smiling and laughing occurs, eye contact accompanies these behaviours.

4.5 Conclusions

As the results of this case study indicate, the examination of the relationship between speech and visual behaviour can offer insights into the processes involved in the child's developing social and communicative skills.

We may approach the functions of visual behaviour from three perspectives: the point of view of the listener (mother), speaker (child) and researcher. From the perspective of the listener, the child's use of eye contact signals that her message is socially intended and directed to a specific person. Often, the very act of looking at an adult elicits a response or inquiry. Looking, therefore, is a signal indicating interest and readiness, whereas not looking can be an indicator of disinterest. A look from the child can indicate to the listener that she is expected by the child to respond.

From the point of view of the child/speaker, looking at and watching the listener during conversations functions to monitor the facial expressions and to collect information regarding the listener's understanding of and attitudes towards what the child is saying. In these four video-tapes there is substantial evidence of Allison's increasing capabilities along these lines. This is most clearly indicated where Allison uses eye contact across-speaker turns and socially marks requests and conversation with her gaze.

From the perspective of the researcher, gaze direction can provide supporting evidence for determining the pragmatics of speech events. Gaze direction is an important indicator of the intentionality of a child utterance, for example IV:16 and IV:19. Over time, the increase in eye contact during situations of pretence indicates the child's growing awareness of the different levels of activity she is involved in. In addition, the use of eye contact may be seen as part of the growing communicative competence of the language-learning child, and can provide supportive evidence for such phenomena as differing structures in speech events, as proposed by Bloom (1973).

To date, research on the relationships between talking and looking is very much in the early stages. We know that there are significant cultural differences in the ways that gaze behaviour is used (Byers and Byers, 1972). Excessive gaze aversion is a primary indicator of infantile autism (Hutt and Ounsted, 1966). Scaife and Bruner (1975) have demonstrated that prelinguistic infants could follow another person's line of regard to an object. Prior to 11 months of age, infants were aided by pointing and vocalizations, but after 11 months, they were able to follow the adult's eye movements alone. As Scaife and Bruner point out, 'It is possible that the ability to orient with respect to another has implications for Piaget's more complex notions of the egocentric child. In so far as mutual orientation implies a degree of knowledge in some form about another person's perspective then the child in its first year may be considered as less than completely egocentric' (p. 266). As Bruner (1980) points out, these behaviours must be conventionalized and rule governed in order to become communicative later on. But at this time we do not know how young children develop and use gaze behaviour in conversation. The conventions of use have not yet been documented. However, by exploring the use of visual behaviour vis-à-vis the speech situations in which it occurs, we can come to know more about the ways in which children learn to initiate, maintain, and terminate conversational exchanges using both their non-verbal and verbal skills.

Notes

1. Many thanks to Lois Bloom for helpful suggestions on an earlier draft of this paper.
2. Transcription conventions for all examples follow Bloom and Lahey, 1978. Child speech is on the right and uses a slash (/) to indicate utterance boundaries; X/ indicates repetition. Mother's speech and all contextual information is on the left.
3. Examples taken from *One Word at a Time* (Bloom, 1973) are marked by sample number (Roman numeral), speech event number, and age (in months and weeks) in parentheses.

5

Topic as a discourse notion:
a study of topic in the conversations
of children and adults[1,2]

E. Ochs Keenan and Bambi B. Schieffelin

5.1 Orientation and goals

Topic has been described as a discourse notion (see, for example, Chafe, 1972; Li and Thompson, 1976). However, there has been no systematic study in linguistics of the way in which topics are initiated, sustained and/or dropped in naturally-occurring discourse. This paper addresses itself to this concern. It draws from notions developed by sociologists engaged in conversational analysis and integrates them with our own observations of the conversations of children and adults. Our observations include nonverbal as well as verbal contexts in which topics are entertained by interlocutors. On the basis of this record, the prerequisite steps for getting a topic into the discourse are characterized and a notion of discourse topic is defined.

In everyday conversations much of the talk that occurs concerns propositions about persons, objects or ideas. Moreover, when individuals, objects, etc., are not known to the hearer, the hearer initiates a series of fairly predictable exchanges directed at clarifying and locating the referent about which some claim is being made.

Consider, for example, the following exchange in which the speakers are eating dinner:

(1) a. Bambi: *It's coming out fast.* (shaking salt on food)
     b. Elinor: *What's coming out fast?*
     c. Bambi: *The salt.*

In this exchange, Bambi assumes that Elinor is attending to her actions and is able to locate in the environment the referent of 'it'. Elinor, however, has not been attending to Bambi's action and cannot identify that referent. Further, Elinor had no clues from prior discourse; Bambi did not precede the utterance with talk about salt, e.g. 'Pass me the salt.' In other words, Elinor had no source for identifying the referent, and consequently, she did not understand what Bambi was talking about.

Clark and Haviland (1977) have pointed out that when speaker-hearers engage in talk, they abide by a 'Given-New contract', that is, the speaker is responsible for marking syntactically as 'Given' that information that he thinks the listener already knows, and marks as 'New' what he thinks the listener does not know. For example, it is appropriate for the speaker to use syntactic devices such as definite articles, pseudo-cleft constructions and anaphoric pronouns when he thinks the listener knows the referent. Indefinite articles and cleft constructions appropriately mark the information that is New to the listener. The appropriate marking of Given and New is critical to the listener's comprehension of particular utterances. Information marked as Given leads the listener to search for its 'unique antecedent' in memory or in the ongoing situation. The listener 'then integrates the New information into memory at that point' (Haviland and Clark, 1974, p. 513).

Analyses of spontaneous conversations show that listeners demand that the Given-New contract be adhered to. That is, listeners will not accept as Given referents that they cannot identify in terms of general knowledge, prior discourse or present context. Speakers make an effort as well to insure that listeners can identify what or whom they are talking about. One device employed by the speaker (in English) is to describe an object or individual using rising intonation. Sacks and Schegloff (1974) call such a construction a 'try-marker'. The speaker leaves a short pause following this construction in which the listener can evidence his recognition or non-recognition of the referent. Absence of a positive listener response (uh huh, head nod, etc.) in this pause indicates non-recognition. This in turn leads the speaker to offer further try-markers in an attempt to elicit a positive listener response.

(2) a. A: ... *well I was the only one other than than the uhm tch* Fords?, *Uh Mrs Holmes Ford? You know uh// the the cellist?*
   b. B: *Oh yes. She's she's the cellist.*
   c. A: *Yes*
   d. B: *Ye//s*
   e. A: *Well she and her husband were there ...*
      (Sacks and Schegloff, 1974, p. 6)

Another such device is to overtly introduce a referent into discourse such as 'Do you remember Tom?' or 'Do you remember the guy we met in Paris?' 'You know those boots we tried on yesterday with the fur lining?' or 'Do you see that chair over there?' and so on.

The point to emphasize here is that speakers are reluctant to make claims involving individuals or objects that have not been or cannot easily be identified or recognized by the hearer. That is, they are reluctant to add New information to the discourse if the objects or individuals to which they are referring cannot be established as Given.

The phenomenon that we have been describing — establishing referents — is a prerequisite for successful collaboration on a *discourse topic*. We take the term discourse topic to refer to the *proposition* (or set of propositions) about which the speaker is either providing or requesting new information, e.g.

(3) Allison III, 20,3½ months
   a. Mother: (trying to put too large diaper on doll, holding diaper on) *Well we can't hold it on like that. What do we need? Hmm? What do we need for the diaper?*
   b. Allison: *pin/*

In (3) the mother is requesting New information about the proposition 'we need something for the diaper'. The proposition thus constitutes a discourse topic. When Allison says 'pin', she is providing the New information requested. The proposition attended to in both the question and the answer is the same: thus the discourse consisting of that Question-Answer pair has a single discourse topic.

When speaker and hearer are directing their utterances to a particular proposition of this type, they are collaborating on a discourse topic. To collaborate on a discourse topic, the hearer must know what proposition the speaker is adding new information to or requesting new information about. If the speaker wants collaboration, he must select a discourse topic that takes account of the listener's knowledge. That is, he must insure that the proposition that constitutes the discourse topic is known to or knowable by the listener. There are several things the speaker can do to this end: he can draw on general background knowledge he shares with the listener; or he can draw on information available in the interactional setting; or he can draw on prior discourse in the conversation at hand (Garfinkel, 1967).

In practice we find that much conversational space is taken up by exchange in which speaker and hearer attempt to establish a discourse topic. In these exchanges, the speaker tries to make the discourse topic known to the hearer.

We propose here a dynamic model of the way in which speakers establish a discourse topic. The model represents the initial work involved in making a discourse topic known. We suggest that getting a discourse topic established may involve such basic work as securing the attention of the listener and identifying for the listener objects, individuals, ideas, etc. (Atkinson, 1979) contained in the discourse topic.

The model is based on child–adult and child–child conversations. However, the application of the model is not limited to these interactions. The model can be applied to adult–adult discourse as well. Child language simply offers abundant and salient instances of this behaviour.

5.2 Data base

The data used in this study are drawn from three major sources. The first source consists of six 30-minute videotapes of a mother and her child, Allison (16,3 months–34 months). The first four of these tapes have been analysed by Lois Bloom in *One Word at a Time* (1973). The second major source consists of 25 hours of audio- and videotaped interactions of twin boys with one another and with adults. The tapes were made over a period of a year, from 33 months to 45 months (see Chapters 1, 2 and 3; Keenan and Klein, 1975, for other analyses of this material). Transcriptions of the videotaped data included extensive nonverbal information. The contextual information forms an integral part of our analysis. The third major source consists of transcriptions of audiotaped conversations between five adolescents and a therapist in five group therapy sessions (GTS). These tapes were transcribed by Gail Jefferson.

In addition, we wish to acknowledge several other sources: L. Tweed has provided transcriptions of audiotapes of monolingual and bilingual children interacting with adults (Infant Development Study, UCLA). E. Schegloff and members of his graduate seminar on conversational analysis have provided illustrations from adult–adult discourse.

5.3 Defining discourse structure

Before defining discourse topic more formally, let us describe in brief the context in which discourse topics emerge, i.e. the discourse itself. For the purpose of this analysis, we take a discourse to be any sequence of two or more utterances produced by a single speaker or by two or more speakers who are interacting with one another (at some point in time and space). Discourses may evolve or develop in several ways.

For example, a stretch of discourse may contain a series of linked discourse topics. The discourse topics are linked in the sense that the propositional content of each is drawn from one or more of the utterances already produced in the discourse. These utterances, unless otherwise challenged (Givon, 1975a), form a 'presupposition pool' (Venneman, 1975) out of which discourse topics are selected.

The discourse topics may be linked in at least two ways:

1. Two or more utterances may share the same discourse topic. This is the case in question-answer pairs (for example see (3)), and in some repetitions, e.g.

   (4) Allison IV, 22 months
       a. Allison: (looks in box, finding calf) *cow/*
       b. Mother: *A cow!*
       c. Allison: (holding calf) *moo/↑*[3]
       d. Mother: *Moo, cow says moo.* ↓

In this example the same discourse topic is sustained from speaker to speaker in lines (4)a and (4)b. Both utterances provide new information relevant to an object Allison is attending to, the new information being that the object that Allison has noticed is 'a cow'. Likewise, utterances in (4)c and (4)d appear to address the same discourse topic, i.e. 'The cow (Allison is holding) makes some sound.' Allison provides the information that the cow makes the sound 'moo' and her mother confirms this claim in her subsequent utterance.

We refer to a topic that matches exactly that of the immediately preceding utterance as a *collaborating discourse topic*. Sequences in which a discourse topic is sustained over two or more utterances are *topic collaborating* sequences. (For other examples of topic collaborating sequences see examples (3) and (5).)

2. Discourse topics may take some presupposition of the immediately preceding discourse topic and/or the new information provided relevant to the discourse topic preceding (all part of the presupposition pool) and use it in a new discourse topic. For instance, the dialogue between Allison and her mother in example (3) continues as follows (we repeat the initial turns for convenience):

   (3) (continued)
       a. Mother: *Well, we can't hold it on like that. What do we need? Hmm? What do we need for the diaper?*
       b. Allison: *pin/*

    c. Mother: *pin. Where are the pins?*
    d. Allison: *home/*

Here, the discourse topic is established at (3)a ('we need something for the diaper') and is collaborated on in (3)b. In (3)c Allison's mother poses a different but related question (of immediate concern). It is related in the sense that the proposition about which information is being elicited, 'the pins are somewhere', presupposes that 'there exists pins', a presupposition that is assumed as well in Allison's preceding claim 'pins/ (are needed for the diaper)'. This new discourse topic becomes collaborated on in (3)d by Allison's providing the new information requested.

We refer to a topic that uses the preceding utterance in this way as an *incorporating discourse topic*. Sequences in which a discourse topic integrates a claim and/or presupposition of an immediately prior utterance are *topic-incorporating* sequences.[4]

We refer to stretches of discourse linked by topic collaboration and/or topic incorporation as *continuous discourse* (see Table 5.1).

Table 5.1

Continuous discourse	
Collaborating discourse topic	Incorporating discourse topic

On the other hand, we may find discourse in which the discourse topics of each utterance are not linked in any obvious way, i.e. where the discourse of one utterance does not draw on a claim and/or presupposition of the preceding utterance. In these discourses a speaker disengages himself from a set of concerns addressed in the immediately preceding utterance and turns to an unrelated set of concerns (see Examples (8), (9), (14). We refer to such stretches of discourse as *discontinuous discourse* (Keenan and Schieffelin, 1975).

Discontinuous discourse may have two types of discourse topic. The first type reintroduces a claim and/or a discourse topic (or part thereof) that has appeared in the discourse history at some point prior to the immediately preceding utterance. (It could draw from the discourse topic and/or claim of the last utterance but one.) We call such discourse topics *re-introducing topics*. Constructions such as 'concerning . . .', 'as for . . .', 'as far as . . . is concerned (goes)', may mark this sort of discourse for adult English speakers, along with remarks such as 'getting back to . . .', 'like you said before . . .'.

Table 5.2

Discourse			
Continuous		Discontinuous	
Collaborating discourse topic	Incorporating discourse topic	Re-introducing discourse topic	Introducing discourse topic

A second type of discontinuous discourse topic introduces a discourse topic that is in no way related to the preceding utterance, and does not draw on utterances produced elsewhere in the discourse. We refer to such topics as *introducing discourse topics* (see Table 5.2).

5.4 Defining discourse topic

We turn our attention now to a more detailed definition of discourse topic. As noted previously, a discourse topic is a proposition (or set of propositions) expressing a concern (or set of concerns) the speaker is addressing. It should be stressed that each declarative or interrogative utterance in a discourse has a specific discourse topic. It may be the case that the same discourse topic is sustained over a sequence of two or more utterances. We have described these as topic collaborating sequences (see 5.3 above). On the other hand, the discourse topic may change from utterance to utterance, sometimes drawing on the previous utterance (incorporating topic) and sometimes not (introducing topic, re-introducing topic).

In determining the discourse topic of an utterance, it is useful to determine the purpose or reason behind each utterance. Why did the speaker say what he did? Although we may never have access to the more remote or global motivations underlying a particular utterance, we can make some headway by determining what low-level, immediate considerations the speaker may be attending to.

These low-level considerations are found in the utterance context (verbal and nonverbal). For example, an utterance may be produced in response to something heard (prior utterance) or in response to something witnessed or noticed. We may think of some utterances as providing an answer to some specific question related to something in the utterance context. For example, if a speaker hears a crashing noise, he may respond 'An accident.' This utterance may answer the implicit question, 'What was that noise?' Similarly, when in (4) Allison notices an object and says 'cow/', she may be answering the question, 'What is this object?'

The listener 'constructs' questions of this sort in interpreting utterances addressed to him: the listener takes the utterance and relates it to some aspect of the utterance context. For example, in (4) Allison's mother takes Allison's utterance 'cow/' and relates it to the nonverbal context, in particular to what Allison is noticing. The listener then must ask how the utterance is related to that feature of the context, that is, the listener asks 'What is the speaker informing me of? Is the speaker providing me with an explanation of some phenomena? An evaluation of some phenomena? A description of some phenomena? An identification of some phenomena? Or what?'

Another way of putting this is to say that the listener tries to determine what question the speaker may be answering. For example, in interpreting Allison's utterance 'cow/', Allison's mother tries to construct a plausible question Allison may be providing the answer to. In this case, the mother interprets Allison's utterance 'cow/' as possibly an answer to the question, 'What is the object?'

Of course what the listener considers to be the question the speaker is answering may not always correspond to the question the speaker believes he is answering. In conversations between adults and children, it is often the case that an adult will not be able to determine exactly what question the child is addressing (see section 5.5.2). Or, a child may not understand the point, i.e. the question behind an adult's utterance, and so cannot respond relevantly. Adults often have to make their questions explicit. We treat this behaviour in fact as a defining characteristic of speech directed to small children (section 5.5.5 considers this and related behaviours).

We will refer to the question (or set of questions) an utterance is a response to as the *question of immediate concern.*

In many cases the question of immediate concern is explicit, i.e. a question actually appearing in the discourse. The question can be produced by one conversational partner and answered by the same speaker. For example:

(5) Allison V, 28 months
   a. Allison: (looking into box) *What's in here?/*
   b. Allison: (reaching into toy box) *It's a pig!/*

On a more abstract level, the question of immediate concern can be treated as a theoretical construct. The linguist may use it to explain more precisely what a discourse topic is: the discourse topic is based on the question of immediate concern. It is the proposition or set of propositions that the question of immediate concern presupposes. It has been shown (Keenan and Hull, 1973) that such a set of propositions can always be represented by a single one, one that implies all the others. Let us call this presupposition the *primary presupposition*. Hence, in Example (3)a, the discourse topic is derived from the question, of immediate concern, 'What do we need for the diaper?' The discourse topic is the primary presupposition of this question, namely 'we do need something for the diaper'. And in Example (4)a, the discourse topic is the primary presupposition of 'What's in here?', namely, that 'something is in here'.

Questions of immediate concern themselves request specific information about the primary presupposition (the discourse topic). Informative responses to these questions presuppose the primary presupposition (the discourse topic), and provide new information relevant to the question posed. For example, in (3) Allison's response (3)b presupposes the primary presupposition ('we need something for the diaper') of the question, and adds the new information 'pin/'. In (5), Allison's response (5)b presupposes the primary presupposition 'something is in here' of the question asked and adds the new information that that something 'is a pig'. The discourse topics for these responses are the primary presuppositions of the questions of immediate concern.

Declarative = (response)	New information + relevant to Q of immediate concern	Primary presupposition of Q of immediate concern (discourse topic)

5.4.1 Determining the question of immediate concern

Of course, not all questions of immediate concern appear overtly in a discourse. A declarative utterance may address itself to some *implicit* question of immediate concern. In this case, the linguist may not have access to the information needed to determine the question. In many instances the question of immediate concern may be understood by speaker and hearer because it arises from their shared background knowledge. Where a declarative utterance initiates a social interaction, the linguist may have no clue whatsoever as to what the discourse topic is. If A says to B: 'Tom called today', the question of immediate concern may be 'What happened today?' or 'Who called today?' or

'What did Tom do today?' or 'What's the good news?' or some other question relevant to speaker and/or hearer.

The more information about the speaker's and hearer's shared knowledge the observer has access to, the easier it will be for him to determine the question of immediate concern and the discourse topic. Given that questions of immediate concern may be drawn from both verbal and nonverbal dimensions of the immediate situation, it is to the advantage of the observer to have available the most complete record of the situation.

5.4.1.1 Nonverbal context

For example, interlocutors often make reference to some nonverbal action or event that they are observing or experiencing, or that they have just observed or experienced. Speakers assume that listeners perceive these occurrences. They treat these occurrences as old or Given information for the listener, and base questions of immediate concern on them. If the listener has not in fact perceived the event or activity in question, he will not be able to determine the discourse topic. For instance, in (1) above, Bambi incorrectly assumed that Elinor was aware that Bambi was putting salt on her food (with a salt-shaker). Bambi's discourse topic was something like, 'It (the salt) comes out (in some manner).' The question of immediate concern was, 'In what manner does it (the salt) come out?' However, Elinor could not reconstruct the discourse topic because she had not noticed, i.e. identified, the referent of 'it' and so did not understand exactly what claim is made by the primary presupposition 'It (the salt) comes out (in some manner).'

Just as interlocutors may fail to determine the discourse topic, because they have not attended to a relevant phenomenon, so the linguist may repeat this experience if he does not have access to a visual record. The need for a visual record is, in fact, critical for under-standing children's utterances in these terms. In interpreting the com-municative intentions of young children, others (adults and other children) make full use of ongoing context. What constitutes the discourse topic may only be reconstructable on the basis of observing what the child is doing, where the child is looking, and so on.

(6) Allison IV, 22 months
   (Mother and Allison are sitting on a big chair)
   a. Allison: (pointing at TV monitor, seeing herself) *Baby Allison/*
   b. Mother: *Do you see Baby Allison?*

For instance, in (6), it is critical to take into account Allison's pointing at the monitor, seeing herself, in interpreting her utterance 'Baby Allison/'. Among other things, her pointing indicates she is aware of something being at a designated location. Allison's utterance provides the information that that something is 'Baby Allison/'.[5] We can think of 'Baby Allison/' as new information being added to the discourse topic 'Something is there (where I am pointing).' If we or her mother did not know that Allison was pointing, we would not be able to reconstruct the discourse in this way. The discourse topic could be different if Allison were patting herself, playing with her doll or reaching for a cookie as she produced her utterance.

5.4.1.2 The verbal context

Another resource available to speakers for determining discourse topic is the ongoing discourse itself. That is, speakers often draw discourse topics from the dialogue as it proceeds. They base their discourse topic on some proposition (or set of propositions) that has been produced in the course of the conversation. In so doing, they may employ either a topic-collaborating or a topic-incorporating strategy.

(7) Adolescents, GTS 4
     (pause)
     a. Ther: *There are such things as con-artists.*
     b. Jim: *I'm one.*
     c. Ther: *Are you?*

For example, in (7), Jim employs a topic-incorporating strategy. He uses the immediately prior proposition 'There are such things as con-artists' as a discourse topic. He adds the new information that he is one of these 'things' called con-artists. (The proposition at (7)a represents New information with respect to a prior discourse topic.)

This process of formulating discourse topics from prior propositions is part of what it means for a speaker to make his conversational contribution *relevant* to the current state of talk (Grice, 1975). Grice states that interlocutors usually expect one another to make their utterances relevant. Interlocutors use the history of the discourse in making sense of a particular conversational contribution. From our point of view, interlocutors make use of the discourse history in reconstructing one another's discourse topics. At least, a listener assumes that a discourse topic is some proposition relevant to the ongoing talk, because the listener assumes the speaker is following the conversational norm of relevance. For example, in (7), Ther assumes that Jim's discourse topic is drawn from his own (Ther's) prior proposition because he assumes Jim is responding relevantly to his utterance.

The constraints on when a relevant response is to be provided will vary across cultures and across situations. For example, Philips (in press) notes that Wasco Chinook Indians, in speaking English, do not necessarily expect each turn in a conversation to be relevant to an immediately prior turn. Speakers often provide a relevant response to some proposition long after the proposition first appeared in the discourse (and after numerous intervening turns) without marking it in any overt way.[6]

5.4.1.3 'Breaking and entering'

If a speaker is conforming to the convention of making his utterance relevant to those that precede his, then he normally assumes that the listener can compute his discourse topic. That is, he can assume that the listener knows to turn to the discourse history to locate the discourse topic. The speaker does not have to mark the discourse topic explicitly.

When a speaker produces a conversational contribution that he realizes is not relevant to the discourse history (i.e. an introducing discourse topic) or may not seem relevant (from the listener's point of view), then he is under some constraint to make the discourse topic known to the listener. Typically, the speaker marks a break in the continuous discourse, alerting the listener to the fact that the discourse topic may not follow from previous discourse. Speakers often announce a break with some metalinguistic remark such as 'I am sorry to change the subject but ...' or 'Not to change the subject but ...', and so on. These remarks are often accompanied by attention-getting devices, e.g. 'hey!', 'listen!', 'look!', 'wait!' (see sections 5.5.2 and 5.5.4) along with hesitations and word searches (Sacks, 1968).

(8) Adolescents, GTS 3
   (pause)
   a. Ken: *E-excuse me changin' the subject but didju hear anything about what happened Monday night?*
            (pause)
   b. Dan: *no, w-weren'tchu uh –*

    c. Louise: *What happened Monday night?* (pause)
    d. Ken: *Oh I came in here y'know, Mom and Dad decided*
             I should . . .

Other remarks of this ilk are, 'Before I forget, I have to tell you something' or 'Hey, I heard a good joke.'

  (9) Adolescents, GTS
     (pause)
     a. Ken: *hey, wait. I've gotta – I've gotta joke.* (pause)
            What's black 'n white 'n hides in caves? (pause)
     b. Roger: *a' right I give up, what's black 'n white// 'n hides*
             in –
     c. Al: *a newspaper.*
     d. Roger: *hhhh.*
     e. Ken: *no,* (pause) *pregnant nun.*

In addition, discourse topics may be explicitly introduced into the discourse by the speaker. The speaker may, for example, pose a question that has as its primary presupposition the intended discourse topic.

  (10) Allison IV, 22 months
     (Allison had been wiping a chair, is now sitting with fingers in
     mouth, staring at the camera)
     a. Mother: *What were we gonna do?*
     b. Allison: *eat/ ↑cookies/*

In (10) Mother initiates a 'new discourse topic' ('we were going to do something') by proposing a question of immediate concern that is not contingent on prior discourse.

In Example (8), Ken introduces the discourse topic 'something happened Monday night' as a *secondary presupposition* of the question, 'Did you hear anything about what happened Monday night?' (The primary presupposition is that 'you (the addressee) either did, or did not, hear something about what happened Monday night'.) This strategy is a common one for speakers of English. Speakers often introduce discourse topics as secondary presuppositions of yes–no questions such as 'Do you know what happened today?' 'Did you see in the paper where Tom Dixon resigned?' and the like. Used in this way, these questions function primarily to direct the listener to attend to a 'new' proposition.

The main point to be made here is that the speaker, in order to communicate felicitously, should make sure that the listener has sufficient resources to reconstruct the discourse topic. One body of resources is the discourse history itself. The speaker may assume that the listener knows this history as a co-creator of it (or witness to it). As long as the speaker bases his discourse topic on the preceding talk, he may assume his discourse is reconstructable. If the speaker wishes to focus on a concern that is not part of the discourse history, he may not be certain that the listener will realize what this concern is. In this case, it may be necessary for the speaker to:

1. alert the listener that the speaker is turning to a different set of concerns;
2. introduce this set of concerns explicitly as a presupposition of a new question of immediate concern.

5.5 The model

5.5.1 Prerequisites for establishing a discourse topic

The model we present here represents the interactional work involved in getting a discourse topic known to a listener. We claim that in order to determine a particular discourse topic the hearer minimally must:

1. be attending to the speaker's utterance;
2. decipher the speaker's utterance;
3. identify those objects, individuals, ideas, events, etc., that play a role in the discourse topic;
4. identify the semantic relations obtaining between referents in the discourse topic.

We may rewrite these prerequisites for topic establishment from the perspective of the speaker in the form of steps the speaker must take to make a discourse topic known to the listener:

1. the speaker must secure the attention of the listener;
2. the speaker must articulate his utterance clearly;
3. the speaker must provide sufficient information for the listener to identify objects, etc., included in the discourse topic;
4. the speaker must provide sufficient information for the listener to reconstruct the semantic relations obtaining between referents in the discourse topic.

Steps 1 and 2 are general requirements of any successful communication. Steps 3 and 4 are more specifically prerequisites of topic establishment and might be restated as Felicity Conditions on the successful establishment of a discourse topic.

The steps described here may correspond to actual moves taken by speakers. These moves may take up varying amounts of conversational space. For example, if the attention of the interlocutor has already been secured prior to the utterance, if the utterance is comprehensible, and if relevant objects, persons, ideas, etc., and their semantic roles are known to the hearer, then all four steps may be completed in a space of a single utterance:

(11) Adolescents, GTS
 (in context of a discussion on the merits and dismerits of smoking cigarettes)
 a. Roger: *Cigarettes aren'* (very) *healthy*
   (pause)
 b. Roger: *You shouldn't be smokin' Ken.*
   (short pause)
 c. Ken: *So the coaches tell me.*

For example, in (11)b, Roger has addressed Ken specifically; therefore Ken at (11)c can assume that Roger will be attending to his response. Hence step 1 is taken care of for Ken. Second, because the interlocutors are engaged in face-to-face verbal interaction, with no concurrent distracting activity, they can assume that their utterances will be heard and decoded without interference; that is, they can operate on the assumption that the noise to signal ratio is low. Hence, step 2 is satisfied for Ken. Third, Ken's discourse topic at (11)c 'that Ken should not be smoking', is drawn from Roger's assertion ((11)b, topic-incorporating). Ken can assume that Roger knows the referents specified in the discourse topic on this basis. In fact, Ken can assume that Roger knows the discourse topic itself. Hence, steps 3 and 4 are accomplished. However, it is often the case that several utterances or even several conversational turns will be needed to take care of these steps.

(12) Adolescents, GTS 4
 a. Ken: *Uh Pat McGee. I don't know if you know him,*
   he – /he lives in// Palisades.
 b. Jim: *I know him real well as a matter of fa*(hh) (he's)
   one of my best friends.
 c. Ken: *He – he used to go to the same military school*
   I did.

For example in (12), two turns, (12)a and (12)b, are taken up with insuring that a referent (critical to the topic) is known to the listener.

It sometimes happens that one or another step is never completed and the discourse topic is dropped by the speaker:

(13) Toby and David at 36 months, in the bedroom.
(calling out to mother who is not present)
a. David: *Honey!/ calling honey!/ honey!/ we lost our blankets/*
b. David and Toby: *honey!/ honey!/ honey!/*
c. David: *honey!/*
d. Toby: *honey!/ honey!/*
e. David: *honey!/* (4 sec. pause) *where are ya/*
f. Toby: *no/ mummy/* (gloss: no, she's not called Honey, she's called Mummy)
g. David: *no/ honey/ honey/ honey/*

In (13), step 1 is never satisfied as the intended addressee (the mother) never responds to either the vocative ((13)a–e) or the question ((13)e) directed to her. It is difficult to assess exactly what constitutes the discourse topic for the utterance 'we lost our blankets/', as the utterance attempts to initiate the interaction with the mother. There is no preceding context from which a discourse topic can be determined (by an outsider). We suggest that the discourse topic associated with such discourse-initial assertions (i.e. an introducing topic) is of the general form 'something happened'. This discourse topic is dropped, as step 1 is unsuccessful. Having failed to secure the attention of the mother, the children redirect their utterances to one another, and engage in a different discourse topic, roughly 'what name to use in calling mother'. By (13)g this new topic becomes collaborated on, as Toby has secured David's attention, David has indicated that he has understood ((13)f) and has accepted it as discourse topic by adding new information to the discourse topic proposed by Toby.

(14) Allison III, 20,3½ months
(Prior context: Mother had brought out glass of juice set into a stack of paper cups. Allison had commented '*glass/*' since she had previously been served juice in either a paper cup or a can)
(Allison eats cookie, looking at cookie)
a. Allison: (putting cookie in her cup like the way the glass of juice was in the cup) *glass/↑↓*
b. Mother: *Well, what did you do?*
c. Allison: *glass/*

d. Mother: *What did you do? Where's the cookie?*
e. Allison: *cup/*
f. Mother: *In the cup.*

In this Example, Allison makes eye contact with her mother, helping her to secure the attention of the mother (step 1 is taken care of), and mother does not question Allison's articulation (step 2 is taken care of). However, step 3 is unsuccessful for a number of reasons. The mother cannot identify the specific object referred to by Allison's utterance 'glass/'. From Allison's point of view 'glass/' is part of a comment on her nonverbal activity, i.e. that the cookie in the cup is like the glass in the cup witnessed earlier. But because the specific referent of 'glass/' never becomes known to mother, neither 'glass/' or the event that it relates to becomes part of an established discourse topic.

Our model for proceeding through conversational space is basically an interactional one. The amount of conversational space taken up with completing these steps is related to the kind of response the speaker receives from the hearer. If the speaker receives a positive response from the listener, then he can assume that the steps for topic establishment have been satisfied. On the other hand, if at any point the speaker gets negative feedback, then he will have to do more interactional work, take up more conversational space, to complete steps. For example, the listener often will question some assumption of the speaker: if the speaker believes that he has secured the attention of the listener but in fact has failed to do so, then the listener may respond 'Who me?' or 'Are you talking to me?', etc. If the attention of the listener has been secured, but he has not heard all or part of the speaker's utterance, he may request a second hearing, or he may state 'I didn't hear you,' 'I didn't quite catch that,' and the like. If the speaker believes that the identity of the referents of the discourse topic are known to the hearer, but, in fact, their identity is not known, then the hearer may challenge the speaker's belief and/or request further information concerning these referents.

The dynamic model for establishing a discourse topic can be represented as in Fig. 5.1.

The interactional work described here is similar to material described by sociologists involved in conversational analysis. In particular, the work of correcting misunderstandings and mishearings is tied to the notion of *repair* in conversation (Schegloff, personal communication). The work of *repairing* some communication involves minimally a *repairable*, the item or set of items that need to be corrected, and a *repair response*, in which the source of misunderstanding or mishearing is attended to. The repair response may or may not actually repair the misunderstanding or mishearing. If it does not, it may in turn be treated as a repairable, requiring some further repair response.

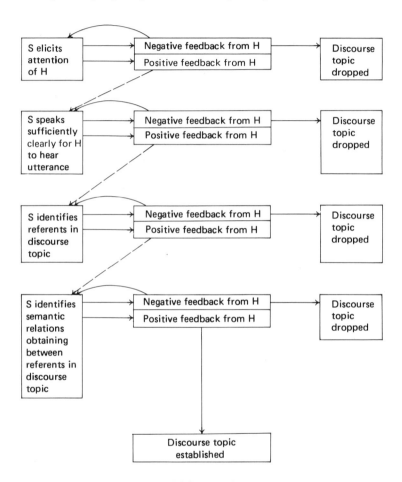

Fig. 5.1 Dynamic model for establishing a discourse topic.

Two major types of repair are relevant to establishing discourse topic. First, there are cases in which the speaker who produces the repairable perceives the repairable and repairs it. These are *self-initiated repairs*, and they normally occur within the space of a single conversational turn.

(15) Adolescents, GTS 3
   a. Louise: *Doc – Mister Cheibe – when're ya gonna be a doctor?*
(16) Toby, 45 months
   a. Toby: (looking at his mother) ↑*daddy/ uh mommy/*
   b. Mother: *yeah?*
   c. Toby: *Are we gonna go↓ now?/*

Examples (15) and (16) illustrate self-initiated repairs on the vocatives used to elicit the attention of the addressee.

In addition, we find many examples in our data of *other-initiated repairs*. In this type of repair, someone other than the speaker who produces the repairable indicates that some repair is necessary. This type of repair may take up several turns. For example, one interlocutor may produce a repairable in one turn, a second interlocutor evidence his misunderstanding or mishearing in the next turn, and in a third turn, the first interlocutor may produce a repair response. Example (17) illustrates such an exchange:

(17) Toby, David, 35 months, bedroom
   a. David: (drawing on misty window) (?) *moon/ I make moon/*
   b. Toby: (pointing to window) *there?/*
   c. David: *there/*

In this exchange, Toby indicates that he needs further information about David's utterance; he needs to know which of David's drawings is the moon. David repairs Toby's misunderstanding by indicating the location of the moon drawn. Example (1) also illustrates this type of repair. In (1) Elinor indicates her lack of understanding, and Bambi repairs this misunderstanding by providing a more explicit referent for 'it' ('the salt').

It is not always the case that other-initiated repairs are repaired by the speaker producing the repairable. The 'other' can repair the repairable of a conversational partner directly in the next turn:

(18) Allison IV, 22 months
   (Allison starting to eat cookie)
   a. Allison: ↑*chocolate↓chip↑cookie/*
   b. Mother: *Chocolate chip cookie? I think that's just a chocolate cookie.*

In (18), Allison's mother points out an error in Allison's identification of the cookie ((18)b) and then repairs the error in her subsequent utterance. Schegloff (personal communication) has pointed out that repairs of this sort frequently appear in adult–child discourse. Adults feel they have a responsibility (or right) to correct judgments of a child. In talking with one another, however, adults show a preference for giving the individual who produced the repairable an opportunity to correct himself. These latter alternates are face-preserving (Goffman, 1963) and hence more polite than direct repair of another's error.

Integrating the notion of repair into our model, we can say that repair procedures tend to be inserted into conversational space when one or more of the four steps have not been satisfied by a speaker. For example, in (15) and (16) the speakers introduce repair machinery to secure the attention of the intended addressee (step 1). In (1), the speaker repairs her utterance so that the addressee can identify an important referent in the discourse topic (step 3).

On a more general level, repair machinery tends to be introduced when an interlocutor has misjudged the communicative needs of a conversational partner. Sacks and Schegloff (1974) refer to the shaping of utterances to meet these needs as 'recipient design', the 'recipient' being the intended conversational partner. When some utterance fails to meet the needs of a partner, then that utterance has poor recipient design.

The notion of recipient design is useful to the analysis at hand. From our point of view, collaboration on a discourse topic demands good recipient design on a number of levels. Utterances must be designed so that the recipient knows he/she is being addressed and so that the recipient can hear the utterance. Good recipient design is also needed to insure that the recipient can identify who or what is being talked about (Sacks and Schegloff, 1974). In the discussion to follow, we consider recipient design in developmental terms. The bulk of our data shows that young children experience communicative difficulties because their utterances have poor recipient design.

5.5.2 *How to secure the attention of the hearer*

Atkinson (1979) explores the use of attention-drawing devices used by small children (look! see! – pointing) which demonstrate to the listener which persons, objects or events the child wishes the listener to focus on. If both participants focus on the selected object, it can be presumed that the speaker has obtained the attention of the hearer, as well as directing him to a specific object. Here we discuss only the first of these procedures: attention-getting.

Before any communication can take place, the speaker must secure the attention of the hearer. This is done in a variety of ways and is one of the earliest acts a child must learn. Crying and other distressful sounds usually bring attention to the infant, indicating that 'something is the matter'. Gazing at the other is also one of the earliest ways to secure his/her attention (Stern, 1974). These acts may not be intentional at the age of 3 months, but by 1 year of age, the child starts using these as conscious devices (see Chapter 4).[7] Smiling plus gazing, as well as laughing while gazing at the other, often elicits not only the attention of the hearer, but a query from the hearer, e.g. 'What happened?' or 'What's so funny?' They elicit attention to self even if that is not what is always intended.

Smiling and laughing are thought of as social phenomena. People feel that they can ask another individual why he/she is laughing — especially if the context does not provide an explicit explanation or source. Presumably one is laughing about something — laughing being a comment or new information about a proposition.

Other nonverbal means of getting a listener to attend to the speaker are touching the listener, tugging, poking, turning towards the listener, getting closer. These behaviours as well typically elicit such queries such as 'What do you want?', etc.

In addition to several nonverbal means of securing the attention of a specific individual, the child develops verbal ways of performing the same act. While crying and other distressful sounds do not specify who should attend, the use of vocatives, i.e. 'Mama' and 'Papa', etc., do. The number of times a name will be called out repeatedly, the pitch and loudness of the calls depend on the utterance context and the desires of the individual. For instance in Example (13) the mother does not respond to her children's calls since she doesn't hear them, and subsequently she is not involved in the interaction. By way of comparison:

(19) Maria, 24 months, Spanish-speaking
   (in same room with mother)
   a. Maria: *mommy/*
   b. Mother: *¿Qué? ¿Qué quieres?¿ Huh?*

Maria succeeds in calling attention to herself in one turn, and her mother indicates that she is attending to the proposition that 'Maria wants something' with her response.

In the next example, Maria has assumed that the attention of the listener has been secured, when in fact it has not.

(20)(several people present in the room)
  a. Maria: *siéntate acá/ siéntate acá/ siéntate acá/*
  b. friend (2;6): *¿mi?/*
  c. Maria: *siéntate acá/*
  (transcribed by L. Tweed)

Not only must children learn to secure the attention of the listener, but when several potential respondents are available, they must select explicitly. For example:

(21)(dinner table, three adults, three children (aged 4 years), noisy)
  a. Zachary: *You know what I saw today?*
  b. David: *What?/*
  c. Zachary: *↑Not you, I'm talking to my mom↓/ ↑Mommy?/*
  d. Mother: *↑yeah?*

These problems also face adults in conversation with each other. Using vocatives also serves as a check on the other's attention, during conversation, and is one of several devices available to maintain the attention of the listener, e.g. 'George, George, are you there?' used when one suspects that the listener has not been completely attending. Other devices used are expressions like, 'hey!' or 'wait!' plus eye contact and touching the individual. Both children and adults use as well expressions such as 'You know what?' or 'Guess what' to shift attention to themselves (see section 5.4.1.3).

Another way to call attention to oneself (used by both adults and children) is to use one of the many expressive particles such as 'uh oh', 'oh dear', 'ouch', 'woopsey', 'wow', etc. Placed in the beginning of an event, the listener hearing such an exclamation will usually look to the speaker and inquire 'What happened?' or 'What's wrong?', in an attempt to find out what has caused such an outburst. The occurrence of one of these expressions during an ongoing interaction usually draws the focus away from what is happening and causes a shift in attention to occur. These particles can simultaneously draw attention to the speaker and the event that he is commenting on. Schegloff (personal communication) treats these expressions as a 'pre' to a 'noticing' by a co-present individual or individuals. That is, they are expressions that elicit a 'noticing'.

5.5.3 *On articulating utterances for the listener*

To collaborate on a discourse topic, a listener must have received a minimally comprehensible message from a speaker. Adults in talking with one another may miss part or all of an utterance if it was delivered too quickly or too softly or if noise from the context interfered with the signal. The problem of poor articulation is even more apparent in interactions involving children as interlocutors.

For example, young children often distort the phonological shape of their utterances to the extent that conversational partners cannot interpret them as meaningful strings in the language. It is often necessary for young children to repeat their utterances several times to get them understood at this basic level. In many cases, the utterance is not deciphered and the topic is dropped:

> (22) Toby, David, 33 months
> (eating midday meal, facing caretaker, Jill)
> (Jill has just asked if Toby and David would like a banana in jelly (British term for jello))
> a. Toby: *no no jelly/* [tɨnkɛl] /
> b. Jill: *You eat your dinner then.*
> c. Toby: [tɨnkɛl] /
> d. Jill: *What?*
> e. Toby: [tɨnkɛl] /
> f. Jill: *tinkle?*
> g. David: *yeah*
> h. Toby: *no tinkle/* [tɨnkɛl] (repeats)/
> i. Jill: *You're a prack.*

In this example, Toby repeats his utterance but with little success. He never get his message across. It is possible that '[tɨnkɛl] /' is intended as 'tin of jello' (unclear), but in any case Jill interprets the utterance as a distortion of 'tinkle', a lexical item which makes little sense in this context. This example illustrates as well the use of repair machinery to achieve comprehensibility. Jill initiates repair procedures twice ((22)d and (22)f) to this end.

At the one-word stage, children experience even greater problems in articulating their utterances with sufficient clarity. Scollon (1976) has documented the way in which many of these early utterances are lost on co-present adults:

For example, one day, this little child (20 mos.), whose name is Brenda, said to me, [kʰa] [kʰa] [kʰa]. I didn't understand and said 'What?'. She then said [gɔo] [go]. The next thing I said cannot be heard clearly enough on the tape to transcribe, but Brenda then said [bəis], nine times. I still didn't understand what she was saying and said 'What? Oh, bicycle? Is that what you said?' Her answer was [na']. I said, 'No?'. She, [na']. I, 'No – I got it wrong.'

When Scollon listened to his recording of this conversation, he heard the sound of a car passing just before Brenda started to speak. On this second hearing, he realized that [kʰa] was Brenda's equivalent of 'car', [gɔo] corresponds to 'go' and [bəis] corresponded to 'bus'. Scollon's analysis illustrates the point that caretakers and others rely heavily on utterance context in interpreting phonologically ill-formed utterances of children. Where no salient referent in the immediate environment can be isolated, adults find it difficult to understand what a child is saying.[8]

We can well imagine that these early attempts to communicate are laced with repair machinery. In fact, Scollon reports that the one-word period is 'cluttered' with self-repetitions on the part of the child and attempts at clarification by a co-present adult. The child repeats a lexical item over and over until he/she receives some sort of assurance from the adult that the utterance has been deciphered.

Scollon observes that the child may repeat an utterance with or without a verbal prompt from the adult. From our point of view, even when there is no verbal repair-initiator such as 'What?', 'Hm?' or trial repetition of the child's utterance, absence of a verbal response from the adults may count as a negative response for the child. That is, silence on the part of a conversational partner may initiate a repair from the child. When the child does not get an immediate verbal confirmation, the child attempts to clarify the utterance (repair) through repetition.

Aside from problems of phonological distortion, the communications of young children may suffer because the child's voice is too soft or too low:

(23) Allison VI, 34 months
  (Allison climbs up on a big chair, trying to move bars into their holes)
  a. Allison: *I'm-I'm put-putting these bars in there/*
  b. Mother: *I can't hear you.*
  c. Allison: (pointing to holes) *in these holes/*
  d. Mother: *What honey?*
  e. Allison: (moving hand up and down bars) *ə these bars/*
  f. Mother: *What about these bars?*
  g. Allison: (trying to move bars) *I'm trying to put them in*
          these hole – mommy?/ I can't get it in these holes/

In many instances, the child may not in fact be directing utterances to others present. The child may be speaking softly because he is engaged in some activity and talking to himself. Others overhearing such talk may try to re-direct it so that it includes themselves. In these cases, the child is not 'guilty' of poor recipient design. Rather it is the co-present other who demands to be recognized as the recipient.

It is important to note that adults regularly apply repair machinery to these communication roadblocks and that very young children respond appropriately to this machinery. That is not to say that young children respond exactly as an adult would respond. Adults tend to treat a mishearing as a misunderstanding and offer an alternate phrasing of their original utterance (Schegloff, personal communication). Children up to about 2½ years of age tend to repeat what they uttered previously. However, they do recognize that a re-delivery is appropriate when a repair initiation is addressed to them.

In many cases, children do provide a clearer articulation of the utterance in the repair response. In her study of peer interaction, Garvey (1977a) found that children 34–67 months regularly altered such 'repeated' utterances. In contrast to the original formulation (i.e. the repairable), these utterances (i.e. the repair responses) were marked by:

1. reduction in tempo, e.g. clear separation of syllables;
2. increase in precision of articulation, e.g. release of final consonants;
3. increase in volume;
4. use of contrastive stress on portion of the queried segment.
   (Garvey, 1977a, p. 85)

Before the age of 3 years, then, a child evidences some sensitivity to, and use of, 'recipient design'.

5.5.4 On identifying referents in the discourse topic

The Given–New contract (Clark and Haviland, 1977) requires that speakers refer to individuals, objects, events, etc., in such a way that the listener can mentally identify the referent. Applied to discourse topic, this means that the speaker should take into account the listener's knowledge or awareness of a particular object in making reference to that object within a discourse topic.

The speaker can misjudge the listener's knowledge/awareness in two ways. It is possible that the speaker may underestimate the listener's knowledge. He may, for example, describe an individual without naming him with the mistaken belief that the listener does not know that individual or at least does not know the name of that individual. In these instances, the listener may indicate his knowledge of the referent's name, e.g. through comments such as 'You mean John?', 'Oh yeah, John', 'Are you talking about John', etc.

In many cases, such errors on the part of the speaker are taken as 'talking down' and insulting by the listener. In 'talking down' the speaker believes that the listener is not informed about some individual, event, process, etc., to the extent that the speaker is. For example, a speaker might say, 'Do you know what John Kennedy, a famous president who was assassinated, once said? "Ask not what your country can do for you, but what you can do for your country."' The discourse topic, 'You (the addressee) do or do not know what John Kennedy, a famous president, who was assassinated, once said,' makes explicit that John Kennedy was a famous president who was assassinated. In cases where the listener already knows this information, the listener may feel that the speaker has underestimated the state of his general knowledge. In other words, the speaker should have presupposed more.

Far more often are cases in which the speaker overestimates the speaker's knowledge or awareness of a referent. We have discussed this behaviour with respect to Example (1). In cases such as this, the listener will not be able to understand what claim is being made or elicited. And, in our society at least, such overestimations of the listener's knowledge provoke some sort of clarification request (repair initiator) from the listener, e.g., 'Who?', 'What?', 'What comes out fast?', etc.

The speaker, then, must take steps to aid the listener in identifying particular referents within the discourse topic. This is part of good recipient design (Sacks and Schegloff, 1974). In identifying requests, speakers appeal to two major sources. First, there are appeals to the physical setting in which the communication is conveyed. Second, there are appeals to the listener's background knowledge. In the first case, the speaker directs the listener to locate the referent in *physical space*. In the second case, the speaker directs the listener to locate the referent in *memory space.*

Let us consider the way in which young children aid the listener in locating particular referents within discourse topic.

5.5.4.1 How to locate a referent in physical space
Overwhelmingly, the conversations of young children are about objects, people, or events that are present in the utterance context. Further, from a very early point in their development, children employ a variety

of devices to direct the listener's attention to these entities. These devices include both verbal and nonverbal behaviours.

Nonverbal means for locating a referent (X) include:

1. *Looking* at (X):   *Commentary*

    (24) Allison II
       (Allison had been pointing
       to mike on her mother)

       a. (Allison looks at hanging   referent = object looked at
          mike)

       b. Mother: *That's another*   referent identified by listener
           microphone.

2. *Holding* (X):

    (25) Toby and David, 35 months
       a. David: *oh dear/* X/[9]
          (sitting up, looking at his   referent = object looked at
          blanket)
          (picking up blanket,
          facing Toby) *that messing*
             up/ this/ 2X/don't
             mess it up/ you mess
             it up/ like this/

       b. Toby: *mummy did/*   referent identified by listener
           mummy did/

       c. David: *yes/*

(See also Examples (30), (32).)

3. *Reaching* for (X):

    (26) Allison III
       (Allison and mother had been
       talking about putting a diaper
       on the baby doll)

       a. Allison: (reaching for doll)   referent = object reached for
           baby doll/

       b. Mother: *Oh, there she is!*   referent identified by listener

4. *Offering* (X):

    (27) a. (Allison offering cookie   referent = object offered
          to mommy) ↑*mommy/*

       b. Mother: *Oh, thank you.*   referent identified by listener

5. *Pointing* at (X):

(28) Allison II
   a. Allison: (crawling into mother's
      lap and pointing to   referent = object pointed at
      microphone) *man*/
   b. Mother: *The man put the*   referent identified by listener
      microphone on.

(See also Example (6).)

6. *Touching* (X):

(29) Allison III
   a. Allison: (touching overhead   referent = object touched
      mike)   *mike*/
   b. Mother: *That's the*   referent identified by listener
      microphone.
   c. Allison: (turns to mother,   referent = object touched
      touching her mike)
   d. Mother: *Mommy has a*   referent identified by listener
      microphone.

From the single-word stage on, the child does not rely on nonverbal means alone to locate referents for the listener (Schieffelin, 1975). As Atkinson (1979) points out, nonverbal means are efficient only when the listener is already visually attending to the speaker.

In the data at hand we find that gestures such as reaching, pointing, and the like are accompanied by verbal means of expression; or verbal means can be used to direct the listener to the relevant referent.

The child can locate a referent verbally (with or without accompanying nonverbal devices) by using:

1. *Notice verbs* (look, see, etc.)   *Commentary*
   (Atkinson, 1979; Keenan and
   Klein, 1975):

(30) David and Toby, 35 months,
   in bedroom
   a. David: (standing, facing
      Toby, David holding up
      a battery) *a battery*/ *this*   referent = object held and
      is battery/ X/   identified
      look I find battery/

b. Toby: *I see: that Jiji's/*   referent identified by listener

2. *Expressive particles* (see section
   5.5.2):

   (31) Allison III, 20, $3\frac{1}{3}$
       a. Allison: (noticing that
                   mother's juice has spilled)   referent = object/event noticed
                   uh oh!/
       b. Mother: *uh oh.*   referent (implicitly) identified
                                          by listener
       c. Allison: (smiling, looking
                   at juice spilled on floor)
                   mommy/
       d. Mother: *What did mommy
                   do?*
       e. Allison: ↑*spill/*↓   reference identified explicitly

3. *Deictic particles*:
(a) Declarative:

   (32) Allison V, 28 months
       a. Allison: (holding truck)   referent = object being held
                   *This is a dump
                   truck/*
       b. Mother: *This is a dump   referent identified by listener
                   truck. Yeh.*
   (33) David and Toby, 35 months
       a. David: (pointing out moth   referent = object pointed at
                  in room) [i] [10] *moth/* 2X/
       b. Toby: *I see/* (*put out   referent identified by listener
                  window*)/
       c. David: *yes/*

(b) Interrogative:

   (34) David and Toby, 34 months
        eating dinner
       a. David: (looking at his bowl   referent = object looked at
                  of food) *what's zis?/*
       b. Toby: *kamoniz/*   referent identified by listener
       c. David: *no macaroniz/*
                 sketiz/

4. *Descriptive or identifying* Noun Phrase (NP)

In many cases, the child identifies a referent for a listener (or himself) by 'naming it'. This is the case in (29), (30), (32), (33), etc. In some instances the child is not secure about the appropriateness of his identification, and waits for a confirmation of the identification from the listener. In other cases, as Atkinson (1979) points out, the child may be secure about his identification, but may not be sure that the *listener* has identified the item. Often the child may refer to the item but wait for evidence that the adult has identified the object, action, etc., before going on to supply new information about it. Atkinson calls this behaviour *priming*. Priming gets the listener to focus on what the speaker wants to talk about.

As is evident in these examples, several means may be employed by the child to locate a referent in physical space. (Of course adults use these same devices when interacting with children as well as when interacting with each other.) A child may first try to locate the referent with an identifying NP, then follow this NP with a string of notice verbs, pointing, showing, etc.

We do not want to imply that every time a child touches, holds, points, or names some entity that he is trying to locate a referent for the listener. Indeed, at the one-word stage, children often employ these behaviours in the course of their own exploration of the environment. The adult may simply be an observer of this process. And if the adult wishes to enter into the interaction with the child, he may use one or another of these behaviours to locate exactly what the child is talking about.

In many cases, however, the child wants a listener to attend and acknowledge the claim he is making about some discourse topic. In these cases, the child employs means such as those described above.

The variety of means and the frequency with which they are employed suggest that young children are often sensitive to the fact that listeners must be able to identify specific entities addressed in a discourse topic proposition. This sensitivity is evidenced as well by the number of tries the child will produce to get the referent located. In many cases the child will repeat a try nine or ten times, stopping only when the listener evidences verbally that he is attending to the child's focus of attention.

(35) David and Toby, 35 months   *Commentary*
     (David holding a truck, picks
     up rabbit. Toby whistling on

pretend flute continuously,
while facing David)

a. David: *rabbit/ X/* referent = object being held
I find truck/
rabbit/ (?) as
like rabbit/
truck/ rabbit/ 2X/
truck truck rabbit/
truck/ rabbit/
(showing truck and rabbit
to Toby) *truck/ rabbit/ 2X/*

b. Toby: *truck/ rabbit/* referent identified by listener
(continues whistling)

c. David: *let me blow?/*

(For other examples, see Chapters 2 and 3)

The listener indicates that he has identified the referent in question by repeating the identification of the referent (Examples (4), (14), (32), (35)) by offering an alternate identification of the referent (Examples (18), (34)) by explicitly stating that he 'sees' the object, etc. (Examples (30), (33)) or by providing some other comment concerning the referent (Example 25). These responses are characteristic of both the child–adult and child–child discourse under study.

On the other hand, there is a way of evidencing awareness of the referent in question that is characteristic of adult behaviour only. An adult may state explicitly the question of immediate concern, addressed by the child, and in so doing specify the object, event, process, etc., pointed out earlier by the child. For example, in (31) Allison notices that her mother did something and directs her mother to notice this action (specifically the result of this action). Allison's mother shows that she has noticed in two ways: First, she repeats Allison's comment, 'uh oh!/', and second, she formulates a possible question of immediate concern, 'What did mommy do?' This question has as its discourse topic 'Mommy did something', a proposition that expresses what Allison noticed.

Although in the discourse described above, the child is relatively successful in calling attention to a referent, there are cases in which the child does not provide adequate cues. In these cases, the referent is located only after one or more repair initiators by the listener; or the referent is never located at all, and the communication fails. In our data, the listener's difficulties in locating referents in the discourse topic derive from at least two major sources:

1. First, the child may confuse the listener by providing *conflicting nonverbal cues*. For example:

(36) Allison II, 19,2 months   *Commentary*
     (sitting on mother's lap)
     a. Allison: (pointing towards   referent = object pointed at
        photographer, touching
        her mouth) *man/*
     b. Mother: *mouth?*   repair initiator on identity of
                              referent
     c. Allison: (pointing to her
        tongue) ↑(?)/↓(whimpers)
        down/
                              (referent not identified by
                              listener)

In (36)a, Allison incidentally touches her mouth as she is pointing out the photographer. At (36)b, Allison's mother is misled by Allison's touching her mouth, and tentatively interprets her utterance as 'mouth', not 'man'. The utterance 'mouth?' requests clarification (initiates a repair) but Allison interprets her mother's utterance as a question about her mouth, e.g. 'where is your mouth?' Step 3 of the prerequisites for establishing a discourse topic is, then, not successful, and the discourse topic is dropped.

In other interactions of this sort, the child may be looking at one thing, and holding up another, and commenting on just one of these things.

(37) Allison IV, 22 months   *Commentary*
     (Allison has taken a calf then
     a cow out of a box. She has
     called the calf 'cow/' and the
     cow 'big cow/') she then,
     a. Allison: (looks at calf,   referent = object looked at
        holding up cow) *tiny ku/*↑↓
     b. Mother: *what?*   repair initiator on step 2
     c. Allison: (looking at cow)   repair response on step 2
        tiny cow/
     d. Mother: *Where's the tiny*   repair initiator on identity
        cow?   of referent
     e. Allison: (showing mother
        calf, holding it next to cow,
        then lifting it up)

        right here/   repair response
  f. Mother: *Right,↑↓*   referent identified by listener
        that's the tiny cow.

In (37), the adult is using the child's gaze direction as a cue in helping to locate what the child is referring to. At (37)d, the adult initiates a repair to establish the unique referent of 'tiny cow'. (The adult knows which object is the tiny cow; she does not know which object the child is calling a tiny cow.) At (37)e Allison is able to repair this misunderstanding through nonverbal and verbal means.

2. A second source of confusion for the listener stems from the child's *failure to specify the referent in a precise enough manner.* Again, in many of these cases, the communication was never intended as social and so not oriented to listener needs. In other cases, however, the child does want to convey the discourse topic and locating a key referent for the listener is a means to this end.

    In the data at hand, vagueness is a result of a failure to provide sufficient nonverbal cues, and/or sufficient verbal cues. For example, we find that a child will often look at an object or an event, or hold an object and refer to it as if it were already identified by the listener. In many cases, the child looks at or touches something present in the environment, and refers to it by some deictic term, such as 'this', [i], 'it'. This is illustrated in a different 'spill' sequence from that in Example (31).

(38) Allison V, 28 months   *Commentary*
    (Allison had been eating a
    cookie, drinking juice, she
    spills some juice from her
    mouth)
    a. Allison: *uh/* (looks at her
       dress, purposely pours juice
       onto it)
    b. Mother: *Oh, what happened?*
           What did you do?
           What did you do?
    c. Allison: (touching her knee,
       looking at original spill)
       spill something/
    d. Mother: *What did you do?*
    e. Allison: (holding up cookie,
       scraping it with her finger)

	it came down from	referent = objects being
	ə ↑cookie/↓	scraped (cookies)
f. Mother:	*What?*	repair initiator on step 2
g. Allison:	(rubbing her dress)	repair response
	it came ↑on my	
	dress/	
h. Mother:	*It came on your*	
	dress. It didn't come	
	on the cookie. ↓Oh	
	means we better wipe	
	you off.	
		(referent not identified by
		listener)

In (38)d Allison's mother is eliciting information about the spilling of the juice by Allison. Allison, however, turned her attention to something else that fell on her dress along with the juice, that is, cookie crumbs. Her utterance at (38)e is a claim that the crumbs ('it) 'came down from a cookie'. The discourse topic is something to the effect, 'The crumbs came from somewhere'. But, because Allison did not clarify sufficiently the referent of 'it', Allison's mother takes the term to refer to the juice, rather than the crumbs. This is evident at (38)f when Allison's mother comments, 'It came on your dress. It didn't come on the cookie'.

Under-specification may also result from a child's deletion of a lexical item, or items within an utterance. Greenfield and Smith (1976) have observed that children in the one-word stage delete certain 'presupposed' information and make explicit what they consider to be important or noteworthy, i.e. 'informative'. Often the information deleted concerns an individual(s) or an event(s) about which the child's utterance provides a 'comment'. We find that deletion of taken-for-granted material continues, but to a lesser extent, throughout our child data sample. (In fact, adult discourse is laced with these deletions as well.) In some contexts, the deleted referent (or set of referents) is not altogether obvious to the listener, and the listener initiates a repair on this referent.

		Commentary
(39) Allison IV, 22 months		
(Allison seeing herself on the		
TV monitor)		
a. Allison: (putting hand to		
her head) *comb hair/*		referent = agent

b. Mother: *Comb hair?*	repair initiator on step 2
c. Allison: *Baby Allison comb hair/*	repair response
d. Mother: *Baby Allison comb hair?*	repair initiator on steps 2 and 3
e. Allison: *yeah/*	repair response (referent identified by listener)

Notice that the child is able to repair the unclarity and successfully locate a critical referent. We find that children at the single-word stage can repair misunderstandings related to referents located in the present *physical space*. However, the same cannot be said for their ability to initiate repairs on locating referents in the utterances of other children or adults. We found no instances of such repair initiators in the Allison Bloom sample, ranging from age 16 months to 28 months. Repair initiation of this sort starts at 35 months in the Toby and David sample (see Example (17)). However, it is a rare occurrence (see Chapter 6). Much more frequent in the Toby and David sample is repair initiation on step 2, articulation (see Garvey (1977a) for a careful discussion of this phenomenon).

We have seen, then, two striking differences between adult–child and child–child discourse. The first is that the adult often explicitly reconstructs a question of immediate concern on the basis of a referring expression by the child. The second is that the adult initiates a repair from the child if a referent is insufficiently located. These observations need to be confirmed by looking at a wider sample of children's discourse.

5.5.4.2 *How to locate a referent in memory*
We have stated that most of the claims made or elicited by young children concern entities that exist in the physical environment of the verbal interaction. However, even very young children sometimes refer to events or individuals that are not present in the ongoing setting. Some of these references are fictitious events or individuals (fantasy) and some are actual individuals or events known to the child from some prior experience. We find child–child discourse up to 37 months to include primarily the first of this type of 'non-situated reference' (fantasy), whereas child–adult discourse contains primarily the second type of these references.

Both types of reference are usually provoked by some object or event, or individual that *is* situated in the ongoing physical context.

In the case of fantasy, something noticed in the setting is associated with some imaginary entity. For example, a battery picked up from the floor by David at 35 months of age is identified first as a battery, and then as a steam roller. Subsequent stretches of discourse use steam roller in various roles within a discourse topic. In the case of 'real world' non-situated reference, some event, etc., triggers off a remembering by the child of a similar entity in the past.

We find that before the age of three, children experience enormous difficulty in getting 'real world' non-situated events, individuals, etc., established as a discourse topic. Typically, the transition from the here and now to past experience, is not clearly communicated by the child. In adult–child interaction, the transition often takes the adult by surprise, and the referent in question cannot be determined. Example (14) illustrates this type of communication roadblock. Here the particular 'glass' being referred to by Allison cannot be identified by the listener, and so 'glass' is not included in subsequent discourse topics.

There are numerous reasons, why these referents are often not identified by the listener. To sort out these reasons, it is useful to compare means available to the child for locating referents in physical space with those available for memory searches:

1. Salient from the video record is the fact that *children rely heavily on nonverbal cues to locate what they are talking about.* This is true both in initial identifications of referents, and in responses to repair initiators. These cues are appropriate to the here and now context, but ineffective in locating objects in the listener's memory. Thus, one important class of 'locators' play no role in helping the listener to retrieve the referent from memory space.

2. Second, although the children in this study use 'notice verbs' such as 'look' and 'see' to direct the listener to an object in physical space, *they do not use these notice verbs to locate referents in memory.* Adults, in contrast, often direct the listener's attention to some individual or event not present through such utterances as '*Look* at what happened to Joe . . . he got a very raw deal from that company.' In certain Scots dialects the verb *see* is used in this way. Atkinson (1979) quotes Macrae as saying that sentences of the form, 'See Jimmy? See chips? He likes 'em' are perfectly appropriate even when 'Jimmy' and 'chips' are not present in the speaker's or hearer's environment.

   Additionally, adults have several other notice verbs that are used to focus attention on a referent in memory (Atkinson, 1979). As discussed in section 5.1, adults often explicitly request the listener to search in memory for some particular referent. They ask the listener if he 'remembers' or 'knows' or 'recalls' a particular individual, object or incident before going on to say anything about it (e.g. Example (2)). The use of these verbs is not evident in the children's discourse under study.

3. A further impedance to locating referents in the listener's memory is the *late development of old information markers* in the speech of young children. The use of anaphoric pronouns, for example, is not part of the child's competence until his average utterance length is at least 2.5 morphemes (Bloom, Lightbown and Hood, 1975), i.e. the child is regularly producing three-word utterances. Before this point, a child may use pronominal forms, but they are used deictically, i.e. to point out things present in the environment, rather than anaphorically. The same can be said of definite articles. Their use in referring to entities not present is not part of the child's competence before 32 months (Maratsos, 1974). Relative clauses as well do not appear anywhere in our corpus of children's utterances.

Thus it is difficult for the young child to mark specifically that he/she is talking about something that he/she has already experienced. Allison at 20,3½ months has no way of marking that the glass she is referring to (Example (14)) is *that* or *the* glass *that was set in the cups.*

4. It is also important to note that the transition from present to prior experience is confounded by the child's non-existent or (later) inconsistent *use of tense marking.*

In general, referring to objects, persons, etc., not contextually situated puts a greater burden on the child's verbal resources. The child must rely exclusively on verbal means to locate the referent in question. In many cases, the listener can simply not determine this referent, as adequate syntactic and semantic marking has not yet emerged in the child's speech. Adults often treat these references of the child as coming 'out of the blue' or irrelevant. They may initiate repairs on the referent, e.g. 'where is the X?' or shift the discourse to a discourse topic that can be determined by both conversational partners.[11]

5.5.4.3 *Identifying referents and old information*

Our observations of adult–adult, adult–child, and child–child conversations indicate overwhelmingly that objects, events, and persons, etc., that play a role in a discourse topic are known to or knowable by the listener as well as the speaker. This is evidenced in two ways.

First, in adult-child discourse, if a child refers to some entity that cannot be located by the adult in physical or memory space, the adult listener usually initiates a repair in an effort to elicit information that will facilitate an identification.

Second, both adult and child speakers are reluctant to use a referent in a discourse topic without confirmation that the referent is known to, or knowable by, the listener (see also Sankoff and Brown (1976) for a discussion of this phenomenon in Tok Pisin). We have provided numerous examples in which young children wait for confirmation from the listener that the relevant referent is identified. And, while adults in talking to one another elicit such confirmation less often, at times they spend considerable efforts in insuring that the entity that they are referring to is a piece of 'shared knowledge'. The following conversation illustrates the amount of conversational space that a speaker can take up with this endeavour.

(40)(Two women in a dress shop)   *Commentary*
Marie tapes (transcribed by
Françoise Brun-Cottian) (pause)
a. Marie: Hah-Hah-Ha
               Remember that red
               blazer you got on the
               other – you had on
               the other day?
               (pause 3 sec.)
b. Dottie: *Me?*
c. ⌈Marie: *Yah that r//ed*
d. ⌊Dottie: *Sweater?*
e. Marie: *Ya that red* – (0.6
               sec.) *thing that uh*
               (1 sec.) *that uh keeps*
               the cold out (but)
               (2 sec.) *The red one*
               (it's –) (2 sec.)
               thin thin thin
               (7 sec.)
f. Dottie: *You mean with the*
               roun' neck? (2 sec.)
               (what cha) *talking*
               about (0.4 sec.)
Marie turns to third woman
and discusses a dress for

several turns. She then
returns to her conversation
with Dottie.

e. Marie: (finds object in
shop shows to Dottie)
This. (1.2 sec.)

h. Dottie: *Oh the red one*   referent identified by listener
I had on// ya:h

i. Marie: *Yeah uh –*
somebody wanted
one, who wanted it.

5.5.5 Identifying the discourse topic proposition

When adults talk to one another, they may not always be certain of the discourse topic addressed by a speaker. That is, the speaker may not always state the discourse proposition as part of an explicit question of immediate concern. On the basis of the utterance itself, prior utterances exchanged and other shared background knowledge, however, the listener may reconstruct a plausible discourse topic addressed by the speaker. On the basis of this reconstruction, the listener then provides (what he perceives to be) a relevant or appropriate response.

There are a number of reasons why this reconstruction process for the listener is easier in adult–adult conversations than in adult–child or child–child conversations.

As noted earlier, adults usually conform to the conversational convention of making their utterances relevant to the current discourse (unless otherwise marked). If an adult (in this society) is attending to a discourse topic that is not tied to the prior discourse topic and/or claim (introducing topic, re-introducing topic) then he is expected to mark this break in some overt manner, e.g. through expressive particles ('Hey', 'Oh no', 'I forgot', etc.), explicit topic-switching expressions, or explicit questions of immediate concern (see sections 5.3 and 5.4.1.3).

This convention is not well-established for young children, particularly those at the one- and two-word stages. There are several reasons for this:

1. First, children at this point in their development have a *more limited attention span* than do older children and adults. This limitation makes it difficult for them to collaborate on or incorporate discourse topics for an extended period of time. At a point of topic exhaustion

(Keenan and Klein, 1975) the child may suddenly turn to a radically different focus of attention.

2. Second, the child is *easily distracted by some new thing he/she has noticed* in the physical environment. In producing an utterance, the child may be focusing on a novel entity rather than on a discourse topic or claim in some last utterance.

3. Third, the child may not provide a relevant next utterance because he *does not understand the point (the discourse topic) of the preceding utterance.* This is particularly the case where the preceding utterance is a declarative one produced by another speaker. In declarative utterances, the question of immediate concern is implicit. In contrast to explicit questions of immediate concern, the child must construct for himself the concern underlying a declarative. This process may often be too difficult for the child, leading him to produce an irrelevant next utterance.

4. Fourth, the child may not respond relevantly to a preceding utterance because he *had not attended to it in the first place.* The child may, for example, be absorbed in his own description of some activity and not attend to utterances directed to him from a conversational partner. This behaviour is characteristic of egocentric speech, what Piaget (1926) calls 'collective monologues'. Thus, if an adult directs a question to a young child, the subsequent utterance by the child may not be a response to that question but a comment relative to the child's previous discourse.

In many cases, the conversational partner realizes that the child has not attended to the immediately preceding utterance but to some other concern. In other cases, however, the child does not provide sufficient cues that his/her attention is directed to some utterance other than the preceding one. For example, attention to a novel object in the environment may be marked only by a shift in gaze direction. The listener is often not aware of this nonverbal behaviour. Thus he is not aware of the concern the child's utterance addresses.

In some cases, the child provides no salient cues whatsoever that his attention has shifted, e.g. where the child is referring to some past experience. For example:

(41) Jason, 24 months
    a. (Jason falls on floor)
       Mother: *What happened?* (2X)
       (long pause)
    b. Jason: *book/*

c. Mother: *Is that a book?*
d. Jason: *me/*
e. Mother: *This isn't your book. Where's your book?*
f. Jason: *me/*
g. Mother: *Where's your chicken book?*
h. (Jason picks up book)
     Mother: *No, that's Gramma's book.*
i. Jason: *me/*
j. Mother: *You can't read Gramma's book.*
k. Jason: *yeah/*
l. Mother: *No. Where's your book?*
m. Jason: *me/*
n. Mother: *Where's Jason's book?*
o. (Jason looks at book)
     Mother: *Gramma's book.*
p. Jason: *me/*
q. Mother: *Oh, what did you hurt?*
r. Jason: *nose/*
s. Mother: *Oh, you hurt your nose.*
t. Jason: *bleed/*
u. Mother: *Oh, does your nose bleed?*
v. Jason: *yeah/ nose*
(transcribed by L. Tweed)

In (41), Jason falls down but does not respond immediately to his mother's query about the fall. He turns his attention to a book in the room. This shift is perceived by the mother, and she directs a number of utterances to Jason concerning the book. However, by (41)d Jason shifts the focus of attention back to himself. The mother, however, continues to interpret Jason's utterance 'me/' in terms of the immediately preceding focus of interest, identification of the book. For example, Jason's utterance at (41)d is treated as a response to (41)c, and it is corrected by the mother at (41)e. For the bulk of the discourse, two distinct concerns are being handled by child and mother. In addition to the mother's (and occasionally Jason's) concern with the book, Jason is apparently saying something about his fall in uttering 'me/' ((41)d). He is not replying to his mother's question. This becomes clearer when Jason stops repeating 'me/' and answers his mother's question at (41)q. This question articulates Jason's concern (his discourse topic), i.e. 'Jason hurt something (some part of himself).' He collaborates on this discourse topic at (41)r and from this point on in the discourse, matters relating to this proposition are addressed.

The misunderstanding in (41) prevails for an extraordinary number of turns.[12] We find nothing of this length in the Allison tapes, for example. The length of this confusion was probably affected by Jason's occasional verbal and nonverbal collaboration on/incorporation of his mother's discourse topic and claim ((41)h, (41)k, (41)o).

A second problem in determining the discourse topic proposition of a child's utterance is linked to the child's limited syntactic/semantic competence. It is usually much more difficult for a listener to determine the discourse topic for utterances that express only part of a claim than for utterances that express a claim explicitly. For example:

(42) Allison II, 19,2 months
    a. Allison: (crawling into her mother's lap and pointing to
               microphone) *man/*
    b. Mother: *The man put the microphone on. Right.*

In (42), it is more difficult to reconstruct the discourse topic for Allison's utterance ((42)a) 'man/' than it would be if the utterance were syntactically and semantically more complete. At (42)a the child conveys only that 'man/' is somehow related to the object she is pointing to (the microphone). If the utterance were more complex, then the listener would have a clearer idea of the claim being made by the child and would be better equipped to determine the question of immediate concern being addressed.[13]

Faced with utterances such as these, the listener has to bring in a great deal of contextual knowledge to reconstruct the question of immediate concern (see section 5.4). The listener considers plausible questions that the communicative act (pointing at one object and uttering 'man/') could be a response to: is the child telling me (the listener) 'what a man did' (discourse topic: 'the man did something'); or 'who did something to the microphone' (discourse topic: 'someone did something to the microphone'); or what? When Allison's mother *expands* (interprets) Allison's utterance as 'The man put the microphone on,' she creates a range of possible questions of immediate concern that Allison's utterance might be a response to, e.g. 'What did the man do?' 'Who put the microphone on?'

Expansions can be seen as one of several means of delimiting possible discourse topics addressed in a child's communicative act. An expanded interpretation can be expressed as an assertion or, more tentatively, as a clarification request (repair initiator). The first alternative assumes that unless otherwise challenged, the expansion (interpretation) is plausible. The second alternative requests an explicit confirmation check (repair response) from the child.

As noted previously, an additional means for arriving at the intended discourse topic of the child is to propose it as a primary presupposition of an explicit question of immediate concern. This response is illustrated in Examples (31) and (38). This alternative differs from expansions in that the speaker commits himself to a specific discourse topic. In expansions, the speaker merely reduces the number of possible questions the utterance is relevant to. On the other hand, questions of immediate concern share certain characteristics of expansions used as repair initiators. They both generate a *topic-collaborating* sequence of utterances. In both cases, the listener is eliciting information about a particular proposition, and the child (speaker) is providing information relevant to that *same* proposition.

5.6 Implications for the notion of competence in child language

The four steps described here for establishing a discourse topic are fundamental to successful communication. Children must develop means to accomplish each of these steps, if they are both to contribute to, and sustain, a coherent discourse. We propose that the extent to which a child is capable of completing these steps is an important measure of the child's developing communicative competence. We say communicative, rather than strictly linguistic, because the child relies on both verbal and nonverbal means for accomplishing these steps.

We need to examine the visual and verbal records of children's speech to determine:

1. *Which steps are taken by the child.* For example, the first analysis of children's speech at the one- and two-word stage shows that steps 1, 2 and 3 are taken by the child. Children at this point in their development can point out referents that are relevant to a discourse topic proposition, but they do not specify the semantic roles of such referents in the discourse topic (step 4). As we have seen, the listener is left to reconstruct the proposition on the basis of the referent located, and shared background knowledge.

2. *How much conversational space (number of utterances, number of turns) is taken up with satisfying each step.* One of the most important things to consider here is the context in which the interaction is occurring. The amount of conversational space taken up depends on the number of individuals present, the extent to which they are attending to the child, and the extent to which they are familiar

with the child and his experiences. In addition, it is important to consider whether the intended listener is an adult, an older child, or a peer. The same string of sounds could be successfully interpreted in one context, yet not understood at all in another context. Those who are intimate with a child may compensate for poor articulation, idiosyncratic expressions, and 'out of the blue' references.

Contexts in which the listener is not intimate with the child reveal more clearly the child's competence. In these contexts, the child must work harder to accomplish these steps. Further, these contexts generate repair procedures. These procedures make explicit what information the child can and cannot provide at each step.

It would be useful to examine adult speech to children to see the extent to which adults initiate repairs on each of these steps. It may be the case that adults only request repairs on those steps the child is capable of carrying out. In this case, we would see a shift in the nature of the repair initiator over time. (This shift would also be affected by what needs to be repaired, e.g. as the child articulates his message more clearly, there should be fewer repair initiators on step 2.)

3. *The means employed by the child for implementing each step.* Although speakers never stop relying on nonverbal means in conveying messages, the extent of their reliance varies developmentally. That is, children come to rely more and more on verbal means to convey their messages, and this in turn provides more explicit cues as to what discourse topic is being addressed. This process has often been noted, but only recently has documentation of this process begun (Greenfield and Smith, 1976).

Looking to verbal means, we need to examine developmental changes in the child's ability to refer to entities in both physical and memory space. And we need to document when and how a child makes it explicit (verbally) that he is introducing a novel topic, or re-introducing a topic addressed earlier.

5.7 Comprehension

A further dimension in the development of competence concerns the extent to which a child is able to determine the discourse topic of a conversational partner. As has often been noted, the relationship between comprehension and production at any one point in time is difficult to determine. However, we can get some indication of what the child is understanding from observing two kinds of responses:

1. When an adult does not understand an utterance, he has the option of initiating a repair on that utterance. It would seem reasonable to look at the child language data for these responses. We find, however, that children initially do not evidence their misunderstanding in this form. As noted, we find no such verbal repair initiators in our data until the child is almost 3 years of age. Once they have emerged in the child's speech, it is important to document the changing character of the repair-initiators, that is, the order in which repairs on each step emerge.

2. The second response that may be said to indicate comprehension on the part of the child (listener) is topic collaboration. This is clearest in question–answer topic-collaborating sequences. To answer a question, the child must locate the discourse topic of the question (i.e. the proposition about which information is requested) and use this discourse topic in his/her answer (see Examples (3), (10), (13), (14), (34)).

It is necessary to examine the child's ability to both collaborate on 'old' topics and initiate 'new' topics in the discourse. We find in our data that asking questions is a speech behaviour more character-istic of adults speaking to children than children speaking to adults, or to each other. A consequence of this is that children often col-laborate on a discourse topic proposed by an adult. We expect to find variation in the extent to which one child can introduce a discourse topic rather than collaborate on a discourse topic. In many of the interactions between adults and children, for example, the adult controls the direction of the conversation by repeatedly initiating discourse topics which the child is then expected to respond to (Corsaro, 1979). This is particularly characteristic of experimental situations, where a question–answer tactic is employed. In these situations, only the child's ability to determine the discourse topic proposition is evident. The child's ability to establish new discourse topics cannot be observed.

5.8 Why discourse topic?

Our treatment of topic as a discourse notion should be considered as distinct from other descriptions of topic in the linguistic literature. From our point of view, topic is not a simple NP but a proposition (about which some claim is made or elicited). In the linguistic literature, left dislocation of an NP (e.g. 'This paper, it's almost done.') has been treated as a topicalization device (Gruber, 1967; Gundel, 1975). From our point of view, these left dislocated NPs vary in the roles they play with respect to discourse and discourse topic.

For example, unstressed left dislocated NPs preceded by *as for* or *concerning* typically retrieve earlier discourse material. In our framework, these constructions mark re-introducing topics. The construction brings a prior proposition or a referent within a prior proposition back into focus. This function might explain why the NPs appearing after *as for* or *concerning* are not drawn from an immediately preceding utterance. For example, a sequence such as 'Where is John?' 'As for John, he's at home' seems inappropriate. It is inappropriate, because there is no need to retrieve or foreground the referent. This function explains as well why *as for* constructions followed by stressed NPs are used to contrast or emphasize referents or propositions, e.g. 'Mary said she wouldn't help, but as for *me*, I'm willing.'

Left dislocated NPs not preceded by *as for* or *concerning* are considerably less restricted in discourse. We find that these constructions may both introduce novel referents and propositions or reintroduce previously mentioned referents and propositions. We find that in many cases the left dislocated NP may be part of the new information or comment on a discourse topic, e.g. 'What's the matter?' 'My father, he's bugging me again.' Here the left dislocated NP is part of the new information provided about the discourse topic proposition, 'Something is the matter.' The NP 'my father' is the 'centre of attention' (Li and Thompson, 1976) of the sentence in which it is couched. *It is not the 'centre of attention' of the discourse in which the sentence is couched.*[14]

It would be valuable to have some understanding of discourse dynamics in topic-prominent languages (Li and Thompson, 1976). In languages where topic-comment constructions alternate with subject-predicate constructions, e.g. Chinese, the use of topic constructions may be contextually constrained. It would be useful to examine spontaneous conversational discourse in these languages to determine the functions of the topic construction in the discourse context. Can these constructions re-introduce, introduce, collaborate, incorporate discourse material? Or is their use restricted to some of these functions only? Where topic-constructions are aways the norm, we would like to determine as well:

1. if all these functions are handled; and
2. if the language differentiates these functions morphologically or syntactically.

In general, we want to establish a framework for comparing topic constructions in their discourse contexts across languages.

We offer here a baseline description of topic in discourse. We refer to this notion as discourse topic, because it is usually discourse-generated (relevant) and often discourse-generating.

Notes

1. We would like to thank the following kind people for their assistance in and patience throughout the formulation of this paper: Edward L. Keenan, Edward L. Schieffelin, Rich Frankel, Gillian Michell, Martha Platt, Sharon Sabsay, Jim Heringer and Emanuel Schegloff.
2. This research was supported by a grant from Social Science Research Council grant no. HR/2941/1.
3. For the Allison data, only gaze directed to the mother is marked. ↑ = child makes eye contact with mother. ↓ = child terminates eye contact with mother.
4. This notion is very close to that of *topic-shading* as discussed by Schegloff and Sacks (1973, p. 305): 'One procedure whereby talk moves off a topic might be called "topic shading" in that it involves no specific attention to ending a topic at all, but rather the fitting of differently focused but related talk to some last utterance in a topic's development.' We do not employ the same term, as the co-creators of it may not agree with the notion of discourse topic developed in this paper.
5. Greenfield and Smith (1976) have discussed the notion of informativeness for children at the one-word stage. In their framework, the child tends to encode that aspect of a situation that the child considers to be the least certain. For example, in volitional acts (requests, demands), 'When the object is securely in the child's possession . . . it becomes relatively certain and the child will first encode Action/State . . . . When the object is not in the child's possession, it becomes more uncertain, and his first utterance will express the object' (Chap. 4).
6. Anglo speakers of English, of course, also 're-introduce' concerns discussed at some prior time. The difference between the two cultures is that Anglo speakers of English mark these re-introducing topics in formal social contexts with constructions such as 'As for . . .', 'Concerning . . .', etc., whereas Indian speakers do not. In less formal contexts, Anglo speakers too are under less constraint to mark overtly that they are addressing their utterance to a prior concern (not addressed in the immediately preceding utterance).
7. For children of 13+ months the establishment of eye contact is one of the most reliable measures of having secured the attention of the listener (Huttenlocher, 1974).

8. These utterances are typically omitted in developmental psycho-linguistic literature. They are characterized as unintelligible. From our point of view, they are often *unreconstructable*, from the hearer's point of view.

9. /X/ = repetition of prior utterance.

10. [i] = general deictic particle for 'there', 'it', 'this', etc.

11. Frequently the adult can reconstruct what the child is talking about despite the child's inability to provide adequate information. The amount of shared experience is critical in this reconstruction process. Someone who spends many hours a day knowing what the child has been doing can often understand an 'out of context' utterance to a much greater extent than an investigator making infrequent visits.

12. It is difficult to say to what extent the child has designed his communication to meet the recipient's needs without access to a video record of the event. The child might have been giving additional cues that the mother didn't attend to.

13. There is adequate evidence prior to this utterance that Allison knows the appropriate label for 'man' and for 'microphone'. Her utterance combined with the pointing can be assumed to be an intentional linking of man and microphone.

14. We wish to point out that a left dislocated simple NP may be either an explicit 'representation' of an implicit proposition or a referring expression only: 'Champagne, that's a fantastic idea' vs 'Champagne, it makes me feel fine.'

6

Questions of immediate concern

*E. Ochs Keenan, Bambi B. Schieffelin
and Martha Platt*

6.1 Propositions and utterances

Fundamental to communication is the capacity both to articulate intentions in such a manner that they are understood by a listener and to interpret the intentions of those addressing us. When we consider the emergence of language in young children, we document the development of this capacity. Until recently, this documentation took the form of a description of the child's utterance; we would ask questions such as: Is the utterance single- or multi-word? Does the utterance display formal organization, i.e. use of word order, inflection? (Bloom, 1970; Bowerman, 1973). Is the utterance a directive, a description, a piece of sound play, or what? (Bloom, 1970; Ervin-Tripp, 1976; see also Chapter 1). In all of these endeavours, the investigator treats the utterance as a viable unit in much the same way as the sentence is a viable unit in adult speech behaviour. The child is portrayed as encoding ideas or propositions into utterances in roughly the same manner as the adult encodes propositions or ideas into sentences. The utterance may correspond more or less perfectly with the comparable adult sentence.

Considerable understanding of language acquisition has been gleaned from the research strategy outlined above. In the past three years, however, the notion that an utterance in child language is always comparable semantically to a sentence in adult language has been questioned (Bloom, 1973; Greenfield and Smith, 1976; Keenan and Klein, 1975; Scollon, 1976; see also Chapter 3). The transcription of utterance contexts while recording children's speech has led some researchers to believe that the child relies heavily on the immediate environment in expressing her/his concerns. This is not an absolute difference between adults and young children; it is rather a difference of degree. Children in the initial stages of language development rely much more heavily on the utterance context in conveying their wants, needs, beliefs than do adults. For example, Greenfield and Smith (1976) point out that a child often deletes a contextually highly predictable piece of information from an utterance. The addressee (if there is one) makes sense out of the utterance by relating the utterance to obvious features of the context. One finds, for example, that simply an action or event has been encoded in an utterance while the relevant agent must be inferred from the situation at hand.

The same argument can be used in relating the child's utterance to its *verbal* environment. In much the same way that the child exploits the nonverbal context to make a point, the child exploits the discourse context to communicate an intention. The discourse exploited may be the child's own prior utterance or the prior utterances of a conversational partner. Further, this sort of exploitation is frequent from the single-word utterance stage (Atkinson, 1979; Scollon, 1976; Bloom, 1973) up through the period when children regularly produce multi-word utterances (e.g. mean number of words per utterance is 2.9) (see Chapter 3). Indeed, we find that adults often build on antecedent utterances in such a manner (Jefferson and Schenkein, 1977). Again we emphasize that the difference between adult and child usage lies in the extent to which such a manoeuvre is employed. For example, children at the single-word stage rely *heavily* on previous utterances in encoding a proposition. Scollon (1973) calls the resulting propositional sequence a 'vertical construction'.

Example (1) illustrates such a construction.

(1) Brenda, 20 months 21 days (Scollon, 1973)
    (Brenda lifts foot over tape recorder, pretending to step on it)
    tape/
    step/

In this example, Brenda uses a sequence of two utterances to partially encode an idea she wishes to communicate. The idea or proposition could be glossed roughly as 'I am pretending to step on the tape recorder' or 'I am going to step on the tape recorder.' However, again the entire proposition is not encoded verbally. Much information is conveyed by Brenda's actions.

Data of this character have been observed and reported by Bloom (1973) as well. Bloom refers to such constructions as 'holistic' constructions. Both Bloom and Scollon report that these constructions appear later in the single-word stage than utterances that do not build on prior talk. The data collectively suggest that children at first build on the nonverbal context and later come to incorporate the verbal context of their utterances (Greenfield and Smith, 1976).

From this point of view the development of linguistic competence consists of the eventual move away from heavy reliance on context (verbal and nonverbal) towards greater reliance on utterance-internal formal devices. In the case of verbal context, the move is away from reliance on *discourse* to convey a proposition towards greater reliance on *syntax* to carry out this task.

We have argued in an earlier paper (Keenan, Schieffelin and Platt, 1979) that the proposition, not the utterance, should be the basic unit of analysis in developmental studies of language. Taking the proposition rather than the utterance as one's basic unit turns out to be productive in understanding the speech of caretakers as well as the speech of language-acquiring children. Our data indicate that caretakers often structure their speech in such a way that a message is conveyed over the space of several utterances rather than within a single utterance. Each utterance in such a sequence carries out a specific task. For example, one utterance may express something the caretaker wants to talk about, and a subsequent utterance may express the predication concerning that something. The predication may concern something the caretaker wants the child to do, a reporting of some event, a description, an offer, and so on.

We argue here that the utilization of discourse in this way is a characteristic feature of caretaker–child interaction in this society. More generally, we argue that this use of speech represents an adjustment to perceived communicative distress (Sabsay, 1976). The sources of the distress may vary depending on the competence of speaker and hearer and on the speaker–hearer relationship. For different reasons, the structuring of propositions across discourse may be a defining feature of interaction between adult and child, between native speaker and second-language learner, or between normal speaker and language-impaired speaker. In the work to follow we examine the nature of these sequences in the speech of caretaker to child.

In looking at propositional sequences, we focus on one heavily employed utterance type, the interrogative. A frequently observed characteristic of caretaker speech in western societies is a heavy reliance on interrogatives; interrogatives can account for up to 50 per cent of the adult speech corpus (Newport, 1976; Corsaro, 1979; Scollon, 1976). We claim that the prominence of interrogative constructions in adult speech to children is linked to the strategy outlined above. In particular, we claim that interrogatives are used to articulate something the caretaker or child wishes to attend to (Atkinson, 1979) or talk about, i.e. they articulate conversational topics (see Chapter 5). They initiate a stretch of discourse in which a proposition is constructed co-operatively by caretaker and child or by one speaker alone. We consider below particular reasons why the interrogative is employed to this end and the types of interrogative sequences employed by caretakers in this speech community.

6.2 Data base

The data used for the present research are drawn from three primary sources. The first source consists of transcriptions of six 30-minute videotapes of a child, Allison Bloom (aged 16–34 months), interacting with her mother. The first four of these tapes have been analysed by L. Bloom in *One Word at a Time* (1973). The second source consists of transcriptions of audio- and videotaped interactions of a caretaker with twin boys, Toby and David Keenan (aged from 33 to 35 months). These transcriptions are part of a larger corpus collected by E. O. Keenan (Keenan and Klein, 1975; see also Chapters 2 and 5). These sources are supplemented by three 60-minute audiotapes of three mothers interacting with their 24-month-old children in home settings. These tapes were transcribed by L. Tweed for the UCLA Infant Studies Project under the direction of D. Parmalee.

6.3 The work of interrogatives

6.3.1 The interrogative as a directive to attend

6.3.1.1 The child as listener
Normally utterances produced by a speaker are directed to some listener or set of listeners. In these cases, the speaker intends that his/her utterance produce some effect in the listener (e.g. to alter his state of knowledge, to alter his future behaviour, to ratify speaker–listener ties, and so on). In order for such an effect to take place in the listener's mental or physical behaviour, the speaker must ensure that certain prerequisites for successful communication have been met. One of these prerequisites is *that the listener is actually attending to the speaker.*

In most face-to-face interactions, interlocutors do not take for granted that conversational partners are attending to them and their utterances. We find in adult–adult as well as in adult–child and child–child discourse that speakers periodically elicit evidence of attentiveness from a listener. Speakers elicit feedback through a range of devices, including vocatives, confirmation checks (e.g. 'right?' 'y'know?' 'mmm?'), invitations to notice something (e.g. 'look!' 'uh oh!' 'oh dear!'; laughing, crying, screaming), pauses in the discourse, eye contact with the listener, and other nonverbal actions.

Some of these attention-getting devices may draw attention to the speaker only: for example, vocatives. In other cases, the attention-getting device may be used to direct the listener to some event or object the speaker wishes to comment on. For example, a speaker who exclaims 'Uh oh!' may cause a co-present person to search for the topical item(s) that provoked the exclamation. If no such item is immediately apparent, the exclamation may elicit queries concerning the nature of the topical item, e.g. 'What is it?' 'What happened?' 'What's the matter?' etc.

The problem of securing the listener's attention is particularly acute in cases where the listener is a child. The child's inattention may stem from any one of a number of sources.

1. For example, the child may have been attending to what the speaker was attending to but, because of *his/her limited attention span*, shifted to other interests. For example, in (2) Allison and her mother had been attending to and commenting on a picture of a girl for over two conversational turns. At this point (line 4), Allison appears to lose interest, whereupon (line 7) her mother directs Allison's attention to a new topical item (something Mommy found, i.e. car).

(2) Allison, 16,3 months
   1 A (drops picture; picking it up): *uh uh no widə/*
   2   (turns picture so she can see girl): *there/*
   3 Mo: *There.*
   4 A (trying to get off chair): *down/*
   5 Mo: *Down.*
   6 A: *widə/*
   7 Mo: *Hey. Look what Mommy found. Look what I have in the*
   8   *car* [sic]. *Look what else I have in the bag.*
   9 A: ... / *car/* ... /
   10 Mo: *Car.*

2. In other cases, the child does not attend to the speaker's concerns because the child is absorbed in his/her own activity.
3. A third source of inattention stems from the child's unwillingness to co-operate in talk (Grice, 1975). In many cases, the child simply does not want to attend to the topic addressed by the speaker. This

is often the case when the caretaker wants the child to carry out some act that the child does not want to perform. Example (3) illustrates this common phenomenon.

(3) Ronnie, 24 months (L. Tweed)
     (R with three caretakers [C1, C2, C3])
1   C1: *Ronnie.*
2   C2: *Ronnie, get back over here.*
3   C1: *Ronnie.*
4   C2: *Ronald, get outa that gutter!*
5   C2: *Come here.*
6   C3: *You wanna fight, Ronnie?*
7   C1: *Ronnie.*
8   R: *no/*

For all the above reasons — memory limitations, egocentrism, unco-operativeness — caretakers need to insure that a child is attending when directing an utterance to him/her. In many cases, if the caretaker were to introduce an informative statement abruptly into the conversation, the information contained in it would not be decoded or understood by the child. The child, otherwise absorbed, may not even hear the utterance. Or, even if the utterance is heard, the child may not be sufficiently aware of the utterance environment to identify what the speaker is making a claim about.

6.3.1.2 *Attention-getting strategies of the caretaker*

Our observations of the six caretakers in this study indicate that adults are sensitive to the child's wandering attention. The adult uses a variety of verbal and nonverbal behaviours to focus the child's attention on the speaker and what she wants to talk about. (See also Atkinson, 1979.) For example, in the case of very young children, the adult may pick up some object in the environment and move it in such a way that the child begins to attend to it (Lewis and Lee-Painter, 1974). Or the adult may point to the object. In other cases the adult may touch the child or use eye gaze to secure eye contact (Stern, 1974) from the child before speaking or performing some action.

Normally these nonverbal devices accompany verbal means of secur-ing the child's attention. We find that among the possible verbal means available, caretakers rely primarily on vocatives, imperatives and inter-rogatives. Many of the imperative and interrogative constructions are explicit directives to notice or attend to some object, event or state of affairs. These directives contain what we have referred to elsewhere as 'notice verbs' (see Chapter 5). Frequently used notice verbs include the verbs *look* —

(4) Allison, 16,3 months
1   Mo: *Look what Mommy has.*
2   *Look what I have* (Mo showing a picture of a girl)
3   A: *girl/*
4   Mo: *Girl. That's a picture of a girl.*

(5) Toby and David, 33 months, with caretaker
1   C: *She's havin' her dinner, look.*
2   T: *yah/*

(See also Example (2).)

(6) Angelique, 24 months, with caretaker (L. Tweed)
     (A and C constructing toy with felt and glue)
1   C: *Stick it like this and then it'll stay on.*
2   C: *See that?*
3   C: *Do it like this.*
4   C: *Angelique, when it comes off, put it back on. Like this.*
5   A (has sticky hands): *Mommy my-hand/*

know and *remember* —

(7) Allison, 16,3 months
1   Mo: *You know what Mommy has?*
2   Mo: *I have something you've never seen before.*
3   Mo: *We have some bubbles.*
4   Mo: *Would you like to have some bubbles?*
5   Mo: *Remember bubbles in the bath?*
     (A and Mo walk away; Mo gets bubble liquid; Mo sits down on floor)

(8) Allison, 28 months
     (Mo putting mike on A)
1   Mo: *You know what this is called?*
2   A: *something/*
3   Mo: *See, it's a microphone.*
4   Mo: *There.*

and *think* —

(9) Allison, 19,3 months
1   Mo: *Do you think there's another baby in your bag?*
2   Mo: *Allison.*
     (A steps in truck but looks towards bag)

3 Mo: *Do you think there's another baby in your bag? Go get the bag.*
4 A (goes to bag, pulling out another doll): *more/*
5 A: *there/*
6 A: *there/*
7 Mo: *There.*

as well as *watch* and *listen.*

On the other hand, an imperative or interrogative may carry out the same communicative work without using a notice verb. For example, in (10) the caretaker uses an interrogative to draw attention to what she is saying.

(10) Toby and David, 33 months, with caretaker
(D, T at dinner table, playing with teddy-bear when they should be eating)
1 T: *Teddy-bear goin' chair (?) chair/*
2 D: *no/*
3 C: *Mmm! you got carrots.*
4 C: *Mmm?*
5 C: *Have you got carrots?*
6 D: *mm mm/*

Here the caretaker uses the interrogative to draw the children's attention away from what they are presently doing and towards what they ought to be attending to, i.e. the food in front of them. Similarly, in (11) the caretaker uses an interrogative to draw attention to something the caretaker once said, something the child should have remembered:

(11) Allison, 28 months
1 A: *oh I don't want drink it out cup/*
2 A: *ǝ want drink it out can/*
3 Mo: *Oh, what did I say about that?*
4 Mo: *What did I say about drinking it out of the can?*
5 A (pointing to can) : *I want drink it out can/*
6 Mo: *Aw, well that's not such a good idea, honey.*

In many cases the caretaker uses an interrogative to draw attention to something the child has just said. The caretaker typically repeats the child's utterance with a question intonation and then goes on to offer some comment relevant to that utterance.

(12) Allison, 28 months
(A has been running around Mo)

1   A (stopping, pushing Mo out of her way): *and move it/*
2   A: *I run around you/*
3   Mo: *You wanna run around me?*
4   Mo: *Well I'm sorry, I'm very comfortable here.*

Here the caretaker does not assume that the child is not attending to her own utterance. Rather, the caretaker uses the interrogative to draw *added* attention to the utterance. In this example, added attention was motivated by disagreement, but we can find this same format motivated by surprise, disbelief, uncertainty and agreement (cf. Jefferson, Sacks and Schegloff, 1976).

Over and over in our transcripts we find caretakers using interrogatives in this way. Further, reports by Atkinson (1979), Newport (1976), Holzman (1972, 1974), and Ervin-Tripp (1976) indicate that interrogatives are widely used among caretakers as attention-getting devices. While interrogatives are used as indirect requests for action, they appear rarely as true requests for information in caretaker speech to children. Typically the adult has prior knowledge of the information she/he is requesting. Many of the interrogatives appear to be rhetorical questions (Newport, 1976) or test questions (Holzman, 1972, 1974).

6.3.2 Interrogatives as questions of immediate concern

Beyond functioning as attention-getting devices, a common characteristic of these interrogatives is that they articulate an *immediate concern* of the speaker. We refer to these interrogatives generally as *questions of immediate concern*. The immediate concern appears in the interrogative (and also in the imperative) as a presupposition of the interrogative/ (imperative). Thus the interrogative in (11) 'What did I say about drinking it out of the can?' presupposes the immediate concern 'I said something about drinking it out of the can.' The interrogative in (7) 'You know what Mommy has?' presupposes the immediate concern 'You do or do not know what Mommy has.'

We suggest that these two functions − articulating an immediate concern and drawing a listener's attention to it − are basic functions of the interrogative. They are basic in that they cut across other uses of the interrogative. Requests for information, requests for confirmation, and requests for future action all express an immediate concern. Further, all are attention-getting devices by virtue of their being requests for some sort of verbal or nonverbal response. A prerequisite for responding appropriately to an utterance is that the addressee shall have attended to that utterance.

We can consider an interrogative as having a number of functional features. It may function as a request for information or action, as a directive to attend, and as an expression of an immediate concern. Any one of these functional features may motivate the use of an interrogative.

For example, a caretaker in asking a question that she intends to answer herself uses only the features of attention-drawing and articulating a concern. This is the case in Example (7), where Allison's mother uses the interrogative only to draw Allison's attention to the object she is holding (bubbles). In cases where the caretaker expects a response from the child, all the functional features are utilized.

The fact that the use of an interrogative may involve certain features and not others helps to explain how young children use interrogatives in the early stages of language development. Atkinson, in an interesting article called 'Prerequisites for reference' (1979), reports that children use interrogatives as attention-getting devices from the time interrogatives first emerge in their speech corpus. For example, one of the children looked at a picture of a cat and commented 'What that pussy', looked at a clock and commented 'What that clock', looked at a flower and commented 'What that flower.' Similar examples have been reported by Griffiths (1974) and Carter (1975). Carter, for example, reports that the child in her study first used the interrogative pronoun 'where' to announce that he had just located the object he was looking for.

Examples (13) and (14) illustrate this use of interrogatives in the speech of Allison, Toby and David.

(13) Allison, 28 months
    A: (looking at TV monitor) *where Allison right there/*
    Mo: *There you are.*
(14) Toby and David, 35 months
    D: (rolling battery across T's pillow, T sucking thumb)
        it's comin'!/
        it's comin'!/
        it's comin'!/
        up there it's comin'!/
        steamroller's comin'!/
        up and eeeuuuuuu/
        what Toby up so high there/
        up top/

In (13) Allison, while looking at herself on the video monitor, exclaims, 'where Allison right there.' In Example (14) David is pushing a battery across Toby's pillow and fantasizing that it is a steamroller. Toby does not acknowledge David's actions, however. And at this point David actively solicits Toby's attention. He first uses utterance repetition, and when this fails he uses the interrogative construction 'what Toby up so high there.'

In all of these examples, the child knows the answer to the question she/he is posing. In Example (14), David provides the information requested ('steamroller's comin'') before he poses the interrogative ('what Toby up so high there'). In Example (13), Allison provides the answer at the same time as the interrogative is produced, i.e. in the same utterance. These interrogatives, then, do not make sense as sincere requests for information. *They do make sense as attempts to get a co-present person to notice something the speaker is concerned with.* Language-acquiring children appear to grasp this basic function of interrogatives and apply it systematically from the first appearance of interrogatives in their speech.

This strategy does not appear to be limited to first-language acquirers. In her study of a six-year-old Persian child learning English as a second language, Gough (1975) reports that the child used an interrogative construction while naming objects, offering objects and protecting objects. For example, in (15), the child, Homer, tells a playmate to watch out for the tunnel he is constructing. He uses the interrogative 'what is it tunnel!' to perform this function:

(15)Homer, 6 years (Gough, 1975)
   (H was annoyed at boy who insisted on pushing sand into his
   newly created tunnel)
   H: *what is it tunnel!* (= stop pushing sand in my tunnel!)

Gough glosses this construction as 'Stop pushing sand into my tunnel!' In the framework which we share with Atkinson, the utterance could be glossed simply as 'Look, it's a tunnel', just as 'where Allison right there' could be glossed 'Look, Allison's right there.'

6.3.3 Interrogatives in propositional sequences

We turn now to the role of interrogatives in the construction of propositions. We suggested earlier that not only the child but the caretaker as well spread the construction of a proposition over a *sequence* of utterances. This behaviour, we claimed, is a defining feature of distressed communication in general and caretaker speech in particular. In the previous section, we have provided at least one reason why the caretaker would use more than one utterance to convey her idea, namely that the child is not always attending to what the speaker is concerned with. The speaker needs to insure that the child is aware of her/his concerns before she/he can successfully communicate further information relevant to those concerns.

We find in the caretaker discourse, then, sequences in which an immediate concern is articulated in one utterance, and new information relevant to that concern is provided in a subsequent utterance. In the examples at hand, the immediate concern is expressed as a presupposition of an interrogative, and new information relevant to the speaker's concern is expressed in subsequent responses to the interrogative. For example, in (11) the speaker's immediate concern is with Allison's drinking juice out of the can, and the fact that she has already said something about that. She expresses this concern as a presupposition of the interrogative 'What did I say about drinking it out of the can?' The new information relevant to this concern is expressed in the caretaker's subsequent utterance, 'That's not such a good idea, honey.'

In logical terms, the interrogative presents the major argument of a proposition, while subsequent responses predicate something of the argument. The interrogative–response pair constitutes a single, sequentially expressed proposition. In (11), the proposition is (roughly) 'What I said about drinking juice out of the can is that it is not such a good idea.'

The propositional character of interrogative–response pairs is more clearly evident where a child responds to an adult's interrogative. The child's elliptical response cannot be understood in isolation. Rather, the child's response provides a predication (new information) relevant to the caretaker's immediate concern. For example, consider the following exchange between Allison and her mother:

(16) Allison, 16,3 months
   Mo: *What's in the bag?*
   A: *horse/*

Here Allison is predicating something about the concern 'Something is in the bag.' The caretaker's interrogative and the child's response together express a single proposition 'What's in the bag is a horse.'

In sequences of this sort, caretaker and child *collaborate* on the linguistic expression of a proposition. The caretaker specifies an event, an object or a state of affairs about which the child subsequently provides relevant new information. We suggest that it is through interactions of this kind that young children learn how to express complex propositions.

We can see as well that the use of interrogatives in caretaker speech is motivated by several areas of communicative distress. Caretakers may use interrogatives not only in response to the child's inattentiveness but in response to the child's inability to articulate an entire proposition on his/her own.

Part II
Using discourse and syntax
to express propositions

7

Planned and unplanned discourse

E. Ochs

7.1 Introduction

In studies of child language, there is an implicit assumption that the child produces an imperfect version of the adult code. The adult code represents the target towards which the child's language is developing. In this perspective, the child moves through a series of 'stages' (Brown, 1973) until he[1] achieves 'competence' (Chomsky, 1965) in the language of the adult speech community. For example, recent literature on the 'single-word stage' suggests that the child at first deletes certain highly predictable information, then, at some later stage, the child expresses that information in the utterance itself (Bates, 1976; Greenfield and Smith, 1976). Another development noted during this period is the movement away from the sequential expression of a proposition towards the syntactic expression of a proposition (Atkinson, 1979; Bloom, 1973; Keenan and Klein, 1975; Scollon, 1976). The child points out some referent in one utterance and predicates something of that referent in a subsequent utterance. The child uses discourse to convey the proposition, producing what Scollon calls 'vertical constructions'. Over time, the child comes to encode argument and predicate in the space of a single utterance, utilizing syntactic rather than a discourse means. The literature on multiword utterances suggests again that the child moves through a series of stages in which not only utterance length but also syntactic complexity of the child's speech corpus is increased (Bloom, 1970; Brown, 1973; Brown, Cazden and Bellugi, 1969; Slobin, 1973a).

This paradigm may lead one to assume that stages are transitory phenomena. As the child moves from one stage to the next, he does not 'go back' to utilize strategies developed at an earlier developmental period. Rather, strategies emerging at a later period are seen as replacing earlier strategies. The present chapter examines this assumption. It suggests that language development be viewed alternatively as the development of certain linguistic *potentialities*. Becoming more competent in one's language involves increasing one's knowledge of the potential range of structures (e.g. morphosyntactic, discourse) available for use and increasing one's ability to use them. In this view, communicative strategies characteristic of any one stage are not replaced. Rather, they are retained, to be relied upon under certain communicative conditions. The retention of emerging communicative strategies goes on not only during language acquisition but also throughout adult life.

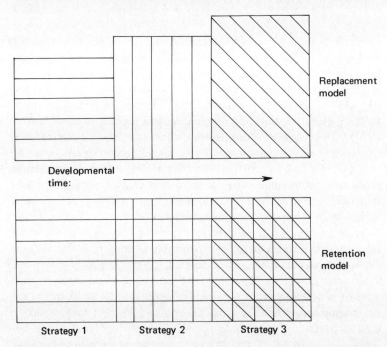

Fig. 7.1 Difference in the two perspectives on language development. Horizontal lines indicate Strategy 1; vertical lines indicate Strategy 2; diagonal lines indicate Strategy 3.

The difference in the two perspectives on language development is represented visually in Fig. 7.1. The replacement model sees language development as stepwise in nature; each step takes the child closer to the adult norm. Hence, auxiliaries at some point are permuted in interrogatives; agreement is marked; plural suffixes emerge (Brown, 1973); and so on. With the exception of severe physical damage or extreme environmental interference, these processes do not reverse themselves. The view of language development as a broadening of knowledge of the language's potential expressive power is better visualized as a series of textures in which developmentally prior communicative patterns coexist with more recently developed patterns (retention model). The extent to which earlier patterns continue to remain prominent (i.e. are used) depends upon the linguistic structures under consideration and the developmental period observed.

We present an alternative model for language development as a vehicle for understanding not only child language but adult language as well. It is not only in the course of becoming competent that developmentally earlier communicative strategies are retained. We also rely on a number of these same strategies as adult communicators, as well as under certain contextual conditions.

A major condition affecting adult reliance on early communicative patterns is the extent to which the communication has been *planned* prior to its delivery. We find that adult speech behaviour takes on many of the characteristics of child language, where the communication is spontaneous and relatively unpredictable. For example, spontaneous dialogues and multiparty conversations among adults evidence greater reliance on developmentally early communicative strategies. Similarly, stream-of-consciousness writing, casual letter-writing, and so on display this reliance. On the other hand, more planned communicative behaviour makes greater use of more complex structures and of strategies developed later in the child's life. Formal expository writing, for example, or presidential addresses to the nation display this kind of speech behaviour.

This claim has interest for those oriented towards integrating psychological and sociological dimensions of language behaviour. Traditionally, notions such as 'spontaneous', 'casual', and 'planned' have been the concern of sociologists of language. Here we suggest that they may have a psychological basis as well. That is, we suggest that, when speakers have not planned the form of their discourse, they rely more heavily on morphosyntactic and discourse skills acquired in the first 3-4 years of life.

The counterpart of this suggestion is that more planned language use draws on knowledge that is acquired or learned (Krashen, 1976, 1977) later in life. In the case of our own society, the suggestion is that more planned uses of language draw upon knowledge transmitted through formal education. This knowledge includes use of complex syntactic structures (e.g. complementation, cleft constructions, certain types of relative clauses, passives) and more formal discourse devices (e.g. use of textual cohesion and transitional terms such as *for example*, *that is*, *furthermore*, *on the other hand*, and the use of topic sentences to open paragraphs in written discourse).

We make this claim on the basis of speech behaviour characteristics of middle-class American adults (Anglo). It may be the case that unplanned and planned discourse can be so characterized only for this population. In this case, we would be offering a culture-specific description of American English varieties. We may find, on the other hand, that, if we looked at unplanned discourse across a number of societies, it would be characterized by a greater reliance on structures acquired early in language development. To the extent that these early-acquired structures transcend particular languages, we may find certain features of unplanned discourse that are common to diverse speech communities.

7.2 Data base

In the present chapter, we present our research to date concerning planned and unplanned discourse. Generalizations drawn in this paper are based on analyses of several types of communicative situations: child–child (Keenan 1974a; Keenan and Klein, 1975; see also Chapter 5), child–adult (Bloom, 1973), and adult–adult (Jefferson, transcriptions; Schegloff, transcriptions; Shimanoff, transcriptions). We have examined relatively informal conversations among adult speakers of English, both native speakers and second-language learners (Brunak, transcriptions). Additionally, we have looked at personal narratives delivered under two conditions by the same speakers. In the first instance, the speaker related the narrative without preparation, orally, within a classroom setting. Second, the speaker wrote the narrative and turned it in as a class assignment (two days later). The first context displayed relatively unplanned discourse, the second relatively planned discourse. The narratives obtained in this manner were transcribed and analysed as a joint project by the 1976–7 discourse seminar of the Department of Linguistics at the University of Southern California. Members of the seminar included T. Bennett, J. Brunak, P. Giunchi, B. Kroll, C. Lehman, S. Peck, S. Shimanoff, S. Staron, S. Tenenbaum, and J. Walcutt (with E. Ochs as director).

Our data reflect a variety of speaker–hearer relationships, topics, genres, and modalities (speaking–writing). We have not, however, covered all the relevant contexts for understanding planned and unplanned communication. In particular, we lack material to date on

unplanned written discourse and planned spoken discourse. Our generalizations are, then, necessarily preliminary.

7.3 Dimensions of planned and unplanned discourse

7.3.1 Definition

Before proceeding, let us establish a working definition of *unplanned*
and *planned* and set out contexts relevant to these concepts.

At the heart of our notion of planning is the idea of *forethought*.
Unplanned discourse is talk that has not been thought out prior to its
expression. In this sense, it is spontaneous. Second, our notion of
planning involves the idea of a *design* or *organization*. In unplanned
discourse, the communicator has not organized how an idea or set of
ideas is going to be expressed or how some speech act (Searle, 1969)
or event (Hymes, 1972a) is going to be performed prior to the time of
communication.

We have arrived at two working definitions:

1. *Unplanned discourse* is discourse that lacks forethought and organiz-
   ational preparation.
2. *Planned discourse* is discourse that has been thought out and organized
   (designed) prior to its expression.

Clearly, these definitions characterize extremes of the concept of
planning. At the one extreme, we have unplanned discourse that
evidences not a shred of preparation or an attempt to structure in an
effective and appropriate manner the verbal act. The result is a string of
nonsensical, haphazard sounds. At the other extreme, we have planned
verbal behaviour in which every idea and every lexical item and every
structure in which the idea is to be expressed is considered and designed
in advance.

Most of the discourse we encounter in the course of day-to-day
communications falls at neither extreme. We usually find ourselves
producing and listening to language that is relatively unplanned or
relatively planned. We shall address ourselves primarily to these less
extreme expressions of discourse planning in the discussion at hand,
since they more accurately represent the data we have examined. We
do not wish to give the impression, however, that the extremes are never
observed. Anyone who has worked on a transcript of young children's
speech can find numerous instances of speech in which predications are

not thought out in advance, in which the informational needs of the intended addressee are not taken into consideration at the time of utterance production, and so on (Atkinson, 1979; Scollon, 1976; see also Chapter 5). On the other hand, we can find extreme examples of total discourse planning when we deliver or listen to a speech that has been written down in advance and has been read aloud.

7.3.2 *Referential and nonreferential dimensions of planning*

Nearly every endeavour that addresses itself to pragmatic considerations of language recognizes that language serves a variety of ends (Austin, 1962; Grice, 1975; Hymes 1962, 1972a; Jakobson, 1960; Searle, 1969; Silverstein, 1976). Language is used not only to articulate propositions (arguments and predicates) but also to display deference, to control the interaction at hand, and to persuade, comfort, antagonize, intimidate, impress, and so on. We have adopted Silverstein's view that all of these uses are social in the sense that 'they get some socially constituted "work" done; they accomplish or "perform" something' (1976, p. 18). Indeed, earlier work on the expression of propositions among young children and caretakers indicates that reference itself is subject to negotiation, checking, confirmation, and the like (Atkinson, 1979; Keenan and Klein, 1975; see also Chapters 5 and 6). Reference in these contexts is characteristically *interactionally accomplished.*

In our discussion of discourse planning, we need to address this multiplicity of social uses of language as well. To characterize a discourse simply as planned or unplanned underrates the social behaviour carried out and the breadth of planning demanded in particular situations. For the purposes of this analysis, we have divided the social uses of language into the two categories suggested by Silverstein (1976). The first category includes the use of language to refer and to predicate, that is, to express propositions. Silverstein calls this use the *referential function* of language. The second category includes all the other uses of language; these uses are referred to collectively as the *nonreferential functions* of language.

A discourse may be planned with respect to all the social functions carried out. On the other hand, it may be planned with respect to certain of these functions but unplanned with respect to others. For example, a speaker may have planned his discourse with respect to referring and predicating but have not planned his utterance with respect to the level of politeness appropriate to the communicative situation. Similarly, a speaker (communicator) may have designed his utterance to meet the politeness norms of the situation but may have failed to take into account the fact that his addressee may not be able to identify a referent specified in the utterance expressed. In this case, the discourse was unplanned with respect to its referential dimension but planned with respect to its nonreferential dimension.

7.3.3 Within and across social acts

A second important context for assessing discourse planning is the verbal unit under consideration. We can discuss planning with respect to individual social acts and with respect to sequences of social acts. We consider a sequence of two or more social acts to constitute a *discourse*. Hence a discourse may consist of two or more descriptions or adjacency pairs (Sacks and Schegloff, 1974), for example, summons–response, invitation–acceptance–decline, greeting–greeting, and so on.

As in our discussion of social functions, we may find that a communication may be planned to varying extents. We can find individual social acts that are well-designed, but the sequence of social acts, the discourse in which they are couched, is unplanned. For example, a speaker may produce a well-thought-out, well-designed predication, but the predication may unintentionally contradict a previous or subsequent predication in the discourse. Similarly, a speaker may have thought out the first part of a riddle sequence but may forget the appropriate response to the riddle. Children are famous for this behaviour.

We do not wish to suggest that planning ends at the level of individual social acts. Planning also takes place *within* individual acts, in the course of their production. Goodwin (1975) has demonstrated that, in multiparty conversations, speakers alter the content of individual utterances according to shifting contextual factors. For example, the speaker may alter what he is saying according to who gives the speaker positive nonverbal feedback. The speaker may start out directing an utterance to one recipient but may fail to get satisfactory eye contact and may move on to another potential recipient.

We can talk about planning, then, on a number of levels. Discourses may vary in the degree to which they are planned. Discourses in which the form of every social act is worked out in advance are the most planned. Discourses in which only certain acts are attended to in advance are somewhat less planned. And discourses in which acts are thought out in the course of their production are even less planned, and so on.

Discourses vary not only in the extent to which they are planned but also in the extent to which they are *plannable*. For example, truly spontaneous conversation is, by definition, relatively unplannable well in advance. Unlike other forms of discourse, in spontaneous conversation it is difficult to predict the form in which entire sequences will be expressed. The content may be even less predictable. Rather, what will be said, the form in which it will be said, and who will say it can be anticipated for limited sequences only (e.g. certain adjacency pairs for certain speaker-hearer relationships). In terms of conversational analysis (Sacks, Schegloff and Jefferson, 1974), spontaneous conversation is 'locally managed'. It tends to be designed on a turn-by-turn basis. Other forms of discourse are more plannable. For example, ritualized speech events tend to have more predictable sequential ordering of social acts and more predictable message content. Communicators can anticipate more what will be said and what their verbal contribution should be. Furthermore, written discourse may be more plannable than spontaneous spoken discourse. In writing, the communicator has more time to think out what he is going to say and how it will be said. Additionally, the writer can rewrite and reorganize the discourse a number of times before it is eventually communicated.

In the discussion of unplanned and planned discourse presented later, we shall consider planning in terms of whether or not the discourse has been planned and in terms of whether or not the discourse is plannable. For example, the spoken narratives in the data base are not planned, in the sense that the speakers did not know in advance that they would perform this task. The spontaneous conversations in the data base constitute relatively unplannable discourse, in the sense previously described.

7.4 Features of children's discourse

In turning to the features of discourse planning, I would like to bring our attention back to the original motivation for this concern. I began this discussion with the remark that relatively spontaneous discourse between adult native speakers of English shared certain properties with the discourse of children. I posited the hypothesis that, in these situations, speakers may rely on certain communicative strategies that emerge in the early stages of language development. I would like now to state more specifically what these strategies and features are.

In pursuing this exercise, let us examine a continuous stretch of discourse produced by two children, aged 35 months, in the course of interacting with one another:

(1) Toby and David (both 2;11), bedroom, early morning
    (An alarm clock rings in the next room)
    DAVID: *bell/*
         bell/
         its mommys/
         was mommys alarm clock/
    TOBY: *bell/*
         (?) it/
         'larm clock/
         yeah/
         goes dindong ding dong/
    DAVID: *no/*
         no/
         goes fip fip/ fip fip/

This passage exhibits a number of communicative features generally characteristic of young children's discourse:

1. On the ideational level, a proposition is conveyed over a series of utterances. Objects and entities noticed in one utterance are subsequently used as major arguments of one or more predications. Here, *bell/* is noticed in one utterance, and subsequently *bell* becomes the major argument for the predications *its mommys/* and *was mommy's alarm clock/*. Similarly, Toby uses the referent of *'larm clock/* as the argument for his subsequent predication *goes ding dong ding dong*, and so on.

   The sequential character of expressed propositions is by now a fairly widely observed phenomenon. For reports of this feature in adult–child discourse, see Bloom (1973), Keenan, Schieffelin and Platt (1979), Scollon (1976), and Atkinson (1979). See also Chapters 5 and 6.

2. A corollary of the sequential expression of propositions is that arguments and their predicates are often tied through their position in the discourse rather than through syntactic means. We relate the two parts of the proposition because they appear in sequentially adjacent positions. We use some pragmatic principle in making the connection. For example, we connect *'larm clock* with *goes ding dong ding dong* because they are in close proximity to one another and because we expect utterances in close proximity to be relevant to one another (unless otherwise signalled) (Grice, 1975; Sacks and

Schegloff, 1974) and because it makes sense to relate the utterances to one another given our knowledge of the world.

At 35 months, it is obviously not the case that all propositions have this status. We get a mixture of syntactically bound propositions and sequentially bound propositions. At the single-word stage, however, the sequential connection predominates. Bloom (1973) calls such constructions 'holistic' and Scollon (1976) calls them 'vertical'. The development of language is seen as a gradual progression away from pragmatic devices towards greater reliance on syntax ('horizontal constructions'). A point I would like to stress here is that the sequential strategy does not eventually disappear altogether. Adult discourse as well evidences this feature under certain conditions.

3. Notice as well in this passage that there is a great deal of repetition. The repetition is of two sorts: self-repetition and other-repetition. In other-repetition, the speaker repeats what someone else previously uttered. Self- and other-repetition carry out a variety of communicative functions, only a few of which are displayed in this example. Self-repetition may be used to draw the hearer's attention to something the speaker has noticed, as in Example (2):

(2) Toby and David (both 2;11), bedroom, early morning
    (D holding a truck, picks up rabbit. T whistles on pretend flute
    continuously while facing D)
    DAVID: *rabbit/ rabbit/ I find truck/ rabbit/* (?) *like rabbit/*
            truck/ rabbit/ rabbit/rabbit/ truck truck rabbit/ truck/
            rabbit/
            (showing truck and rabbit to T)
            truck/ rabbit/ rabbit/ rabbit/
    TOBY: *truck/ rabbit/ let me blow?/*

Self-repetition may also be used to emphasize a point. Example (2) displays both of these uses. Furthermore, self-repetition may be used to clarify or to correct a previous utterance, as in Example (1), where David says *its mommys/ was mommys alarm clock/*. In the second utterance, the tense is changed and utterance is expanded to include the noun phrase *alarm clock*. It is a fuller and more accurate expression of what has happened.

The use of other-repetition has been analysed in some detail in previous papers (Keenan, 1974a; Keenan and Klein, 1975; see also Chapters 3 and 5). Other-repetition is one of the most widely used devices among language-acquiring children. Among other uses, it serves to let the speaker know that the addressee is attending to some object under consideration. For example, in (1) Toby's utterance *bell/* lets David know that he too has noticed/is attending to the bell. In Example (2), Toby finally lets David know he has noticed the truck and rabbit David is holding up. He does this by eventually repeating *truck/ rabbit/*. Similarly, the repetition of propositions or parts of propositions may serve to acknowledge, agree with, disagree with or challenge or question, depending on the nature of the prior communicative act (a request for information, an announcement, an assessment, etc.) and the manner in which the repetition is produced (e.g. the intonation contour).

4. There is a tendency to use lexical items having similar phonological features across a series of adjacent utterances (Keenan, 1974a; Keenan and Klein, 1975; Weir, 1962; see also Chapter 3). In the discourse of young children, we find recurrent use of certain sounds and clusters of sounds. For example, in (2) we see that both *truck* and *rabbit* contain the sounds /t/, /k/, /b/. These sounds all share the features of being *stops*, varying only in place of articulation. On many occasions, the sound patterns themselves become a major focus of attention rather than the literal meaning of the lexical item. This could account in part for why David repeats *truck/ rabbit/* in an apparently tireless fashion. We of course have observed cases in which the focus of the child was exclusively on the sound patterns, where the resulting combinations have no referential meaning whatsoever. Example (3) illustrates such an orientation:

(3) Toby and David (both 33 months), bedroom, early morning
    DAVID: *apple kings/ apple keys/ apple kings/*
    TOBY: *apples/ apples/ apples/ apples . . .*
    DAVID: *gi:naug/ ginɔ:g/ ginɔ:/*
    TOBY: *ginɔ:g/ ginɔ:g/ ginɔ:g/ ginɔ:g/*
    DAVID: (laughs) *ki:tan/ ki:tan/ kakadu/ kakadu/*
    TOBY: *no/ kakadu/*
    DAVID: *kakadu/*
    TOBY: *no kakadu/ wʌps ko:sʌps ko:z/*
    DAVID: *zʌp ko:z ka/*

5. In addition to the aforementioned properties, it is, of course, the case that children use relatively simple morphosyntactic structures. We find reliance on simple, active sentences, or unmarked subject, verb, object (SVO) word order for declaratives. We find reliance on deictic items (this, that, there, here, etc.) rather than on definite articles and relative clauses. We find deletion of major terms of

reference as well as deletion of functor words (articles, prepositions, etc.). In short, we find the kind of morphosyntactic form that characterizes early child language (Bloom, 1970; Brown, 1973; Slobin, 1973a; etc.). Much of the deleted information is, alternatively, conveyed through nonverbal means, such as pointing, touching, reaching towards, gaze direction and the like (see Chapter 5).

7.5 Features of relatively unplanned and planned discourse

I present here a number of features that characterize and distinguish relatively unplanned and planned discourse of English speakers. The principles are by no means exhaustive. They are presented as initial generalizations to be refined and extended over the course of future research. I will relate these features to the strategies of young children. However, my order of discussion will not necessarily follow the ordering of child language features presented before.

Feature 1: In relatively unplanned discourse more than in planned discourse, speakers rely on the immediate context to express propositions.

This principle claims that, in spontaneous communication, speakers (communicators) rely less heavily on syntax to articulate semantic relations obtaining between referents or between whole propositions. That is, along a continuum of use, reliance on context to communicate information falls towards the unplanned pole, and reliance on syntax falls towards the planned pole.

Context is used to link referents (logical arguments) to their relevant predications, and it is used to link whole propositions to one another. Let us consider first the reliance on context to link arguments and predicates.

7.5.1 Argument–predicate relations

7.5.1.1 Referent deletion
One of the observations on child language previously presented above is that children frequently do not articulate the semantic relation of an argument to its predicate through syntactic means. On the one hand, we find reliance on nonverbal means to supply the missing information, for example, the use of pointing, reaching, holding up, eye gaze, etc. Second, we find reliance on the verbal environment to supply the

necessary information. In particular, we observed a pattern whereby the listener has to turn to the previous discourse to locate exactly what the child is referring to. It is the 'nextness' of the referent and the predication that creates the link between the two pieces of information. The link is not made through syntactic means.

We find a similar pattern in the spontaneous discourse of certain speakers. In particular, we find predications in which the major argument is deleted in the current utterance. To locate the relevant referent, the listener must turn back to the discourse history or to the situation at hand. With respect to the situation at hand, it is primarily reference to the speaker and to the hearer that is deletable, as in (4) below:

(4) Two Girls (Schegloff, transcript)
    B: *Uh how's school goin.*
    A: *Oh: same old shit.*
    B: *Hhhh// (really?)*
→ A: *'have a lotta tough courses.*

With respect to the discourse history, speakers will rely on the listener's acquaintance with any referent, regardless of person (third person referents are as likely to be deleted as are first person referents) and number (singular, plural). Examples (5), (6), and (7) illustrate predications that rely on previously specified referents:

(5) Two Girls
    B: *Y'have any cla-y'have a class with Billy this term/*
    A: *Yeah he's in my Abnormal class*
    B: *Oh yeah// how*
    A: *Abnormal Psych.*
→ B: *Still not married*
    A: ((loud)) *Oh no definitely not// (no)*

(6) A Jewish Grandfather (Shimanoff, transcription)
    (G has been talking about the fact that his grandson is difficult to please. He gives one example – oatmeal cereal)
    G: *And **its** uh **got ta good taste**, its good. And the **cereal**-grandma e don't like **cereal** but she **finished** to the last (**dish**) and I enjoy – I like it too. It's tasty! And I uh (1.2) He didn't want the **cereal, doesn't eat**. I said, 'Todd*
    → *it wouldn't **kill** ya, **taste** it!' . . .*

(7) Subways in London (Brunak, transcript) (unplanned version)
    (G has been telling story of how she had to grab hold of a woman to keep from falling off a subway platform. The woman

started to fall back as well but was stopped by a nearby man.)

G: *and it seemed like a long time when it happened but when*
      I look back at it it happened just like that ((snaps his
      fingers)) *this man-this guy there almost* **casually** *looked*
      over at 'er and just **grabbed** *'er arm* (.7) *and pulled 'er back*
→   *up and then I just kind a grabbed her* ((laugh)) *and* **looked**
      at me like I had the **nerve** *to assault 'er, it was like* **how dare**
      you ((high-pitched))

Notice in these examples that it does not seem to matter what grammatical status the previous NP hold. Prior object of prepositions (5),
subjects (6), direct objects (7), and so on may in turn be employed as
deleted subjects of subsequent predications. Deletions such as these do
not appear in more planned, more formal discourse. For example, (7)
is part of the USC seminar project on unplanned and planned narrative
form. In the planned version, the episode was expressed as in (8) below:

(8)   Subways in London (planned).
      The train sped nearer as we were both ready to fall off the edge.
      A friend with whom she had been talking, clutched her other
      arm and steadied her as I pulled on the purse's shoulder strap
      moving closer to her arm. My balance was finally steadied and
      it wasn't until after some exchanges of looks did I move on
      with a quick 'Excuse me.'

We can see here how in the more planned version, the narrator does not
delete any of the referents.

7.5.1.2 *Referent and proposition*

Thus far we have looked at cases in which there is no syntactic relation
between a referent and its predication because the referent is, in fact,
missing. There are, however, other cases in which a referent is specified
initially, and, subsequently, an entire proposition relevant to the referent
is expressed. These contributions have been treated in two earlier papers
(Duranti and Ochs, 1979; see also Chapter 5). We refer to them as
'Referent + Proposition' (Ref + Prop) constructions. They differ from
the previously illustrated sequences in that no referent is deleted. In
certain of these Ref + Prop constructions, it is rather that the semantic
relation between the referent and the subsequent predication is not
expressed. In a certain sense, these initial referents serve as topics (Li
and Thompson, 1976) for the subsequent propositions and imply an
as for or *concerning* relation. This is illustrated in (9) below:

(9) Two Girls (Schegloff, manuscript)
     (Discussing classes at the local university)
                          Ref
→   B: *Ohh I g'ta tell ya one course*
    A: (*incred-*)
                          Ref   Prop
→   B: *The mo- the modern art the twentieth century art, there's*
        about eight books

Here, there is a reference to B's twentieth-century art course, and the
reference is followed immediately by an entire proposition, that is,
there's about eight books. We might paraphrase the sequence *As for one
course, the modern art, the twentieth-century art, there's about eight
books.* However as it stands, there is no explicit *as for* or its equivalent,
and the semantic relation obtaining between the initial three noun
phrases and the subsequent sentence is inferred only from the positioning of these two structures. It is not syntactically expressed. We use the
principle of *nextness* to make the link and associate the referent and
the proposition.

As with the argument–predicate constructions discussed earlier,
these Ref + Prop constructions as well rarely appear in more formal,
prearranged Standard English discourse. Work carried out by Duranti
and Ochs (1979) evidences that this difference is characteristic of
Italian discourse as well. Ref + Prop constructions appear in spontaneous
conversation between intimates but rarely appear in newspaper articles
and magazines, scholarly papers, and so on.

There is a particular type of Referent + Proposition construction
that is more commonly discussed in the linguistics literature. This is
the construction linguists have called left-dislocation (Ross, 1967;
Gundel, 1975). According to Ross, left-dislocation is a transformation
that moves an NP out of and to the left of a clause, leaving in its place
a co-referential pronoun. A series of these constructions is illustrated
in Examples (10), (11), and (12) below:

(10) GTS4:1 (Jefferson, manuscript)
     (K has been talking about the fact that his car radio was taken
     from his car)
     K: *They cleaned me out. And my father oh he's// he's fit to*
         be tied.
(11) GTS4:15
     K: *Uh Pat McGee. I don't know if you know him, he- he lives*
         in// Palisades.

(12)GTS5:35

(Discussing students falling asleep in class)

→   K: *Uh:: this guy, you could yell 'Hey John, Hey Joh-' 'n you c'd go over an' tap him on the shoulder*

     R: *So he's gotta// good imagination*

     K: *That's the only way you c'd snap him out of it.*

In these examples, the left-dislocated NPs are *my father*, *Pat McGee*, and *this guy*, respectively.

The left-dislocations differ from both of the previously discussed constructions in that there is a reference to the relevant referent within the subsequent predication. This reference is through the coreferential pronoun in the predication. The constructions are of interest to us because they otherwise appear to share many of the properties of sequentially expressed propositions. The initial referent appears to be part of a separate utterance, a separate speech act, if you will, in much the same way as the other referents we have considered are. We cannot say that the principle of *nextness* alone encourages the listener to link the initial referent to the subsequent proposition, the copy pronoun does this as well. These constructions, then, stand somewhere between single subject-predicate constructions and discourse. They share properties of both.

A second reason why left-dislocations are of interest to this discussion is that they too rarely appear in highly planned discourse. We rarely find left-dislocations in written prose, for example. On the other hand, we do find left-dislocations or rather constructions like left-dislocations abundantly in the speech of young children producing multiword utterances. For example in (1) David's two utterances *bell/ its mommys/* could be considered as a left-dislocation (see also Gruber, 1967). These constructions may as well be transitional structures anticipating more syntactically coherent sentences. They are not transitional in the sense that they disappear altogether. We have just witnessed that adult speakers produce these constructions when they are speaking under casual, spontaneous circumstances. They may be transitional in the sense that the child may first use this type of construction exclusively to express certain semantic relations. At a later point, the child comes to utilize both the subject-predicate and the left-dislocation construction to express those relations.

7.5.2 *Proposition–proposition relations*

Context may link whole propositions as well as constituents within a single proposition to one another. We may link one proposition to another because they appear next to one another and because we expect sequentially expressed propositions to be relevant to one another. In using context, the communicator does not make the semantic relation obtaining between the propositions explicit. For example, if the communicator produces the sequence *I don't like that house. It looks strange.*, he does not specify explicitly the link between these assessments. As recipients of this communication, we use our knowledge of the world and our expectations concerning the sequencing of talk to relate the two propositions. We treat the second utterance not only as relevant but also as relevant in a particular sense, for example, not only as providing an explanation or basis for the initial assessment.

Our observations of discourse indicate that context is an alternative to syntax and that planned and unplanned discourse differ in their utilization of the two alternatives. Syntax makes the semantic link explicit, for example, *I don't like that house, **because** it looks strange.* It is relied upon more heavily in planned versus relatively unplanned discourse. This association may be due to the possibility that it takes more planning to express a specific semantic relation (using a syntactic term) than to imply only that some semantic relation obtains. In the former case, the speaker's encoding task is greater and may demand greater planning.

The spontaneous conversations and unplanned versions of personal narratives in the data base were laced with contextually linked propositions. As analysis of subordinate and co-ordinate constructions done by Kroll (1977) indicated that, in the unplanned narratives, only 7.1% of the clauses were subordinate constructions, whereas in the planned narratives 20% were subordinate.

To see these two types of propositional links, compare (13) with (14) below. Example (13) presents a portion of a spontaneous narrative. Example (14) presents the same event described in the planned version of the same narrative.

(13) Driving Home (Kroll, transcription) (Unplanned Version)
   [M describes to class (C) how his father nearly crashed into a truck]
   M: *so he decides that he's gonna pass these cars* (?) *and uh (.4) he pulls out in the other lane and starts passin' 'em (.5) and all of a sudden we see this big truck, you know*
   C: (laughter)
   M: *This truck comin' for us and uh (.5) this guy was going pretty fast and (.5) and we had passed one car and there's*

> *no way we can get (in or out) and uhm this trucker's*
> *comin' and he's just sort of bearing down on us and honkin'*
> *his horn. He wasn't slowing down*

C: (laughter)

(14) Driving Home (Planned Version)

> *After some five minutes of tailing these cars, my father decided*
> *it was time to pass the cars.*
> *He pulled into the other lane and accelerated. As we passed the*
> *first car we noticed a large Mack truck coming our way.*

Examples of the immediate context alone linking propositions are provided in (15) and (16):

(15) Two Girls

A: *I'm so ... tired I played basketball today (   ) the first time*
    since I was a freshman in high school

B: *Bask(hh)etb(hhall) heh heh/ heh*

> (versus *I am so tired, **because** I played basketball for the first*
> *time since I was a freshman in high school*)

(16) Jewish Grandfather

G: *Alright, he moved **out**, he's- in fact, **Ruthie**: wro:te to me*
    *e Joseph (hey Pa:) is not good for him to **stay** here. let him*
    *stay here jist **one** weekend to let him get uh (   ) **dormotory***
    *and (for what)- he's earning the **money**. Let him **spend it**.*
    *He'll be too **much** for **you**.*

> (versus *It is not good for him to stay here, **therefore** ... Let him*
> *stay here just one weekend ... **because** ..., etc.*)

Feature 2: In relatively unplanned discourse more than in planned discourse, speakers rely on morphosyntactic structures acquired in the early stage of language development. Relatively planned discourse makes greater use of morphosyntactic structures that are relatively late to emerge in language.

As suggested in the preceding section, in relatively unplanned discourse speakers tend to avoid using grammatical structures that are late to emerge in language development. For example, Limber (1973) indicates that the use of subordinate conjunctions appears later in the child's speech than does the use of co-ordinate conjunctions. In fact, 'The earliest suggestion of conjunction is the grouping of two sentences together without a distinguishable conjoining morpheme. Very often, in listening to tapes made between 2;0 and 2;4, one is apt to perceive a *so*, *and*, or *if*, when, in fact, upon replay there is not any direct basis for this percept [p. 182].'

In addition to the above structures, we find the following morpho-syntactic preferences in relatively unplanned discourse:

7.5.3 Modes of reference

We find a greater reliance on earlier emergent forms of reference in spontaneous discourse. For example, we find frequent use of demonstrative modifiers where definite articles are used in planned discourse. Compare, for example, the unplanned version of a narrative, as in (17), with the planned version, as in (18):

(17)Subways in London (Unplanned)
> G: *I'd done this many times before so I didn't think twice*
> → *about it (I was walk-) I tried to walk between the edge of*
> *this platform (.7) A:nd this group of people*

(18)Subways in London (Planned)
> *Squeezing through narrow spaces and finding my way between*
> → *people I continued in my pursuit of an emptier spot on the train*
> *platform and a woman whose back was turned toward me as*
> *she wildly conversed with some friends.*

Similarly, in reference, there is a reliance on simpler, determiner (demonstrative, definite article, etc.) plus noun constructions in situations in which, in planned discourse, the communicator would use a *relative clause construction*. Compare, for example, the unplanned and planned versions of the narrative 'Subways in London'. In the unplanned version illustrated in Example (7), a character is referred to as *this man-this guy*. The same individual is referred to as *a friend with whom she had been talking* in the planned version, illustrated in (8). Similarly, in the same narrative, the major female character is referred to as *this woman lady* in the unplanned version. This is illustrated in (19):

(19)Subways in London (Brunak, manuscript) (Unplanned)
> G: *So I was walkin' along the edge and uh as I said there were*
> → *these people talkin' and this woman **lady** was describin'*
> *somethin'...*

In the planned version, the same woman is referred to as *a woman whose back was turned*. This is illustrated in (18).

Other alternatives to relative clause constructions found in relatively unplanned discourse include referent + proposition constructions (see *Feature 1*) and noun + propositional phrase constructions.

Schachter (1974) has discussed the avoidance of relative clauses as a strategy of certain speakers learning English as a second language. Here we can see that native speakers as well often rely on syntactically simpler alternative forms of reference. Indeed, in many cases, we can see the avoidance explicitly in unplanned discourse. The speaker starts to use the relative clause construction but cuts the construction off before its completion and reformulates the reference in an alternative fashion. In the example below, the speaker reformulates the relative clause as an independent construction:

(20)Two Girls

B: *This is s- y'know this 'the Indian class an' they stuck us in*
→ *this crazy building- that they j- they're not even finished with it.*

7.5.4 Verb voice

Another area in which relatively planned and unplanned discourse differ concerns the use of active and passive voice. Developmentally, the passive voice is acquired much later than the active voice among English-speaking children (Bever, 1970). We find that the passive voice is rare in both planned and unplanned discourse. However, relative to unplanned discourse, it appears with much greater frequency in planned discourse. Bennett (1977) examined verb voice in the unplanned and planned personal narratives. In the unplanned narratives, the passive accounted for 0.9 per cent of the total verbs. In the planned versions, the passive accounted for 7.05 per cent of the total verbs. The contrastive use of these two voices is illustrated in Examples (7) and (8).

7.5.5 Verb tense

An additional point of contrast between relatively planned and unplanned communication concerns the use of verb tense. Developmentally, the use of the present tense anticipates past and future tenses (Antinucci and Miller, 1976; Brown, 1973). That is, even when the past or future is referred to, children will initially use the present tense. The narratives in our data base all concern past events in the experience of the narrator. In referring to these events, the speaker did not always use the past tense in the unplanned versions. In contrast to the planned versions, the speaker frequently used the present tense in relating past events. Examples (13) and (14) illustrate the different use of tense to relate the same events. Typically, the past is used in the initial part of the narrative, to orient the addressee to the temporal and spatial context of the event related. Once the context is specified, the speaker moves towards greater use of the present tense (Walcutt, 1977). Notice here that this way of marking temporal ordering is similar to that described for certain pidgin-creole languages (Sankoff and Kay, 1974).

Feature 3: In relatively unplanned discourse more than in relatively planned discourse, speakers tend to repeat and replace lexical items in the expression of a proposition (Shimanoff and Brunak, 1977).

In most cases, repetition and word replacement within a speech act reflect trouble spots in the communication. Repetition of a lexical item may be part of the speaker's search for a particular word (Schegloff, Jefferson and Sacks, 1977) or predication. The search may be motivated by the speaker's desire to select a term or construction that is appropriate to the addressee or clear to the addressee. Or the speaker may repeat a term (set of terms) because the speaker feels that the initial term has not been decoded by the addressee. For example, in (13) the speaker repeats *this truck* following the occurrence of laughter simultaneous with the first mention of *this truck*. Schegloff et al. (1977) treat these repetitions as 'repairs' on the occurrence of overlap in conversation. Repetition may also be simply part of the speaker's attempt to think out an idea.

Repetition is a highly versatile device, and it is among the earliest behaviours emergent in the speech of the language-acquiring child (Scollon, 1976; see also Chapter 3).

Word replacement is another example of what Schegloff, Jefferson and Sacks (1977) call 'repair' or error-correction. As with the use of repetition, the motivations for the replacement are diverse. The speaker may replace one term with another because the initial term is inappropriate:

(21) Two Girls
    B: *This fella I have uh "fella" This **man**, he had uh f- who I have for linguistics is*
    A: *Hm hm*
    B: *really too **much***

Or the term (set of terms) initially used may not accurately express what the speaker wishes to convey:

(22) Skiing over a Cliff (Shimanoff, transcription) (Unplanned)
M: *So: I sor:ta rushed myself. And I uh went down (1.1) this this uh (cliff) not really a cliff but it was a very sharp incline of the mountain.*

Word replacement is part of a more general phenomenon characteristic of relatively unplanned discourse–afterthought (Hyman, 1975). The communicator remembers after the relevant point in the discourse that certain information is missing. In many cases, the personal narratives in our corpus contained whole propositions as afterthoughts. The narrator would remember that relevant background information had not been provided. Example (23) below illustrates the appearance of afterthoughts in the unplanned version of a narrative. Example (24) illustrates the omission of such afterthoughts in the planned version of the same narrative.

(23) People Scare Me (Staron, transcription) (Unplanned)
F: *Well (.2) we (   ) came um we stayed across the street from our house. I used to live in Florida an' we stayed across the street cuz my mom was in the hospital an' we were really small.*

(24) People Scare Me (Planned)
When I was ten years old my sister, brother, and I stayed with the neighbours across the street while my mother was in the hospital.

The use of repetition and word replacement for the purpose of improving or correcting some dimension of the communication indicates that planning is going on in the course of the speech act itself. When we speak of these features as characteristic of relatively unplanned discourse, we mean that either the communicator has not planned his communication prior to the individual speech act or the communication was unplannable prior to the individual speech act (e.g. shifting addressees, speaker–hearer roles, etc.).

The use of repetition and other hesitation phenomena, word replacement, and other forms of afterthought and repair lead to lengthy formulations of particular social acts. We find that, in relatively unplanned discourse, the expression of social acts tend to take up more discourse 'space' (see Chapter 5) than in planned discourse. That is, the same social act verbalized in planned discourse will be more compact than the unplanned version. For example, compare the unplanned and planned versions of 'People Scare Me' illustrated in (23) and (24). Other features mentioned in previous sections also contribute to this characteristic of unplanned discourse. The use of referent + proposition constructions rather than subject–predicate constructions and the use of co-ordinate constructions in place of subordinate constructions lead as well to more 'spacious' renditions of descriptions, requests, announcements, and the like. Differences in discourse space created by these alternative constructions are demonstrated in (13) and (14).

Feature 4: In relatively unplanned discourse, the form and content of sequentially arranged social acts tend to be more similar than in relatively planned discourse.

In our discussion of *Feature 3*, we mentioned that unplanned discourse contained repetition within social acts. Here we treat another form of repetition in which parts of previously expressed social acts are incorporated in subsequent acts. The features incorporated may be morphological, syntactic, or phonological. For example, a *lexical item* appearing in one utterance in an unplanned discourse may be repeated in one or more subsequent utterances:

(25) Two Girls (Schegloff ms.)
    A: (*you sounded so// far*)
→ B: *Right/*
    A: *Yeah*
→ B: *See/ I- I'm doin' something right t'day finally*
    A: *Mm*
→ B: *I finally said something right. You are home hh.*

In many cases, the lexical item repeated serves the same grammatical function in the series of utterances in which it appears. We sometimes find the repetition of two or more lexical items, both occupying the same grammatical roles in the sequence in which they appear. Example (26) illustrates such a case.

(26) Jewish Grandfather (Shimanoff, manuscript)
→ G: *So sometimes you know you can lose the letter you can-*
       something can happen in Beverly Hills.

This example as well as Example (6) illustrates how a speaker may become locked into a subject or subject-verb frame. Shifts in perspective are sometimes accomplished only by cutting off an existing frame and recycling (Schegloff, 1972) the speech act using a novel frame, for example, the *you can* frame is replaced by *something can* in (26).

The repetition of prior utterances or parts of prior utterances is a basic characteristic of early child discourse. Scollon (1976) for single-word and Keenan (1974a; see also Chapter 3) and Weir (1962) for multiword utterances show that cross-utterance repetition dominates the earliest discourses of children. An earlier study by the author (Keenan, 1974a; Keenan and Klein, 1975; see also Chapter 3) showed that, over time, reliance on repetition gives way to substitution (*Mommys silly/ Daddys silly/, not sketis/ makaronis, not shoes/ slippers*) and to formally novel means of maintaining continuity across utterances. In the initial period, form and content are maintained across utterances. In the subsequent period, form is maintained, but content changes; and, in the final period, both form and content change. (That is, in each subsequent period an alternative means of maintaining coherence is available; options are increased over time.) It may be the case that it requires more forethought and planning to alter both the form and the content of a message than to alter the content alone. Language development may be linked to an increased capacity of the child to attend to both the form and the content of the propositions they express.

Similarly, in the adult corpus, it may be the case that, when speakers have not previously organized their discourse, they may retain the same morphosyntactic format to express novel content. Hence, stream-of-consciousness writing and on-the-spot working out of a difficult concept may exhibit repeated use of a formal frame.

The similarity in form across utterances in relatively unplanned discourse is not limited to morphological and syntactic form. We find as well similarities in the *phonological* shape of sequentially placed speech acts. For example, in (27)

(27) Two Girls
    A: *Ripped about **four** nails, and oh::ch*
    B: *Fantastic*
    A: *But it was **fun**. Y'sound very far away*

we have repetition of the phone /f/. Furthermore, we have repetition of the phone sequence /f/ + /r/ (*four, far*) and the phone sequence /f/ + /n/ (*fantastic, fun*).

Phonological repetition is a very early feature of children's discourse (Jakobson, 1968; Keenan, 1974a; Weir, 1927). Children at times seem to select lexical items on the basis of their phonological similarity rather than on the basis of their appropriateness to the message conveyed. Previous reports of this phenomenon describe the behaviour as 'language play' or 'sound play'. It has been exclusively associated with the speech behaviour of very young children. In terms of the 'replacement' model, this behaviour apparently disappears in the course of language development. We see here that this kind of behaviour does not in fact disappear. Adults as well appear to select their words at least in part on phonological grounds (i.e. phonological similarity).

Schegloff (personal communication) refers to this phenomenon as 'sound touch-offs' in adult speech. That is, the sound of one item in the discourse may 'touch-off' the articulation of other items sharing those sound patterns. These sound touch-offs represent one type of touched-off behaviour. For example, Schegloff has discussed the phenomenon of lexical touch-offs as well. In certain cases, one lexical item may touch-off another lexical item having a complementary or opposite meaning. We have found, in our spontaneous data, discourse of this character. The speaker mentions a particular lexical item in one utterance, and, in subsequent utterances, its opposite appears. Example (28) illustrates this behaviour:

(28) Skiing over a Cliff (Unplanned)

M: *And we were caught **up** in a snow: storm (1.5) An:d we were skiing **down** the mountain. An:d he was in **front** of me with some other **friend** an:d I had **stopped** at a corner, cuz one of my **bindings** were **broken**, and was trying to git my ski boot back up to the **skii:es**. (1.0) So I wasn uh: very **sharp**, and I'd say about **six** people i:n front of **me** . . .*

Here we find *up* followed by *down* in the subsequent clause and then *up* reappearing four clauses later. Similarly, *front* is followed by *back* three clauses later with *front* reappearing two clauses after that.

From our point of view, we cannot tell if it is always the case that sounds or meanings of lexical items 'touch-off' subsequent items. It may not be the case that the initial item triggered the production of subsequent items. Rather, it could be the case that the speaker (writer) is thinking ahead, projecting what he is going to say next in the course of the current utterance or just before the current utterance. This projection may lead him to produce the initial lexical item in the first place (see Fromkin, 1973).

(29) Jewish Grandfather

G: *So **we** had a **couple** of **skirmishes**. Not only **this** with the **food**, but the you know he's he's hon- you know his he **doesn't trust** people.*

For example, in (29), it does not appear that the initial item *honest* touches off *doesn't trust*. Rather, it appears as if the speaker was thinking about *doesn't trust* but unconsciously articulated a term having its opposite meaning. That is, it is the *future concept* that touches off the initial lexical item.

7.6 Constraints on discourse planning

In this section I ask the question 'What conditions create relatively unplanned discourse?' In previous sections, I have mentioned that planning must be discussed for both referential and nonreferential functions of language. I suggest here that, if one or the other of these functions place heavy demands on the communicator, that relatively unplanned discourse will be produced. That is, in many cases it is because the communicator is attending to ideational or situational demands that he is unable to attend to all dimensions of the message form. Let us consider each of these demands in turn.

7.6.1 Situational demands

In some cases, a communicator cannot plan the form of his communication because the situation in which he is participating requires more or less continuous monitoring. For example, in spontaneous conversation, who will assume the floor, when the floor will be assumed, and what will be communicated is negotiated on a turn-by-turn basis. The participant in such a situation must attend closely to each turn in order to deal with each of these questions. If he wishes to take hold of the floor, he must listen for the first possible moment in which he can appropriately do so (i.e. the first possible 'transition relevance space' – see Sacks, Schegloff and Jefferson, 1974). In previous studies (Duranti and Ochs 1979; see also Chapter 5), we found that referent + proposition constructions (or left-dislocations) appear in the context of such behaviour. In an effort to take hold of the floor, the speaker makes reference to some entity ('referent') initially and only subsequently formulates the predication relevant to the referent. The initial NP acts as a place-holder allowing the speaker to maintain the floor. Where turn-taking is locally managed in this sense; it may take priority over the expression of well-informed propositions for the communicator. The more predictable the sequential ordering of talk, the freer the communicator is to attend to the propositions he wishes to express and the form in which they are to be expressed.

7.6.2 *Conceptual demands*

Just as situational demands may interfere with the planning of propositions, so the demands of expressing a proposition may interfere with the organization of other social acts. Conceptual demands may be of various sorts. For example, a concept may demand the speaker's (writer's) concentration because it is cognitively complex for that individual. The communicator may need to focus primarily on working out the idea and on articulating it. With this priority at hand, the communicator may fail to plan his discourse on other social levels. For example, he may fail to attend to social norms constraining how long a turn at talk should be, how much information should be conveyed, and the appropriate form of expression for that addressee.

This kind of conceptual demand is the basis of *egocentric speech* in young children. Braunwald (1979) observes that young children stop attending to the needs of their conversational partners when they talk about some topic that slightly exceeds their cognitive capacity. So, for example, when children start talking about the remote past, they may not attend to the needs of the intended recipient of the talk. On the other hand, when children talk about topics with which they are familiar and that are within their cognitive capacity, they are much more sociocentric. This study is consistent with the observations of the author of children's discourse. The most highly social behaviour of the children observed involved songs, rhymes, sound play, and topical talk linked to the here-and-now (Keenan, 1974a).

As with other dimensions of language development, we do not see egocentric speech as ultimately replaced by social speech. Rather, egocentric speech persists throughout adult life, appearing under much the same conditions as in child language. When an adult is thinking through a difficult idea, he may 'tune out' the behaviour of others present. Often, for example, the speaker will avoid eye contact. Here, the speaker appears unwilling to establish intersubjectivity and to register additional social demands.[2]

In our discussion of sources of unplanned discourse, we do not wish to suggest that situational demands take their toll only on the planning of propositions and that conceptual demands take their toll only on non referential planning. The demands may affect every dimension of discourse planning. Thus, for example, conceptual demands may lead a communicator not to take into consideration critical informational needs of his listeners (readers) prior to its expression. Similarly, situational demands on the level of turn-taking may lead a speaker to ignore displays of politeness appropriate to that situation.

7.7 Planned unplanned discourse

This chapter would not be complete without some discussion of the self-conscious expression of unplanned discourse features. There are cases in which a speaker or writer will intentionally produce discourse that appears unplanned. For example, a novelist trying to recreate a casual situational context will use many of the features (e.g. left-dislocation, deletion, hesitations) of unplanned discourse in his story. In fact, we regard a novelist highly if she or he is able successfully to reproduce such verbal spontaneity.

Second, we can find planned unplanned discourse in many speeches and lectures of skilled rhetoricians. Journalists, politicians, even academics at times have planned their discourse to appear as if it were being planned in the course of its delivery when, in fact, it has been worked out well in advance.

Third, in the anthropological literature there are accounts of cultures in which lower-status individuals are expected to speak as if they had not or could not organize what they have to say. Albert's study of the Burundi makes this point effectively:

> It would be an unforgivable blunder for a peasant-farmer, no matter how wealthy or able, to produce a truly elegant, eloquent, rapid-fire defense before a herder or other superior. However, the same peasant who stammers or shouts or forces a smile from a superior by making a rhetorical fool out of himself when his adversary is a prince or herder may (elsewhere) . . . show himself an able speaker, a dignified man who speaks as slowly and as intelligently as ever a highborn herder could [1972, p. 83].

We do not have to venture to distant cultures to witness this behaviour. Accounts of lower socioeconomic status groups within our own society describe the same expectations (cf. Abrahams, 1964).

In all of these situations, features of unplanned discourse are exploited for specific ends, for example, to get something. We offer here a framework for describing the distinguishing characteristics of this communicative behaviour, one that is potentially productive for cross-cultural studies of communicative strategies. Future research is needed to assess not only the extent to which features of unplanned discourse are common across languages and cultures but also the extent to which these features match more self-conscious attempts to produce unplanned discourse. Do the screen-play writer, novelist, politician, and Burundi peasant in fact utilize the actual features of unplanned discourse? To what extent have certain features become conventionalized? Are there features of unplanned discourse that have become stereotyped or stigmatized across a number of speech communities?

It is important to distinguish this use of unplanned discourse features from truly unplanned discourse. Simply displaying certain features is not sufficient for a discourse to be unplanned. The discourse must lack forethought and prior organization on the part of the communicator. (See p. 133 for this definition of unplanned discourse.) We can draw an analogy here between this behaviour and that of the sober man pretending to be drunk. He may stagger from pillar to post, roll back his eyes, and slur his speech, but we would not want to say 'This man is drunk.' Similarly, when a communicator self-consciously adopts features of unplanned discourse, we do not want to say 'This discourse is unplanned.'

Notes

1. In English the unmarked pronoun is *he*. However, the reader should bear in mind that the pronoun refers to both males *and* females.
2. We have mentioned only one source of egocentric speech, but there exist other sources as well. For example, the speaker may be concentrating on what he is doing or thinking because it is interesting or is of some importance to him.

8

Foregrounding referents:
a reconsideration of left dislocation
in discourse

E. Ochs Keenan and Bambi B. Schieffelin

8.1 Goals and orientation

In this paper we discuss a set of verbal constructions found in spontaneous conversational discourse. These constructions have in common
the following format: *Referent + Proposition*. That is, some referent is
specified initially and is then followed by a proposition relevant in
some way to this referent.

(1) GTS4–1
   (K has been talking about the fact that his car radio was taken
   from his car)

	Ref	Prop

   K: *They cleaned me out. <u>And my father oh he's-// he's fit to
   be tied.</u>*
   R: *Tell Daddy to buy you some more.*

For example, in (1), 'And my father oh he's-// he's fit to be tied'
represents such a construction. Here the referent expressed by 'my
father' is semantically related to the subsequent proposition 'he-s// he's
fit to be tied.'

Constructions of this type have been previously described as left
dislocations (Chafe, 1976; Gruber, 1967; Gundel, 1975; Ross, 1967, for
example). Left dislocation represents a transformation that moves an
NP within the sentence. The term left dislocation is not entirely appropriate to the constructions considered in the present analysis. First,
although the proposition following the initial referent usually contains
a coreferential pronoun, it sometimes does not. Example (2) illustrates
such a case:

(2) Two Girls; 8
   (in discussion about reading required for courses)

Ref
B: *ohh I g'ta tell ya one course,* ((pause))
A: (incred-)

Ref
B: *The mo-the modern art the twentieth century art,*
    Prop
there's about eight books.

Secondly, left dislocation is a formal operation that transforms one sentence into another. However, many of the constructions in our data look more like discourses than sentences. *That this has not been previously appreciated is due to the failure to examine these constructions in their context of use.*

In the discussion to follow we consider the communicative work being performed in utterances of the form 'Referent + Proposition'. This involves first familiarizing the reader with the discourse contexts in which such utterances are employed. In particular, we turn our attention to the role of the initial referent in the discourse. What is the relation of the initial referent to the discourse history, for example? What is the relation of the initial referent to subsequent discourse? We argue that the status of the initial referent as definite /new or given/new (Chafe, 1976) needs further clarification. Specifically it will be argued that a critical factor is the need of the speaker to provide *appropriate* old information, i.e. old information relevant to the main point expressed about the referent.

After assessing the function of these constructions in the discourse at hand, we present alternative strategies for carrying out the same communicative work. These strategies involve a *sequence* of two or more utterances. In the first utterance, a referent is introduced into the discourse. In the subsequent utterance(s), propositions relevant to that referent are expressed. We argue that Referent + Proposition constructions share many of the properties of these sequences.

8.2 Data base

Our analysis is based primarily on transcriptions made by G. Jefferson of five group therapy sessions (GTS) in which several adolescents took part (approximately 500 pages). Material on children's use of the constructions under study is drawn from transcriptions of the conversations of twins recorded over the period of a year (33-45 months). (Keenan, 1974a).

8.3 Role of referent + proposition in the discourse history

8.3.1 Bringing referents into discourse

What is the speaker doing when he produces utterances of the form 'Referent + Proposition', as expressed in Example (1)? As a first step in answering this question, we construct a series of *hypothetical* discourses. Imagine the following dialogues:

Interlocutor A	*Interlocutor B*
	As for ⎫
* (A) What happened to Tom?	Concerning ⎬ Tom, he left.
? (B) What happened to Tom?	Tom, he left.
(C) What happened to Tom?	His car, it broke down, and he's depressed.

Each of these dialogues varies in its degree of acceptability. Dialogue (A) appears the most awkward, and, in fact, we did not find any instances in the data in which *as for X, concerning X*, appeared following an immediately prior mention of X. (B) as well is odd. The most natural way to utter such a sequence is to utter the second 'Tom' with a question intonation, indicating that perhaps he had not heard the speaker, e.g. 'Tom? He left.' We can imagine, however, that such a discourse is possible if a long pause separates the two utterances and/or if the addressee (B) repeats 'Tom' in the course of searching for an adequate response.

Discourse (C) is by far the most natural of the three presented here. And in fact, constructions of the form 'Referent + Proposition' appear most often in precisely this sort of discourse environment, namely, an environment in which the referent does not appear in the immediately prior discourse. Chafe (1976) discusses the fact that a referent may or may not be presently in the consciousness of the hearer. If a referent is in the consciousness of the hearer, the referent is said to be 'foregrounded'. In English foregrounded information may be syntactically marked by the speaker by use of the definite article, anaphoric pronoun, relative clause and the like. We would like to claim here that in producing constructions of the form 'Referent + Proposition' speakers are performing work of precisely the *opposite* sort: rather than presenting information that is already in the foreground of the listener's consciousness, *the speaker brings a referent into the foreground of the listener's consciousness* (see also Sankoff and Brown, 1976). With respect to the interactional history of the interlocutors, *the referent is usually not currently a 'centre of attention', i.e. not usually the current 'topic'* (in the sense described by Li and Thompson (1976)). In producing constructions of this sort, the speaker makes the referent a 'centre of attention' (see also Payne, 1973).

Typically, the initial referent is some entity known to or knowable by the hearer from the nonverbal context of the utterance from some prior background experience. In other words, it is some entity that the hearer can identify or recognize. The referent may or may not have been discussed at some point in the current discourse participated in by the interlocutors;

1. In many cases, the speaker uses the 'Referent + Proposition' construction to *introduce* discourse-new referents. Examples (2), (3) and (4) exhibit this work:

   (2) GRS4:15

            Ref   Prop

     K: *Uh Pat McGee. I don't know if you know him, he -he lives in// Palisades.*

     J: *I know him real well as a matter of fa*(hh) (he's) *one of my best friends*

     K: *He-he used to go to the school I did// an' he-*

     J: *No, no* (hh)

     K: *He was in the dorm with me, and I was over him- and he-he had a room/ An' he-*

     J: *No!* (hh)// *heh heh*

     K: *-he despised me.*

   (3) GTS1:97

                             Ref   Prop

     L: *yeh, that c'd b e, cawss my sister, 'hh she en her boy friend jus broke up becawss he ast me tu me tuh go out with um:*

   (4) GTS3:62

     (Adolescents discussing how parents treat them)

     K: *Yeah// Yeah! No matter how old// you are*

     L: *Yeah. Mh hm*

                             Ref   Prop

     L: *Parents don't understand. But all grownups w-they do it to kids. Whether they're your own or not.*

2. On the other hand, some referent may have been in the foreground of the interlocutor's mind at some prior point in the conversation but fell to the background subsequently. In these instances, the speaker may use the 'Referent + Proposition' construction to *reintroduce*

a referent into the discourse. It should be emphasized here that a referent may fall into the background rapidly after its first mention. It sometimes happens that a referent must be reforegrounded after one turn or even after one utterance within a turn. Example (5) illustrates a re-introduced referent:

(5) GTS3:37

K: *An' I got a red sweater, an' a white one, an' a blue one, an' a yellow one, an' a couple other sweaters, you know, And uh my sister* loves *borrowing my sweaters because they're pullovers, you know, an' she c'n wear a blouse under'em an' she thinks 'Well this is great'*
(pause)

	Ref	Prop

K: *An' so my* red *sweater, I haven't seen it since I got it.*

8.3.2 *Functions of foregrounding*

Once the global function of these constructions, i.e. to bring into the foreground or focus on some referent (cf. Sankoff and Brown, 1976), is understood, more particular functions of this phenomenon make sense.

1. *Alternatives*: In many cases, the speaker uses this construction to bring in a different referent from one previously specified with respect to some particular predication. The speaker in these cases suggests an *alternative* to that produced in a prior utterance or turn. Example (4) illustrates this usage. We avoid the term 'contrast' to describe this function, as 'contrast' usually implies that the referent brought in in 'contrast' is an alternative considered (with varying degrees of certitude) by both hearer and speaker (Chafe, 1976; Kuno, 1972). The way in which many of these 'Referent + Proposition' constructions is used is much broader than this treatment of contrast. In the data at hand, the speaker may bring in a referent that the hearer has not yet entertained as a viable alternative. For example, in (4) the referent 'all grownups' is not a set that was under consideration by those listening to L.

2. *Particular cases*: The 'Referent + Proposition' construction is used to draw the listener's attention to a particular case of some general phenomenon under discussion or to some particular member of a previously specified set. For example, in (5) the speaker is isolating

'my red sweater' from a previously mentioned list of items. Perhaps the most common use of this construction is to *introduce* referents that further illustrate the current topic of discussion. Note that the referents in themselves do not constitute topics of discussion (discourse topics) but rather are important arguments in a proposition or set of propositions (discourse topic) under consideration in discourse (see Chapter 5). For example, the discourse in (2) is preceded by a discussion about people who do not like one another. The introduction of 'Pat McGee' initiates a case history relevant to the current topic or concern of the interlocutors. Similarly, in (6) below, the interlocutors have been talking about students falling asleep in class and K can't resist bringing in a relevant anecdote:

(6) GTS5:35

            Ref   Prop

K: *Uh:: this guy, you could yell 'Hey Jo:hn, hey Joh-' 'n you*
    c'd go over an 'tap him on the shoulder

R:⌐ *So he's gotta// good imagination*
    ⌊   Prop

K:⌊ *That's the only way you c'd snap him out of it.*

It isn't always the case that the introduction of novel referents as particular cases involves speaker change. In many cases, a speaker may bring up a certain point and use the 'Referent + Proposition' construction to illustrate his/her own point. For example in (7) below, there has been some discussion about how parents never treat their children as mature individuals (see also Example (4)) and L brings up the point that her parents are exceptions to this generalization. By way of illustration, L describes an incident in which her mother plays a major role:

(7) GTS3:63

L: *Well my parents are different. I- it isn't my parents that do*
                            Ref   Ref
    it to me, cause my my mother, like my little sister, she had
      Prop   Prop
    a party. So she says to the girls, 'Just don't get pregnant'
    (pause)

D: *heh heh heh*

Notice here that we have a case of a complex 'Referent + Proposition' construction in which one Referent + Proposition is embedded in another. The 'Referent + Proposition' construction 'like my little

sister, she had a party' is embedded in the Referent + Proposition
construction 'my mother, . . . so she says to the girls, "Just don't get
pregnant"'.

3. *Special emphasis:* In some cases, the 'Referent + Proposition' construction may be used neither to introduce nor re-introduce a
referent but to mention again a referent currently in the foreground
of the interlocutors' minds. We argue that this use is secondary rather
than basic to such constructions. In these cases, the speaker is using
the basic function of focusing the listener's attention on some
referent to amplify the attention paid to some referent under
discussion. In other words, the speaker uses the basic focus function
to give *special emphasis* or importance to a particular entity. Example
(8) illustrates this use.

(8) GTS1:43
   (discussing younger siblings)
   L: *T'know some of 'em are darmn tall and goodlooking they
      could pass for* (t)- *nineteen.// A twelve year old guy comes
      over I say who's y-older brother is he? He's not he's in
      the A7.*
   R: *But they don't-*
   R: *But they don't have a brain to go with it hehh*
          Ref   Prop
   L: <u>*These kids I don't believe it they're six foot.*</u>

This use of 'Referent + Proposition' appears infrequently (6.6 per cent
of adult corpus, $f = 3$) in the data under consideration.

8.3.3 Foregrounding and the topicalization hierarchy

If our suggestion is correct, that is, if the primary function of Referent
+ Proposition constructions is to bring into the discourse a referent that
the speaker believes is not currently in the foreground of the listener's
consciousness, then one would expect that frequently mentioned or
discussed referents would appear infrequently in these constructions.
That is, referents that are high in the sentence topic hierarchy (Li and
Thompson, 1976) should be low in the foregrounding referent hierarchy.
To a large extent, this is, in fact, precisely what occurs.

In this speech community co-conversationalists usually talk about
themselves (Sacks, 1968; Hawkinson and Hyman, 1974). Overwhelmingly, conversations orient themselves to the speaker and/or the hearer.

In terms of the sentence topic hierarchy, then, referents for 'I' and 'you' appear at the top. In the Referent + Proposition constructions collected, we found a number of cases of *indirect* reference to speaker or hearer, reference to others *through* the speaker or hearer, but *direct* reference to the speaker or hearer appeared only once (2 per cent of adult data). Our data suggest that these referents are less likely to be foregrounded or 'topicalized' through such constructions. We can explain their infrequent appearance as due to their near constant presence in the discourse history (see Table 8.1). This observation should be taken into account in comparing topic constructions across languages. Constructions of the Referent + Proposition format have been treated as comparable to topic constructions in other languages (Li and Thompson, 1976). For example, they often appear as glosses for topic constructions in other languages. It is not clear at this point, however, just how such constructions operate in the discourse of different languages. We need to examine the discourse of languages such as Chinese, Japanese, Korean, Lahu and so on to assess the extent to which the informational status of the topicalized referent(s) is the same. In this way we can assure that constructions that appear similar on formal grounds are similar functionally as well.

Table 8.1

Sentence topic	Ref + Prop constructions	
Speaker/hearer	Individuals other than speaker/hearer	High likelihood
Individuals other than speaker/hearer	Speaker/hearer	Low likelihood

8.4 Foregrounding, definiteness and subsequent discourse

Thus far, we have discussed the initial Referent in Referent + Proposition constructions in terms of its status as piece of *given* information in the discourse (Chafe, 1976) and a sentence topic. We turn now to a discussion of its status as *definite*. We use the terms *given* and *definite* in the sense expressed by Chafe (1976). '*Given* refers to referents that the speaker assumes to be in the consciousness of the addressee at the time of the utterance' (Chafe, 1976, p. 7). *Definite* refers to referents that the speaker believes the hearer knows you can identify. The hearer may know the referent through the discourse history or through the nonverbal context or through prior shared experience with the speaker, general knowledge of the world and so on. A piece of information, then, may be definite but not necessarily given. For example a referent may be mentioned in discourse for the first time but may be identifiable by the hearer from other sources.

We find that the initial referent in Referent+Proposition constructions normally is not given information, but it is normally definite. However, in looking over these constructions, we find that the distinctions between given/definite/new are still not sufficient for understanding the status of the initial referent and the form of the Referent + Proposition construction. We find that from the speaker's point of view, what is important is that the hearer knows certain background information that is critical to assessing the subsequent proposition. That is, the hearer must not only recognize or know who the speaker is talking about. The hearer must know certain facts about the referent, facts that are *relevant* to the main predication the speaker wants.

We find that many of the constructions in the data perform just this task. We find that in many cases an initial referent will be expressed; it is then followed by one or more propositions that provide more information about the referent; and this in turn is followed by a major predication relevant to the referent. Examples (9), (10) and (11) illustrate such a construction: Referent + Background Proposition + Main Proposition.

(9) GTS3:70

    (In discussion about attitudes towards young siblings)

           Ref   Background Props

    L: *My sister when we were up in camp when she was twelve.*
       And all the guys were sixteen, (pause) *and fifteen. They*
       don' wanna do out with twelve year olds. So I let everyone
           Main Prop
       know that she was thirteen and a half, almost fourteen.

(10) GTS3:47

           Ref   Background Props

    K: *Y'know, the cops if they see you, and they think 'Well,*
           Main Prop
       he's 18,' A lotta time they'll letcha by, quicker than a 16
       year old or a 17 year old.

(11) GTS3:64

    (L has been talking about how her car broke down)

                                    Ref   Background
K: *Oh-oh wait. In Mammoth my Jeep I've got surf stickers all*
    Props
    over the back windows you know?

L: *Mm// hm*

K: *An' up there they hate surf. Surf is the lowe//st thing, in*
    the world. An' all the adults frown upon it, the kids hate
    'em, they see me, an' they used to throw rocks// you
    know? An' I was avoiding rocks. So I finally decided this
                                    Main Props
    isn't for me y'know, I took razor blades, took all my surf
    stickers off? So it looked like just a normal everyday Jeep
    ...

See also Example (2).

In these cases it appears that the speaker refers to some entity then realized that he must provide additional information. For example, in (11) K has to provide information about his Jeep and about the atmosphere in Mammoth so that the addressee can understand the activity described in the major predication, i.e. that K had to take stickers off the windows of the Jeep in Mammoth. Similarly in (2), K had to provide further information concerning Pat McGee, i.e. that he lived with K, so that the hearer would understand the relevance of the referent to the topic under discussion.

These observations indicate that the Referent + Proposition construction is a form of 'unplanned' speech. In more planned modes of speaking, the interlocutor might present such background information as a non-restrictive relative clause or adverbial clause embedded in a matrix clause. Or the interlocutor might present this information in a *sequence* of well-formed sentences that anticipate the major predication to be made. Before developing further the role of Referent + Proposition constructions, we turn to this latter alternative, discourse, as a means of getting a referent known to an intended listener.

8.5 Alternate foregrounding strategies

8.5.1 'About' questions

A speaker may draw the listener's attention to a particular referent in ways other than by the bald presentation of that referent as in 'Referent +

Proposition' constructions. For example, the speaker may introduce/
re-introduce the referent through the use of an 'about' question:
'How about X?' 'What about X?', where X represents some object,
event, etc. (see also Gundel, 1975). The response to this question
provides a proposition relevant to X (the referent). Here, then, two or
more separate utterances convey what is conveyed in 'Referent +
Proposition' utterances. For example, in (12) an individual named
'Hogan' is introduced by J in an 'about' question. He is identified in
the subsequent three turns, at which point J is able to convey the
relevant proposition ('he's a real bitchin' guy').

    (12)GTS4:21

                        Ref
    J: How about a guy named Hogan?
    K: Bill Hogan?
    J: Bill Hogan
    K: Yeah I know him real well.
           Prop
    J: I do too *he's a//real bitchin' guy*.

In Example (13), D asks his listeners to consider a particular type of
person (rather than some specific individual):

    (13)GTS5:37

       (Talking about self-conscious people)
                   Ref
    D: Well what about the *guy gets up on the dance floor, who
          feels that he can't dance.*
           Prop
    R: *-He's scared.*

8.5.2 Directives to locate referent

One extremely common strategy for bringing a referent into the discourse either as an Alternative or as Particular Case is for the speaker to
request that the listener locate the referent in memory or in the nonverbal context. Here the speaker makes use of one or more *locating
verbs*, for example 'look at', 'see', 'consider', 'turn to', 'watch out for',
'remember', 'know', 'return to', 'check out', 'take a glance at'. Certain
of these verbs are used to locate referents in both memory and visible
environment of the talk taking place. For example, one can ask a listener
to 'look at' some individual not present, using 'look' in a metaphorical

sense and of course one can ask the listener to 'look' at some object present in the physical setting.

Locating Verbs appear in a number of sentence modalities. For example, they may appear in an *interrogative* sentence, as in Example (14):

(14)GTS4:28

                     Ref

  K: (D ju remember) *Kouhalan*?// (Fat kid two oh nine?)

  J: Oh God, yeah, I know that guy.

                     Prop

  K: Did Mc//*McGee hates him.*

  J: That guy's insane we're drivin' down the freeway . . .

(15)GTS1:73

                     Ref

  L: Whaddya think of Paul

  K: Paul the //quiet guy?

                  Prop

  L: *He was the quiet one who never said anything.*

More widespread in conversational discourse is the use of Locating Verb in the *imperative* mode. By far the most commonly used is the verb 'look' or 'look at'.

(16)GRS4:12

                                     Ref   Prop

  T: . . . Look, if I have – for example *Picasso. I think he's an individual, who w-you may classify him as being neurotic or I don't know what, but I don't think he is,* I think he's . . .

                     Ref

  J: (Lookit) the guy *who cut off his ear*

  R: That's another man

  T: That was Van Gogh

                  Prop

  J: Well, *he was nuts*, wasn't//he?

The Locating Verb 'know' does not appear as such in the imperative, i.e. as 'know X!'. We find, however, that the texts are littered with the construction 'you know' (y'know). We argue that 'you know' sometimes operates as a directive to the listener to put himself in the state of knowing X, where X is some referent or proposition conveyed. That is, the speaker is directing the listener(s) to search in memory or in the immediate context for some known/knowable X. In Example (17), we find this use of 'you know' intermingled with other locating verbs used to the same end.

(17)GTS1:73

   (In discussion of picking fights in downtown Los Angeles)

   A: I think-

   R: Yeah *that* was much better man. You know an' -Lookit
       Ref

      these people come walkin down the street (Y'know dey
      oughta be-) *Y'see dis executive, y'know wid his wife*
            Prop   Prop
      y'know *ou'* come up t'him an 'chose'im off, he *doesn't*
      know what de hell's happened . . .

Here we find the speaker making use of the Locating Verbs 'know',
'lookit', 'see'.

If the speaker feels that the listener may not know the information
he wishes to convey, he may use 'know' in either of two ways: he may
ask if the listener knows the entity, proposition to be discussed. This
does the work of making the listener aware that there is something
that he does not in fact know and puts him in a state of readiness to
receive the information (Heringer, personal communication). In many
cases, the speaker does not expect that the listener does know the bit of
information he will convey. Indeed often the speaker makes it impossible
for the listener to know the information at the time of the 'Do you
know?' information request. The speaker may simply ask 'Do you
know what?' or 'Know what?' Here the listener is being informed that
there is something he does not know. He is obliged to respond with the
request for information 'What?' or 'No, what?' This in turn obliges him
to attend to the subsequent response (Sacks, 1968). The question 'You
know what?', then, is a powerful tool for a speaker who wishes to
control the direction of the listener's attention. The question operates
in much the same manner as the use of the 'summons–response' adjacency
pair (Schegloff, 1972). A summons or calling out of someone's name is
usually responded to with some query such as 'Yes?' 'What is it?' 'What
do you want?' Having asked this question the party summoned is
obliged to attend to its response. Given that 'you know' questions are
such effective attention-getters, it is not surprising that they are employed
to shift to a novel topic or introduce anecdote. Examples (15) and
(16) illustrate such uses. Example (18) illustrates a not altogether
successful use.

(18)GTS1:10

   (in course of joke-telling session)

L: *You know what a cute one is? You wanna hear what a*
      cute one is? What's purple and goes bam bam bam bam.
      A four door plum.
      (pause)
K: *Terrific.*

(19)GTS1:54
      (K tasting something)
      K: *Aahh!* ((whispered)) *This is good.*
      L: *You know what my father keeps down in the basement?*
            Cases of champagne.
      A: *What?*
      (K): (I din't hear.)
      L: *Cases of cham//pagne.*

A second alternative available to a speaker who feels the listener
may not know what/who he is talking about is to assert that he, the
speaker, knows this information, i.e. 'I know X.' Example (20) illustrates
this strategy.

(20)GTS1:20
      (In discussion of going to a psychiatrist at an early age)
      K: *Oh he* is *a young 'un hhh*
      R: *Maybe younger I don't really remember*
      L: (If you think-) *I know this guy who has been going since*
            he was eight years old and he's *even worse off than he-when*
            he started.
      R: *I thought you were going to say worse off than me*
            hehhhhehh

The use of Locating Verbs to direct the listener's attention to
something the speaker wants to talk about is common to two sets of
speakers other than adult speakers of English. First of all, we find this
strategy heavily employed by young children acquiring English. Atkinson
(1979) reports that children at the one-word stage use verbs such as
'see' and 'look' to secure the attention of some co-present individual.
Once the attention of the individual is captured, the child may go on to
predicate something of the object of attention. This behaviour is highly
characteristic of the twins' conversations recorded by Keenan (1974a).
The transcripts from 33 months to 37 months are laced with demands
and (later) requests that the conversational partner look at some
object in the room. Often the speaker would repeat the directive over
and over until the other child complied (Chapter 5). Example (21)
illustrates the character of such communications.

(21) Toby and David, 33 months
(T and D have been talking about a scratch on D's back when
D abruptly notices a book on the floor)
D: *See it/ A B C/ See it/ See/ A B C/ Look!/*
T: *Oh yes/*
D: *A B C in 'ere/*

A second group of communicators who employ Locating Verbs in imperative and interrogative utterances to this end are users of American Sign Language. Friedman (1976) mentions that the sign equivalent for 'know' can be used to establish a referent as a 'topic' (p. 28). The sign-equivalent for the sentence 'There's a train that runs between San Jose and San Francisco' begins with the sequence 'You know-that/ train/'. Similarly English sentences containing relative clauses may be glossed in sign by initially asking or telling the addressee to 'remember' or 'know' some referent and then predicating something of that referent, e.g. 'I saw the man who bought the dog' may be glossed in sign 'Remember man bought dog? Saw him (index)' (Brandt, personal communication).

8.6   Left-dislocations or discourses?

The strategies presented above represent discourse strategies for getting the listener to attend to and know a particular referent. The referent is introduced in one utterance, usually a directive. Subsequent utterances provide one or more predications concerning the referent. The major predication may or may not be preceded by background information relevant to the referent and its role in the predication.

We argue that Referent + Proposition constructions perform very similar communicative work. The uttering of the initial referent functions as a directive to attend to that referent. Subsequent propositions provide background information and/or a major predication concerning the referent. In this sense, the Referent + Proposition constructions look more like discourses (a sequence of communicative acts) than a single syntactically bound communicative act. In fact, it is possible to para-phrase many of the Referent + Proposition constructions by placing a locating verb before the initial referent. For example,

'But all grownups w-they do it to kids' = But (look at, consider) all
grownups w-they do it to kids.

Further support for an underlying locating verb is seen in cases in which a pronoun appears as the initial referent. The pronoun appears in the objective case in English in these contexts (e.g. me, him, us, etc.). In these cases as well, the construction could be paraphrased with a locating verb:

Me, I don't wear stockings	=	(Look at) me, I don't wear stockings
Him, he never studies	=	(look at him), he never studies

That the Referent and Proposition function more like a discourse than a single construction is supported by formal characteristics as well.

8.6.1 Prosodic breaks between referent and proposition

We find that in most examples of Referent + Proposition there is an intonational break between Referent and Proposition. In most cases, the referent is uttered with a slight rising intonation (represented by a comma in transcript). This is then often followed by a pause or by a hesitation marker (e.g. uhh). In other cases the referent is expressed with a falling intonation followed by a brief pause.

8.6.2 Interruptions

Another feature that supports the sequential nature of these constructions is the presence of interruptions between referent and subsequent propositions. We find interruptions of two sorts. First, there may be interruptions from a listener (Example (6)). Second, and more interesting, there may be *self-interruptions*. For example, we may consider the cases in which the speaker expresses the referent and then inserts background information about the referent before the main point as self-interruptions (see Examples (6), (7), (9), (10) and (11)).

8.6.3 Loose syntactic ties

The initial Referent is not tightly tied to the subsequent proposition in the same way as sentential subjects are (Keenan, 1976). The initial referent does not control verb agreement for example. Further even the presence of a coreferential pronoun is not always manifest (Examples (2), (11)). We find several cases in which the initial referent is linked to the subsequent proposition simply by juxtaposition. For example:

(22) GTS3:62
   (L has been talking about how her grandmother treats her father as small child)

L: *Oy! my fa- my my-// my grandmother. My father comes in
the house 'Oh my son my son'*

In (22) the referent of 'my grandmother' is linked to the subsequent
proposition as utterances in a discourse are linked, i.e. by the maxim of
relevance (Grice, 1975). We link the two expressions because they
follow one another in real speech time and because we assume that
speakers normally make their utterances relevant to prior talk, and
because it makes sense to link them (given their content and our
knowledge of the world). In such constructions, then, referents and
propositions are linked *pragmatically* rather than syntactically.

In this paper we have displayed many of the discourse properties
of Referent + Proposition constructions. We have argued that formally
and functionally the expression of the initial referent and the expression
of subsequent predications constitute more or less independent communicative acts. We say 'more or less' because these constructions vary
in the extent to which they are formally integrated. For example, (1)
is prosodically and syntactically more cohesive than (22). But we may
say the same for relations between separate utterances within a stretch
of discourse. They may be more or less formally bound through the
use of conjunctions, adverbs, anaphora and the like. When we contrast
discourse with sentence, we are speaking of a continuum. Along this
continuum, communicative acts are morphosyntactically or otherwise
formally linked to varying extents.

We may use such a continuum to characterize properties within and
across languages. For example, written and spoken (particularly informal,
spontaneous) modes of a language may differ with respect to discourse
or sentential strategies for communicating (see Chapter 7). Furthermore,
languages may differ from one another in the extent to which they
rely on sequences rather than single sentences to convey information
(cf. Foley, 1976). For example, topic-prominent languages (Li and
Thompson, 1976) may turn out to be discourse-oriented languages,
whereas subject-prominent languages may turn out to be more sentence-
oriented. Finally, the continuum may be useful in assessing changes
over time within a language. For example, ontogenetic development
of English is marked by a move away from discourse strategies for
communicating towards greater reliance on sentences (i.e. greater
reliance on syntax) (Keenan and Klein, 1975; Scollon, 1976; see also
Chapter 5). Similarly diachronic changes may be marked by syntac-
tization of earlier discourse constructions (cf. Sankoff and Brown,
1976).

Part III
Cross-cultural perspectives on caregiver–child communication

9

Talking like birds: sound play in a cultural perspective[1]

Bambi B. Schieffelin

Sound play has been discussed in terms of the vocal/verbal activity of a single speaker by Jakobson (1968) and Weir (1962). More recently it has been described in dialogic contexts between young children (Keenan and Klein, 1975; Garvey, 1977b). In these exchanges, children pay attention to the phonological shape of one another's utterances and repeat or modify slightly a sequence of sounds just produced. These sequences, which may be referentially meaningless, are nonetheless textually cohesive in that utterances relate, by similarity in phonological shape, to each other. In addition, Keenan and Klein (1975) have pointed out that sound play is coherent on a social level since it constitutes a single speech event.

The occurrence of sound play has been reported in a number of different cultures. Most middle-class American adults usually think of sound play as one of many verbal or vocal activities young children engage in. They are not disturbed by sound play as such, provided the language is not obscene and the activity does not disturb others.

However sound play is not thought of as an innocent or acceptable activity in all societies. I would like to present an example of one such society, where children's sound play is terminated whenever it is heard. In the first part of the paper a spontaneously produced sound play sequence will be analysed in terms of form and content. We shall examine turn-taking procedures for the ways in which play is established and agreed upon by the two young girls involved. The formal features of language which can be played with (pitch, prosody, timing) are discussed. Metalinguistic awareness of conversational conventions, and conversational co-operation are demonstrated in the sequences which bring evidence against Piaget's notion of early egocentrism in speech.

In the second part of the paper I will present a cultural explanation for the adult response which terminates the play. This response is motivated by beliefs about the language acquisition process and the symbolic association between young children and birds. I hope to demonstrate the importance of looking at spontaneous sound play from an ethnographic perspective.

The data are drawn from an ethnographic study of the development of communicative competence among the Kaluli of Papua New Guinea (Schieffelin, in press). The Kaluli, who number about 1200, are traditional, nonliterate, tropical forest subsistence horticulturalists who live in longhouse communities of 60-100 individuals. Unlike many Highlands peoples, Kaluli society has no 'Big Men' and is essentially egalitarian in structure (Schieffelin, 1976).

As part of this study, the spontaneous conversations of four children who were beginning to use syntax were taperecorded for one year. These conversations took place between the child and those people with whom he or she regularly interacted. In this way data on language acquisition could be collected as well as data on the contexts of language acquisition. After recording, the conversations were transcribed by the author and discussed with Kaluli people. In addition to taperecording, extensive observations were made and interviews were conducted in the community.

All of the children in the study were involved in playful interactions with sound play, but there was individual variation in the amount and elaboration of the activities. The sequence which I shall focus on is an interaction between two little girls, Mɛli (age 30 months 2 weeks) and her cousin named Mama (age 45 months). They lived in the same house and played together in other verbal modes: word play, repetition games, singing, as well as sound play.

Mɛli and her cousin Mama are in the house; Mɛli's mother is cooking and engaged in conversation with other adults. The two girls have been in a playful mood all morning, and had been engaged in a repetition game earlier. They are waiting for food. Mama is banging on a water jug.[2]

1. Mama: *Mɛli Mɛli mɛli mɛli mɛli mɛli*

2. Mɛli: *oh*

3. Mama: *oh*

4. Mɛli: *obɛ*

5. Mama: *obɛ*

6. Mɛli:　o͡h

7. Mama:　　o͡h

8. Mɛli:　o͡h

9. Mama:　　o͡h

10. Mɛli:　o͡bɛ:

11. Mama:　　o͡bɛ

12. Mɛli:　o͡o:

13. Mama:　　o͡o:

14. Mɛli:　o͡bɛ:

15. Mama:　　o͡bɛ:

16. Mɛli:　o:h͡

17. Mama:　　o͡h

18. Mɛli:　u͡u

19. Mama:　　u͡u

20. Mɛli:　u͡ʷu:

21. Mama:　　u͡ʷu:

22. Mɛli:　u͡u:

23. Mama:　　u͡u:

24. Mɛli:　u͡bu:

25. Mama:　　u͡bu:

26. Mother: *wai!   to nafa   se sɛlɛiba!   obɛ towɔ we.*
                  (talk good try to talk   bird talk this.)

(1. Mama: Mɛli Mɛli mɛli mɛli mɛli mɛli
  2. Mɛli: *yes?*
  3. Mama: *yes?*
  4. Mɛli: *what?*
  5. Mama: *what?*
  6. Mɛli: *okay*
  7. Mama: *okay*
  8. Mɛli: *yes?*
  9. Mama: *yes?*
 10. Mɛli: *whaaat?*
 11. Mama: *what*

12 to 25 — no English gloss

26. Mother: *Try to talk good talk. This is bird talk.*)

In this sequence we see the transition from language to rhythmic
sound play. It is one of many instances where two children collaborate
and maintain this type of speech activity. Mama's use of Mɛli's name as
a vocative in initiating talk to Mɛli (line 1) is different from the usual
ways in which speakers use vocatives to secure the attention of the
listener in normal conversation. Her calls to Mɛli are accompanied by
rhythmic banging on a water jug and are rapidly repeated six times
without an interval to allow Mɛli to respond. In addition, they are
high-pitched and staccato, and do not follow the usual prosodic contours used in conversation.

While Mama is playing in her opening line, Mɛli responds in her next
turns in usual conversational style. After her name is called, Mɛli
acknowledges Mama (line 2) with *oh*, 'yes?' When Mama imitates Mɛli's
opening acknowledgement (line 3), instead of providing a line of conversation, Mɛli requests clarification with *obɛ* 'what?' Mama again repeats
Mɛli's utterance. Next, Mɛli responds to Mama's turn with a closing
acknowledgement *oh*, 'okay' (line 6), which Mama again imitates. While
Mama's imitations of Mɛli's utterances are playful, Mɛli is in a conversational frame, and is using normal conversational features. However,
when Mama repeats Mɛli's utterance in an even higher pitched voice
with a shorter than usual interval between turns, Mɛli's following response (line 8) is also higher pitched, and the play is on. Thus, the mood
or key initiated by Mama is finally recognized by Mɛli and 'play' is

agreed upon, as indicated by her rise in pitch.

By the tenth turn, there is overlap between the two speakers, with Mama imitating Mɛli's utterances. The overlap is *within* turn pairs, never *across* turn pairs (that is, there is no overlap between turns 13 and 14, only between 14 and 15). As in other play sequences based on words, Mɛli always waits for Mama to complete her turn before starting the next pair.

Up to this point (turns 10–11) the girls are playing with the conventions of opening and closing up talk (Schegloff, 1968). That is, there is a vocative as a summons (Mɛli's name), a response, 'yes?', a clarification request when a message is not forthcoming, 'what?', and the closing confirmation, 'okay'. However, in this sequence there is *no* content, topic or message in between the opening and the closing. There is no transfer of information. Thus, lines 1–11 consist of playing with the formal devices of conversation, only the openings and closing.

Then there is a shift: from turn pairs 12–13 the intervals between the turn pairs become shorter, the pitch becomes higher and the vowels are lengthened, then shifted. What has been a sequence of words dissolves into a sequence of sounds as the girls play with the phonological shape of the words. Here the younger child, Mɛli, takes the lead. From turn pairs 12–17 the prosodic contours remain similar to the opening and closing contours, but from pairs 18–25 they too shift into a playful modality. Other changes occur during these turns. The vowels rise and the turn-taking pattern becomes less conversational and more like the call-response pattern in women's songs. The two little girls started out playing with the words used to signal the openings and closings of talk, correctly sequenced, and then jointly renegotiated the sequence into one of playing with sounds. They co-operated for twenty-five turns, signalling their ongoing agreement to maintain this play/speech activity using features of pitch (high voice), prosody (exaggerated intonation), and timing (shortened within pair turn intervals). Mɛli acknowledges the imitation on the part of Mama as playful as evidenced by her collaboration. In other sequences Mama mocks her speech by imitating it and changing the phonological shape, and Mɛli refuses to respond except in anger.

After turn 25, Mɛli's mother, who had been busy scraping taro and having a conversation with someone else, turns abruptly to the girls and in a loud authoritative voice says, 'wai! try to speak good talk! this is bird talk!' The girls immediately stop and become quiet. Both girls were enjoying this activity so why did the mother respond as she did?

The mother's termination of the sound play was not due to mild irritation caused by the noise the girls were making, since similar noise levels caused by other kinds of verbal activity would never have prompted this reaction. Her particular response, which was consistent with that of other Kaluli mothers in similar situations, has a cultural and symbolic basis, related to Kaluli ideas about language development and the broader notion of taboo.

The Kaluli have a well-articulated notion of how their children learn language — they say that children must be taught to speak (Schieffelin, 1979). This is done principally by the mother. Kaluli use no baby talk (BT) words, nor do they employ other features of BT that some researchers have claimed are universal. This is because Kaluli feel that even young children should not hear or be encouraged to use childish forms, since it is important for them to use 'hard speech' as spoken by adults if they are to learn how to talk. The Kaluli have no lexical item for sound play. When asked about it, they grouped it with babbling; they said it was 'to no purpose'.

The major strategy for teaching young children to talk involves telling the child what to say to someone in ongoing interactions. The mother provides the model utterance, followed by the imperative 'say like that'. By 'prompting' their children, mothers are actively involved in the promotion, support and, as they see it, the facilitation of the child's use of language, primarily in interactions with others. These prompts are not limited to routines, and extend over many turns of connected discourse.

The young child's language is seen as 'soft', that is, it is not well-formed. The process of language development (and development in general) is talked about as a 'hardening process'. The goal of language development is to produce speech that is both well-formed and socially appropriate.

In addition to having ideas about how a young child's language should sound, Kaluli say that birds and children are connected in a number of complex symbolic ways. One area in which this relationship is manifested is the system of food taboos, which prevents the association between children and certain birds. Kaluli say that if young children eat certain pigeons that they too would only coo, and never learn hard language. Thus, this prohibition is necessary to protect the child's developing language (and, by implication, social) ability.

Birds and children are closely associated in other contexts. The calls of certain fruit doves are felt to be similar to the pathetic whining voices of small hungry children. Both are high pitched and repetitive in their vocalizations. Yet another association turns on the fact that upon death a person's soul becomes a bird. (This has been discussed in detail by Schieffelin (1976) and Feld (1982).)

Given these powerful and problematic symbolic associations between birds and young children, the two must be kept separate. This means that children must not only avoid eating certain birds, they must not sound like them either, even in play. Mothers discourage their children from emulating or imitating qualities associated with certain birds. This avoidance is serious, especially in terms of its potential consequences for language development. Thus, in order to ensure that 'hard language' develops, the mother prevents a dangerous association; she terminates the sound play. Furthermore she makes it explicit to the children that they are to speak 'good talk, not bird talk'.

Conclusion

The fact that two children, ages 2½ and 3½, are able to sustain an interaction over twenty-five turns, attending with great detail and precision to each other's utterances, is evidence against Piaget's notion of egocentrism in early language. This is consistent with the findings of other researchers who have looked at spontaneous speech, for example Keenan (1974a), and Shatz and Gelman (1973). In addition, the fact that the children are playing with the formal devices of talk, is evidence of their metalinguistic awareness of such pragmatic phenomena. Perhaps spontaneous sound play is one important area where metalinguistic awareness may be investigated in very young children.

Second, in terms of the methodology the data analysis is a result of a culturally contextualized analysis — detailed ethnographic information from a number of different cultural domains (e.g. food taboos) was used in order to arrive at a description of what the Kaluli think is important. In investigating the development of communicative competence, one must not only look at 'language' data, but contexts in which children play with language as well.

In connection with this it is crucial to understand the role of language in a given society — including the beliefs and practices concerning acquisition. Thus, the notions of 'hard' talk and 'good' talk are related to the expectations of how language is to be spoken. For the Kaluli, language is a major means of social control in an egalitarian society where people essentially make their own way. This is one of the reasons that mothers teach their young children what to say, so that from an early age they will be able to get what they want and express themselves through well-formed, adult-like language. And by examining the contexts of acquisition we see the very important role played by the mother, as she participates in verbal exchanges, shaping interactions that involve her young children, and making sure that nothing, for example sound play, impedes their development. We see how the acquisition of *language* is embedded in *culture*, and as the children are learning one, they are also learning the other.

Notes

1. Excerpted from *How Kaluli children learn what to say, what to do, and how to feel: An ethnographic study of the development of communicative competence* (Schieffelin, in press).

   The research for this study was made possible by grants from the National Science Foundation and the Wenner-Gren Foundation for Anthropological Research, New York. In addition, the invaluable assistance provided by E. L. Schieffelin and S. Feld during the course of the research is gratefully acknowledged.
2. Transcription conventions for this example: lines above utterance show the general pitch contour of the vocalization; : after lexical item = vowel lengthening; double vowels = vowel gemination. Position of word in each turn pair roughly indicates amount of time between termination of first turn and onset of second turn of the pair.

10

Cultural dimensions of language acquisition[1]

E. Ochs

Current work on how children acquire language tells us that caregivers, particularly mothers, are highly instrumental in this process. This is accomplished in several ways: mothers simplify their syntax, reduce their utterance length, reduce their vocabulary, repeat and paraphrase their utterances, when speaking to young childen (Ferguson, 1977; Snow, 1972, 1977, 1979; Newport, 1976; Cross, 1975, 1977).

Further, while mothers don't overtly correct the form of a child's utterance, they will often repeat what the child says, using correct adult syntax. These are referred to as *expansions* in the literature (Brown et al., 1969; Cazden, 1965, 1972; Cross, 1977) and are illustrated in sequences such as the following:

Child: *down/*
Mother: *You want to get down.*

Child: *Daddy go car/*
Mother: *Right. Daddy is going in the car.*

Child: *baby diaper/*
Mother: *Baby is wearing a diaper.*

Another reported practice of mothers is asking the child to clarify unintelligible utterances. In this way, mothers encourage children to express their thoughts more clearly and in a more acceptable form (Scollon, 1976; Atkinson, 1979; see also Chapter 5).

What I want to discuss here is the cultural nature of these observations of the way in which mothers speak to children. I want to persuade you that what has been observed is *not universal*, is *not a fact* about normal mother–child interaction. These observations are largely based on middle-class, Anglo-American mothers or on middle-class European mothers.

If you are an educator or a clinician involved with communicative disorders, it is crucial to separate biological patterns from cultural patterns, to distinguish between a child or a caregiver who does not conform to a cultural norm from a child or caregiver who deviates from a *biological* norm. This is particularly the case when dealing with young children and families of non-Anglo, non-middle-class backgrounds. For these children, it is crucial to know what are the normal and appropriate ways in which young children communicate. Children from different ethnic and class backgrounds may use language in ways that differ from middle-class American children. The diagnosing of their language as disordered or deviant in some way must be based on deviance with respect to their own cultural norms for child language and not with respect to norms of the therapist's or educator's culture, where it differs from that of the child. In other words, it is important to distinguish *difference* from *deviance*.

To this end, I would like to report on an important difference between Anglo-American mother–child interaction and mother–child interaction in a non-Western, traditional society. The society is Samoan, a Polynesian society, and the study is based on 13 months' intensive observation of children's language and socialization in a Western Samoan village. Our study audio- and videotaped twenty-three children under the age of 6 interacting with caregivers and peers.

Samoan traditional caregiving patterns differ significantly from what most Americans are exposed to. Infants and small children are cared for by a wider range of caregivers. A child's mother is the primary caregiver in the first year of life, but typically she is assisted by another, older child within the household. As young children learn to walk and talk, mothers assume fewer caregiving responsibilities and more responsibility is handed over to the older sibling of the child. This type of caregiving is characteristic of over one third of the world's societies, but it has rarely been described in depth and its consequences to the child's cognitive and linguistic competence has been minimally addressed (Weisner and Gallimore, 1977).

As the Samoan child grows somewhat older, around the age of 3, she or he spends most of the day with other children of roughly the same age. These children form age-graded peer groups (*aukegi*) with members drawn primarily from the local extended household.

We should notice right here a major difference between Western Samoan and middle-class American social environments. Americans tend to live in nuclear households (a mother, a father and their direct descendants). Typically there is only one caregiver and typically, in middle-class families, there are fewer than three children.

It is important to point out here that the observations of Anglo-American mother–child interaction from which we have drawn so many conclusions examine one mother interacting with one child. In structured observations by psychologists (e.g. in university observation rooms), the mother has only one personal focus, the child; and the child has only one personal focus, the mother. In naturalistic observations, it is typical for psychologists and linguists to document interactions between a mother and the *first* child. No siblings are present.

This setting contrasts dramatically with that typical of Western Samoan households, where several mothers may be together in a single compound along with nine or ten children in caregiving or cared-for roles. There caregivers must attend to a number of persons and a young child is most often not a central focus of attention.

A second major difference in caregiving concerns the kind of care that mothers are expected to give and the kind of care siblings are expected to provide. In traditional Samoan communities, age is a determinant of status. Older persons have more status than young persons, adults more than children. In the household, *mothers* are high status caregivers and siblings are low status caregivers.

One behaviour that distinguishes high and low status is action, motion, movement, involvement. High status persons ideally remain stationary. Lower status individuals are active and provide most of the physical work within the community. With respect to giving care to children, this means that high status caregivers, e.g. mothers and grandmothers, tend to move very little. It is the *sibling caregiver who provides the more active care*. They are primarily the ones to change wet diapers, dress and undress and clean a young child. They are also the ones to prepare and bring food to a young child.

What are the consequences of this social organization of caregiving to mother–child interactions? The result produces a very different type of verbal interaction pattern than that found in middle-class Anglo-American homes. In middle-class homes, we typically find mother and child engaged in a *dialogue*. If a child is distressed, she voices this distress to her mother, expecting a direct response. Under normal circumstances, the mother does respond directly to the child's communication. This produces a direct, two-party conversational sequence in which child talks to mother, mother talks to child, child talks to mother again, mother talks to child again, and so on (ABABAB . . .).

In the traditional Samoan household, these same expectations and norms do not exist. A child exhibiting some distress – wet diapers, hunger, thirst, etc. – may express this information to her mother. However, typically the mother does not then respond directly to the child. Rather, the mother will turn to an older sibling of the child who is responsible for active care and direct that sibling to respond to the child's distress. At that point the sibling responds verbally or nonverbally directly to the child. Instead of the American mother-child dialogue, we find typically the *child participating in three-party conversations*. Child speaks to mother, mother speaks to sibling, sibling speaks/responds to child (ABCA . . .).

Samoan children, then, have quite different expectations from American children concerning how mothers will respond to their needs. In the American case the mother's response is direct. In the Samoan case the mother's response is mediated through a sibling. In parallel fashion, Samoan children have quite different expectations concerning how and when mothers will talk to them. Samoan children usually do not expect a direct verbal response to a notification of their needs. Indeed under certain circumstances, such as when the mother is talking with another adult, the child learns to expect no response at all from the mother. Under these circumstances the older guest takes precedence over the child in occupying the mother's attention.

Thus far, the discussion has focused on differences in social organization of caregiving and has outlined its effect on child-adult communication. I turn now to another cultural dimension that affects the way in which young children and their caregivers converse with one another. This cultural dimension involves cultural beliefs about the nature of children. It is important to realize that when an American mother responds to her infant in a particular way, she is doing so not because of *innate biological* patterning but because she is acting on cultural assumptions about qualities and capacities of young children.

For example, middle-class American mothers see even very young infants as distinct individuals. These mothers often will look for personality traits in a young infant and interpret behaviours of the infant as expressive of the infant's basic character – easy-going, fussy, serious, pensive, extroverted, excitable, and so on. In this perspective, the child is seen as acting the way he does because of his particular personal nature.

But not only are these infants seen as having individual personalities, they are also seen as capable of acting in a purposeful and goal-directed manner. Middle-class Anglo-American mothers very often interpret infants' verbal and nonverbal behaviours as conscious, motivated, intentional, directed to some end. A hand gesture is interpreted as a reach, an offer, a display. A vocalization is interpreted as a summons to attend, a greeting, a noticing, a request for some object or a rejection and so on.

The child development literature is filled with detailed descriptions of such maternal interpretation of and response to pre-language child behaviours (Stern, 1974, 1977; Bates et al., 1979; Shotter, 1978; Trevarthen, 1979). Trevarthen, who has filmed dozens of British mothers interacting with infants, reports:

> As a rule, prespeech with gesture is watched and replied to by exclamations of pleasure or surprise like 'Oh, my my!', 'Good heavens!', 'Oh, what a big smile!', 'Ha! That's a big one!' (meaning a story), questioning replies like, 'Are you telling me a story?', 'Oh really?', or even agreement by nodding 'Yes' or saying 'I'm *sure* you're right' (1979, p. 340).

Trevarthen and his colleague Sylvester-Bradley see these maternal responses as expressive of their perception of infants. They conclude: 'A mother evidently perceives her baby to be a person like herself. Mothers interpret baby behaviour as not only intended to be communicative, but as verbal and meaningful' (1979, p. 340).

These perceptions of young humans are not, however, shared by mothers in all cultures. The maternal worldview described by Trevarthen and his colleague is not, for example, shared by most Western Samoan mothers living in traditional villages. Concepts of infancy differ radically in Samoan and Anglo-American communities. I have mentioned that American mothers often assign a particular personality to their infant. There is not even a word in the Samoan language for 'personality'. The idea that a given individual has a basic, consistent character is not part of the Samoan worldview (Shore, 1977). People are seen as constantly changing their demeanour, behaviour and mood in response to particular situations. People are said to have many sides (*itū*) and different sides emerge in different events (Shore, 1977). There is no core personality, however, that holds these sides together into a coherent individual.

Further, Samoans generally do not believe that an individual has a strong capacity to control and direct emotions and actions. Emotions and thoughts are often described as 'springing up suddenly' (Shore, 1977), outside the control of the individual. This type of springing up or impulse leads people to act in socially destructive ways — to fight or show disrespect, for example.

This belief contrasts sharply with that of Anglo-American culture.

Anglo-American culture places a strong emphasis on *intentionality*, the ability to act in a self-conscious, goal-directed manner. As a member of this culture, I believe that individuals have the capacity to act *intentionally* as well as *unintentionally*. This distinction and this belief is very important and underlies the way in which members of the culture interpret acts and events. For example, I assess an act in terms of whether an individual acted intentionally or unintentionally. If damage was caused, I excuse it if it were unintentional but not if it were intentional. Our legal code responds to this distinction as well; sanctions are based in part on the extent to which the individual consciously performed the act.

This concern with intentionality is not present to the same extent in traditional Western Samoan communities. In assessing an act of a person, it is not relevant whether or not the person did so intentionally or unintentionally. What counts is the social consequences and the act and its impact on the family and community. An act will be negatively sanctioned if it has damaged the social order, regardless of whether or not the actor did so knowingly, consciously.

This worldview has an effect on the way in which Samoan caregivers interact with their infants and young children. Whereas the Anglo-American mother looks for individual personality traits of her infants, traits that distinguish that child from others, the Samoan mother does not. Whereas the Anglo-American mother responds to her infant as if that young infant were capable of conscious, intentional communication, the traditional Western Samoan mother does not.

The traditional Samoan mother operates in the belief that young children, particularly infants, have no control over their behaviour. They are born with certain natural impulses and it is these impulses that control the child's action. In the first year of life there is very little attempt to constrain the behaviours of the child and very little social instruction is directed to the child. The child, as Margaret Mead discovered, is not considered socially responsive or responsible during this period. Caregivers, then, have little inclination to search for the intentions behind infant behaviours or to engage in the type of pre-language communication reported over and over in the literature on maternal input. In the second year of life, caregivers begin to instruct children in publicly acceptable conduct – how to sit, how to eat, how to interact with siblings and elders and how to speak. This process of socialization produces a communicative relationship in which caregivers introduce and control topics. The very young, language-learning child is neither expected nor encouraged to initiate topics of talk.

What is the import of these behaviours to therapists, clinicians and educators? American society is filled with children of diverse ethnic backgrounds. Many ethnic groups share the cultural patterns just described for Samoan households. These cultural patterns are maintained inside individual households within the United States. The child is socialized inside the household, according to traditional norms and child-rearing practices. But once the child reaches the age of 5 or 6, his days are spent outside the household, in formal classroom settings, where typically someone from outside his culture is the socializing agent. These children find themselves face-to-face with educators who do not share the same expectations as to how children and adults communicate with one another. These children may experience considerable distress in classroom settings or other settings in which they are expected to engage in a direct dialogue with an adult authority figure.

The educator without any background concerning the child's cultural values and norms may see the child's problem as a problem concerning knowledge of *English*. The child's problem is diagnosed as a *language proficiency* problem. The child might then be assigned to a professional who will work on facilitating the child's linguistic competence. Many minority children do have language learning problems. However, in the case at hand, the educator does not grasp the full nature of the minority child's problem. His problem is one of *cultural* interference rather than linguistic interference, a conflict in cultural norms for using language (Hymes, 1974) rather than a conflict in grammatical structure between first and second language.

The transition from monolingualism to bilingualism has been facilitated over the past several years by the availability of numerous language materials that outline points of contrast between a child's first language and English. The number and variety of materials that exist on cultural differences in conversational procedures and conventions is dramatically low. Basic observations have hardly been carried out and those that have been are by and large not communicated to educators and others who interact with ethnically diverse children on a day-to-day basis. Thus the ability of these children to make the transition from monoculturalism to biculturalism is severely hampered.

Note

1. This research is supported by the National Science Foundation, Grant no. 53–482–2480. Principal investigator: Elinor Ochs.

Bibliography

Abrahams, R. (1964), *Deep Down in the Jungle*, Hatboro, PA., Folklore Associates.

Albert, E. (1972), 'Cultural patterning of speech behavior in Burundi', in J. Gumperz and D. Hymes (eds), *Directions in Sociolinguistics*, New York, Holt, Rinehart, & Winston.

Antinucci, F. and Miller, R. (1976), 'How children talk about what happened', *Journal of Child Language*, 3, pp. 167–89.

Argyle, M. and Cook, M. (1976), *Gaze and Mutual Gaze*, Cambridge University Press.

Atkinson, M. (1979), 'Prerequisites for reference', in E. Ochs and B. B. Schieffelin (eds), *Developmental Pragmatics*, New York, Academic Press.

Austin, J. L. (1962), *How to do Things with Words*, Oxford University Press.

Bates, E. (1976), *Language and Context: The Acquisition of Pragmatics*, New York, Academic Press.

Bates, E., Camaioni, L. and Volterra, V. (1979), 'The acquisition of performatives prior to speech', in E. Ochs and B. B. Schieffelin (eds), *Developmental Pragmatics*, New York, Academic Press.

Bateson, G. (1958), *Naven*, 2nd edition, Stanford University Press.

Bennett, T. (1977), 'Verb voice in unplanned and planned narratives', in E. Ochs Keenan and T. Bennett (eds), *Discourse across Time and Space*, Los Angeles, Calif., SCOPIL 5, University of Southern California.

Berger, P. and Luckmann, T. (1966), *Social Construction of Reality*, New York, Doubleday.

Bever, T. (1970), 'The cognitive basis for linguistic structures', in J. R. Hayes (ed.), *Cognition and the Development of Language*, New York, John Wiley.

Bloom, L. (1970), *Language Development: Form and Function in Emerging Grammars*, Cambridge, Mass., MIT Research Monograph 59.

Bloom, L. (1973), *One Word at a Time: The Use of Single Word Utterances before Syntax*, The Hague, Mouton.

Bloom, L. and Lahey, M. (1978), *Language Development and Language Disorders*, New York, John Wiley.

Bloom, L., Hood, L. and Lightbown, P. (1974), 'Imitation in language development: If, when and why', *Cognitive Psychology*, 6, pp. 380–420.

Bloom, L., Lightbown, P. and Hood, L. (1975), *Structure and Variation in Child Language*, Monograph of the Society for Research in Child Development, 40 (2, serial no. 160).

Bowerman, M. (1973), *Early Syntactic Development: A Cross-Linguistic Study with Special Reference to Finnish*, Cambridge University Press.

Braine, M. (1965), 'Three suggestions regarding grammatical analyses of children's language', paper presented at the Tenth Annual Conference on Linguistics of the Linguistic Circle of New York.

Braunwald, S. (1979), 'Forms of children's speech, private, social and egocentric', in K. Nelson (ed.), *Children's Language*, vol. II, New York, Halstead Press.

Brown, R. (1973), *A First Language*, Cambridge, Mass., Harvard University Press.

Brown, R. and Bellugi, U. (1964), 'Three processes in the child's acquisition of syntax', *Harvard Educational Review*, 34, pp. 133–51.

Brown, R., Cazden, C. and Bellugi, U. (1969), 'The child's grammar from I to III', in J. P. Hill (ed.), *Minnesota Symposia on Child Psychology*, vol. 2, Minneapolis, University of Minnesota Press. (Reprinted 'The child's grammar from I to III', in C. Ferguson and D. Slobin (eds) (1973), *Studies of Language Development*, New York, Holt, Rinehart & Winston.)

Bruner, J. (1975), 'The ontogenesis of speech acts', *Journal of Child Language*, 2, pp. 1–19.

Bruner, J. (1980), 'Afterword', in D. Olson (ed.), *The social foundations of language and thought*, New York, W. W. Norton.

Byers, P. and Byers, H. (1972), 'Nonverbal communication and education of children', in C. Cazden, V. John, and D. Hymes (eds), *Functions of Language in the Classroom*, New York, Teachers' College Press.

Carroll, J. B. (ed.) (1956), *Language, Thought, and Reality: Selected Writings of Benjamin Lee Whorf*, Cambridge, Mass., MIT Press.

Carter, A. L. (1975), 'The transformation of sensory motor morphemes into words', paper presented at the Stanford Child Language Research Forum, Stanford University.

Cazden, C. (1965), *Environmental Assistance to the Child's Acquisition of Grammar*, Ph.D. thesis, Harvard University.

Cazden, C. (1972), *Child Language and Education*, New York, Holt, Rinehart & Winston.

Chafe, W. (1972), 'Discourse structure and human knowledge', in R. O. Freedle and J. B. Carroll (eds), *Language Comprehension and the Acquisition of Knowledge*, Washington, D.C., Winston.

Chafe, W. (1976), 'Givenness, contrastiveness, definiteness, subjects, topics and point of view', in C. Li (ed.), *Subject and Topic*, New York, Academic Press.

Chao, Y. R. (1951), 'The Cantian idiolect', *Semitic and Oriental Studies*, II, pp. 27–44.

Chomsky, N. (1965), *Aspects of the Theory of Syntax*, Cambridge, Mass., MIT Press.

Chomsky, N. (1966), *Cartesian Linguistics*, New York, Harper & Row.

Chomsky, N. (1975), *Reflections on Language*, New York, Pantheon.

Clark, E. (1971), 'On the acquisition of "before" and "after"', *Journal of Verbal Learning and Verbal Behavior*, 10, pp. 266–75.

Clark, H. and Haviland, S. E. (1977), 'Comprehension and the given-new contract', in R. O. Freedle (ed.), *Discourse Production and Comprehension*, Norwood, N.J., Ablex.

Coates, B., Anderson, E. P. and Hartup, W. W. (1972), 'Interrelations in the attachment behavior of human infants', *Developmental Psychology*, 6, pp. 218–30.

Cook-Gumperz, J. and Gumperz, J. J. (1978), 'Context in children's speech', in N. Waterson and C. Snow (eds), *The Development of Communication*, New York, John Wiley.

Corsaro, W. (1979), 'Sociolinguistic patterns in adult–child interaction', in E. Ochs and B. B. Schieffelin (eds), *Developmental Pragmatics*, New York, Academic Press.

Cross, T. (1975), 'Some relationships between motherese and linguistic level in accelerated children', *Papers and Reports on Child Language Development*, no. 10, Stanford, Calif., Stanford University Press.

Cross, T. (1977), 'Mothers' speech adjustments: the contribution of selected child listener variables', in C. Snow and C. Ferguson (eds), *Talking to Children*, Cambridge University Press.

Duranti, A. and Keenan, E. Ochs (1976), 'The organization of reference in Italian discourse', paper presented at the Winter Meeting of the Linguistics Society of America.

Duranti, A. and Ochs, E. (1979), 'Left-dislocation in Italian conversation', in T. Givon (ed.), *Syntax and Semantics*, vol. 12, *Discourse and Syntax*, New York, Academic Press.

Durkheim, E. (1938), *The Rules of Sociological Method*, New York, Free Press.

Ellsworth, P. C. and Ludwig, L. M. (1972), 'Visual behavior in social interaction', *Journal of Communication*, 22 (4), pp. 375–403.

Ervin, S. M. (1964), 'Imitation and structural change in children's language', in E. H. Lenneberg (ed.), *New Directions in the Study of Language*, Cambridge, Mass., MIT Press.

Ervin-Tripp, S. (1973), *Language Acquisition and Communicative Choice*, Stanford, Stanford University Press.

Ervin-Tripp, S. (1976), 'Is Sybil there? The structure of some American English directives', *Language in Society*, 5, pp. 25–66.

Escalona, S. (1973), 'Basic modes of social interaction: their emergence and patterning during the first two years of life', *Merrill-Palmer Quarterly*, July.

Exline, R. (1963), 'Exploration in the process of person perception: visual interaction in relation to competition, sex, and need for affiliation', *Journal of Personality*, 31, pp. 1–20.

Exline, R. V. and Winters, L. C. (1966), 'Affective relations and mutual glances in dyads', in S. S. Tomkins and C. Izard (eds), *Affect*, *cognition and personality*, London, Tavistock.

Feld, S. (1982), *Sound and Sentiment: Birds, Weeping, Poetics, and Song in Kaluli Expression*, Philadelphia, University of Pennsylvania Press.

Ferguson, C. (1977), 'Baby talk as a simplified register', in C. Snow and C. Ferguson (eds), *Talking to Children*, Cambridge University Press.

Fillmore, C. (1971), *Lectures on Deixis*, given at University of California at Santa Cruz.

Fillmore, C. (1975), 'Pragmatics and the description of discourse', *Berkeley Studies in Syntax and Semantics*, 1, pp. 1–25.

Foley, W. (1976), Ph.D. thesis, University of California, Berkeley.

Freedle, R. O., Keeney, T. J. and Smith, N. D. (1970), 'Effects of mean depth and grammaticality on children's imitation of sentences', *Journal of Verbal Learning and Verbal Behavior*, 9, pp. 149–54.

Friedman, L. (1976), 'The manifestation of subject, object, topic in American Sign Language', in C. Li (ed.), *Subject and Topic*, New York, Academic Press.

Fromkin, V. (1973), *Speech Errors as Linguistic Evidence*, The Hague, Mouton.

Garfinkel, H. (1967), *Studies in Ethno-Methodology*, Englewood Cliffs, N.J., Prentice-Hall.

Garvey, C. (1974), 'Interactional structures in social play', paper presented at Annual Convention of the American Psychological Association.

Garvey, C. (1977a), 'The Contingent query', in M. Lewis and L. A. Rosenblum (eds), *Interaction, Conversation and the Development of Language*, New York, John Wiley.

Garvey, K. (1977b), 'Play with language and speech', in S. Ervin-Tripp and C. Mitchell-Kernan (eds), *Child Discourse*, New York, Academic Press.

Givon, T. (1975a), 'Toward a discourse definition of syntax', MS.

Givon, T. (1975b), 'Universal grammar, lexical structure and trans-latability', in M. Guenthner-Reutter and F. Guenthner (eds), *Anthology on the Theory of Translation*, Cambridge University Press.

Givon, T. (1975c), 'Negation in language: pragmatics, function, onto-logy', MS., UCLA Colloquium, January.

Goffman, E. (1963), *Behavior in Public Places*, New York, Free Press.

Goffman, E. (1964), 'The neglected situation', *American Anthropologist*, (special publication) 66(6), Part 2, pp. 133–6.

Goffman, E. (1971), *Relations in Public*, New York, Basic Books.

Goodwin, C. (1975), 'The interactional construction of a turn', paper presented at the American Anthropological Association Annual Meeting, San Francisco, California.

Goody, J. (ed.) (1958), *The Developmental Cycle in Domestic Groups*, Cambridge Papers in Social Anthropology, No. 1, Cambridge University Press.

Gough, E. W. (1975), 'Comparative studies in second language learning', Ph.D. thesis, University of California, Los Angeles.

Greenberg, J. (1966), 'Some universals of grammar with particular reference to the order of meaningful elements, in J. Greenberg (ed.), *Universals of Language*, Cambridge, Mass., MIT Press.

Greenfield, P. M. and Smith, J. H. (1976), *The Structure of Communication in Early Language Development*, New York, Academic Press.

Grice, H. P. (1969), 'Utterer's meaning and intentions', *The Philosophical Review*, April.

Grice, H. P. (1971), 'Utterer's meaning, sentence-meaning, and word-meaning', in J. R. Searle (ed.), *The Philosophy of Language*, Oxford University Press, pp. 54–71.

Grice, H. P. (1975), 'Logic and conversation', in P. Cole and J. L. Morgan (eds), *Syntax and Semantics*, vol. 3, *Speech Acts*, New York, Academic Press.

Griffiths, P. (1974), 'That, there, deixis I: that', MS., University of Newcastle upon Tyne.

Gruber, J. (1967), 'Topicalization in child language', *Foundations of Language*, 3(1), pp. 37–65.

Gumperz, J. J. (1977), 'Sociocultural knowledge in conversational inference', in M. Saville-Troike (ed.), *Linguistics and Anthropology*, Georgetown University Round Table on Languages and Linguistics, Washington D.C., Georgetown University Press.

Gundel, J. (1975), 'Left dislocation and the role of topic–comment structure in linguistic theory', *Ohio State Working Papers in Linguistics*, 18, pp. 72–132.

Halliday, M. A. K. (1973), *Explorations in the Functions of Language*, London, Arnold.

Halliday, M. A. K. (1975), 'Learning how to mean', in E. Lenneberg and E. Lenneberg (eds), *Foundations of Language Development: a Multi-Disciplinary Approach*, Unesco/Ibro.

Haviland, S. E. and Clark, H. H. (1974), 'What's new? Acquiring new information as a process in comprehension', *Journal of Verbal Learning and Verbal Behavior*, 13, pp. 512–21.

Hawkinson, A. and Hyman, L. (1974), 'Hierarchies of natural topic in Shona', *Studies in African Linguistics*, 5(2), pp. 147–70.

Hoenigswald, H. (1960), *Language Change and Linguistic Reconstruction*, University of Chicago Press.

Holzman, M. (1972), 'The use of interrogative forms in the verbal interaction of three mothers and their children', *Journal of Psycholinguistic Research*, 1, pp. 311–36.

Holzman, M. (1974), 'The verbal environment provided by mothers for their very young children', *Merrill-Palmer Quarterly*, 20(1), pp. 31–42.

Hutt, C. and Ounsted, C. (1966), 'Biological significance of gaze aversion with particular reference to the syndrome of infantile autism', *Behavioral Science*, 11, pp. 346–56.

Huttenlocher, J. (1974), 'Origins of language comprehension', in R. L. Solso (ed.), *Theories in Cognitive Psychology*, Hillsdale, N.J., Lawrence Erlbaum.

Hyman, L. (1975), 'On the change from SOV to SVO: Evidence from

Niger-Congo', in C. Li (ed.), *Word Order and Word Order Change*, Austin, University of Texas Press.

Hymes, D. (1962), 'The ethnography of speaking', in T. Gladwin and W. C. Sturtevant (eds), *Anthropology and Human Behavior*, Washington, D.C., Anthropology Society of Washington.

Hymes, D. (1967), 'Models of the interaction of language and social setting', *Journal of Social Issues*, 23(2), pp. 8–28.

Hymes, D. (1970), 'Linguistic method in ethnography: Its development in the United States', in P. L. Garvin (ed.), *Method and Theory in Linguistics*, The Hague, Mouton, pp. 249–325.

Hymes, D. (1972a), 'Models of the interaction of language and social life', in J. Gumperz and D. Hymes (eds), *Directions in Sociolinguistics*, New York, Holt, Rinehart & Winston.

Hymes, D. (1972b), 'On communicative competence', in J. B. Pride and J. Holmes (eds), *Sociolinguistics*, Harmondsworth, Penguin.

Hymes, D. (1974), *Foundations in Sociolinguistics: an Ethnographic Approach*, Philadelphia, University of Pennsylvania Press.

Jakobson, R. (1960), 'Linguistics and poetics', in T. A. Sebeok (ed.), *Style in Language*, Cambridge, Mass., MIT Press.

Jakobson, R. (1968), *Child Language, Aphasia and Phonological Universals*, The Hague, Mouton.

Jefferson, G. (no date), *Transcription of Five Group Therapy Sessions*.

Jefferson, G. (1974), 'Error correction as an interactional resource', *Language in Society*, 3(2), pp. 181–99.

Jefferson, G. (1978), 'Sequential aspects of story-telling in conversation', in J. Schenkein (ed.), *Studies in the Organization of Conversational Interaction*, New York, Academic Press.

Jefferson, G., Sacks, H. and Schegloff, E. (1976), 'Some notes on laughing together', *Pragmatics Microfiche* 1.8:A2, Dept. of Linguistics, University of Cambridge.

Jefferson, G. and Schenkein, J. N. (1977), 'Some sequential negotiations in conversation: unexpanded and expanded versions of projected action sequences', *Sociology*, 11(1), pp. 87–103.

Jespersen, O. (1922), *Language, its Nature, Development and Origin*, London, Allen & Unwin.

Kay, P. (1970), 'Some theoretical implications of ethnographic semantics', in *Current Directions in Anthropology, Bulletin of the American Anthropological Association*, 3:3 (Part 2), pp. 19–35.

Keenan, E. L. (1976), 'Towards a universal definition of "subject"', in C. Li (ed.), *Subject and Topic*, New York, Academic Press.

Keenan, E. L. and Hull, R. D. (1973), 'The logical presuppositions of questions and answers', in Franck and Petofi (eds), *Präsuppositionen in der Linguistik und der Philosophie*, Athenäum.

Keenan, E. Ochs (1974a), *Conversation and Oratory in Vakinankaratra Madagascar*, Ph.D. dissertation, University of Pennsylvania, Philadelphia.

Keenan, E. Ochs (1974b), 'Again and again: the pragmatics of imitation in child language', paper presented at the Annual Meeting of the American Anthropological Association, Mexico City.

Keenan, E. Ochs (1974c), 'Norm-makers, norm-breakers: uses of speech
    by men and women in a Malagasy community', in R. Bauman and J.
    Sherzer (eds), *Explorations in the Ethnography of Speaking*,
    Cambridge University Press.
Keenan, E. Ochs and Klein, E. (1975), 'Coherency in children's
    discourse', *Journal of Psycholinguistic Research*, 4, pp. 365–80.
Keenan, E. Ochs and Schieffelin, B. B. (1975), 'Discontinuous discourse',
    paper presented at the Annual meeting of the American Anthro-
    pological Association, San Francisco.
Keenan, E. Ochs, Schieffelin, B. B. and Platt, M. (1979), 'Propositions
    across utterances and speakers', in E. Ochs and B. B. Schieffelin
    (eds), *Developmental Pragmatics*, New York, Academic Press.
Kendon, A. (1967), 'Some functions of gaze-direction in social inter-
    action', *Acta Psychologica* 26, pp. 22–63.
Kendon, A. and Cook, M. (1969), 'The consistency of gaze patterns in
    social interaction', *British Journal of Psychology*, 69, pp. 481–94.
Kingdon, R. (1958), *The Groundwork of English Intonation*, London,
    Longman.
Kluckhohn, C. (1954), 'Culture and behavior', in G. Lindzey (ed.),
    Handbook of Social Psychology, pp. 19–35.
Kohlberg, L., Yaeger, J. and Hjertholm, E. (1968), 'Private speech:
    four studies and a review of theories', *Child Development*, 39,
    pp. 691–736.
Krashen, S. (1976), 'Linguistic puberty', paper presented at NAFSA
    Conference, San Diego, California, May 7.
Krashen, S. (1977), 'The monitor model for adult second language
    performance', in M. Burt, H. Dulay and M. Finocchiaro (eds),
    Viewpoints on English as a Second Language, New York, Regents.
Kroll, B. (1977), 'Ways communicators encode propositions in spoken
    and written English: A look at subordination and co-ordination',
    in E. Ochs Keenan and T. Bennett (eds), *Discourse Across Time
    and Space*, Los Angeles, California, SCOPIL 5, University of Southern
    California.
Kuno, S. (1972), 'Functional sentence perspective', *Linguistic Inquiry*,
    3(3), pp. 269–320.
Labov, W. (1966), *The Social Stratification of English in New York
    City*, Washington, D.C., Center for Applied Linguistics.
Lewis, D. (1969), *Convention*, Cambridge, Mass., Harvard University
    Press.
Lewis, M. and Lee-Painter, S. (1974), 'An interactional approach to
    the mother–infant dyad', in M. Lewis and L. A. Rosenblum (eds),
    The Effect of the Infant on its Caregiver, New York, John Wiley.
Li, C. (ed.) (1976), *Subject and Topic*, New York, Academic Press.
Li, C. and Thompson, S. (1976), 'Subject and topic: a new typology of
    language', in C. Li (ed.), *Subject and Topic*, New York, Academic
    Press.
Limber, J. (1973), 'The genesis of complex sentences', in J. Moore
    (ed.), *Cognitive Development and the Acquisition of Language*,
    New York, Academic Press.

Lyons, J. (1968), *Introduction to Theoretical Linguistics*, Cambridge University Press.

Maccoby, E. E. and Feldman, S. S. (1972), 'Mother-attachment and stranger reactions in the third year of life', *Monograph of the Society for Research in Child Development*, 37(1), serial no. 146.

MacWhinney, B. (1977), 'Starting points', *Language*, 53, pp. 152–68.

Maratsos, M. (1974), 'Preschool children's use of definite and indefinite articles', *Child Development*, 45, pp. 446–55.

Menyuk, P. (1963), 'A preliminary evaluation of grammatical capacity in children', *Journal of Verbal Learning and Verbal Behavior*, 2, pp. 429–39.

Newport, E. (1976), 'Motherese: the speech of mothers to young children', in N. Castellan, D. Pisoni and G. Potts (eds), *Cognitive Theory*, Vol. II, Hillsdale, N.J., Lawrence Erlbaum.

Nielsen, G. (1962), *Studies in Self-Confrontation*, Copenhagen, Munksgaard.

Ochs, E. and Schieffelin, B. B. (in press), 'Language acquisition and socialization: three developmental stories and their implications', in R. Shweder and R. LeVine (eds), *Culture and its acquisition*, Chicago, University of Chicago Press.

Payne, J. (1973), 'Sentence conjunction and subordination in Russian', in *You Take the High Node and I'll Take the Low One*, Chicago Linguistic Society, pp. 305–25.

Philips, S. U. (in press), *The Invisible Culture*, New York, Longman.

Piaget, J. (1926/1955), *(The) Language and Thought of the Child*, New York, Harcourt Brace.

Piaget, J. (1951), *Play, Dreams and Imitation in Childhood*, New York, Norton.

Radcliffe-Brown, A. R. (1952), *Structure and Function in Primitive Society*, London, Cohen and West.

Redfield, R. (1953), *The Primitive World and Its Transformation*, Ithaca, Cornell University Press.

Richards, M. P. M. (1971), 'Social interaction in the first weeks of human life', *Psychiat. Neurol. Neurochir.*, 14, pp. 35–42.

Robins, R. H. (1959), 'Linguistics and anthropology', *Man*, pp. 175–9.

Robson, K. (1967), 'The role of eye-to-eye contact in maternal–infant attachment', *Journal of Child Psychology and Psychiatry*, 8, pp. 13–25.

Rodd, L. J. and Braine, M. D. S. (1971), 'Children's imitations of syntactic constructions as a measure of linguistic competence', *Journal of Verbal Learning and Verbal Behavior*, 10, pp. 430–43.

Ross, A. I. F. (1968), *Directives and Norms*, London, Routledge & Kegan Paul.

Ross, J. (1967), *Constraints on Variables in Syntax*, Ph.D. Dissertation, MIT, Cambridge, Mass.

Ryan, J. (1972), 'Interpretation and imitation in early language development', paper for Conference on Constraints on Learning, Cambridge, April.

Ryan, J. (1974), 'Early language development: towards a communicational analysis', in M. P. M. Richards (ed.), *The Integration of a*

Child into a Social World, Cambridge University Press.

Sabsay, S. (1976), 'Communicative competence among the severely retarded: some evidence from the conversational interaction of Down's Syndrome (Mongoloid) adults', paper presented at the Linguistic Society of America, winter.

Sacks, H. (1968) (unpublished), Lecture notes, Sociology Department, University of California, Irvine.

Sacks, H. and Schegloff, E. (1974), 'Two preferences in the organization of reference to persons in conversation and their interaction', in N. H. Avison and R. J. Wilson (eds), *Ethnomethodology: Labelling Theory and Deviant Behavior*, London, Routledge & Kegan Paul.

Sacks, H., Schegloff, E. and Jefferson, G. (1974), 'A simplest systematics for the organization of turn-taking for conversation', *Language*, 50, pp. 696–735.

Sankoff, G. and Brown, P. (1976), 'On the origins of syntax in discourse', *Language*, 52, pp. 631–66.

Sankoff, G. and Kay, P. (1974), 'A language-universal approach to pidgins and creoles', in D. DeCamp and I. Hancock (eds), *Pidgins and Creoles*, Washington, D.C., Georgetown University Press.

Sapir, E. (1927), 'Speech as a personality trait', *American Journal of Sociology*, 32, pp. 893–905.

Sapir, E. (1932), 'Cultural anthropology and psychiatry', *Journal of Abnormal and Social Psychology*, 27, pp. 229–42 (SWES 509–21).

Scaife, M. and Bruner, J. S. (1975), 'The capacity for joint visual attention in the infant', *Nature*, 253 (5489), pp. 265–6.

Schachter, J. (1974), 'An error in error analysis', *Language Learning*, 24, pp. 205–15.

Schaffer, H. R., Collis, G. M. and Parson, G. (1977), 'Vocal interchange and visual regard in verbal and preverbal children', in H. R. Schaffer (ed.), *Studies of Mother–Infant Interaction*, London, Academic Press.

Schegloff, E. (1968), 'Sequencing in conversational openings', *American Anthropologist*, 70(4), pp. 1075–95.

Schegloff, E. (1972), 'Notes on conversational practice: formulating place', in D. Sudnow (ed.), *Studies in Interaction*, New York, Free Press.

Schegloff, E. (1973), 'Recycled turn beginning: a precise repair mechanism in conversation's turn-taking organization', unpublished manuscript.

Schegloff, E. (1975), lecture notes, unpublished.

Schegloff, E. and Sacks, H. (1973), 'Opening up closings', *Semiotica*, 8, pp. 289–327.

Schegloff, E., Jefferson, G. and Sacks, H. (1977), 'The preference for self-correction in the organization of repair in conversation', *Language*, 53, pp. 361–83.

Schieffelin, B. B. (1975), 'Communicative functions of pointing: a developmental study', unpublished.

Schieffelin, B. B. (1979), 'Getting it together: an ethnographic approach to the study of the development of communicative competence', in

E. Ochs and B. B. Schieffelin (eds), *Developmental Pragmatics*, New York, Academic Press.

Schieffelin, B. B. (in press), *How Kaluli Children Learn What to Say, What to Do and How to Feel*, Cambridge University Press.

Schieffelin, E. L. (1976), *The Sorrow of the Lonely and the Burning of the Dancers*, New York, St Martin's Press.

Scollon, R. (1976), *Conversations With a One Year Old*, University of Hawaii Press.

Scollon, R. (1979), 'A real early stage: an unzippered condensation of a dissertation on child language', in E. Ochs and B. B. Schieffelin (eds), *Developmental Pragmatics*, New York, Academic Press.

Searle, J. R. (1969), *Speech Acts*, Cambridge University Press.

Shatz, M. and Gelman, R. (1973), 'The development of communication skills: modifications in the speech of young children as a function of the listener', *Monographs of the Society for Research in Child Development*, 38(5), serial no. 152.

Shimanoff, S. and Brunak, J. (1977), 'Repairs in planned and unplanned discourse', in E. Ochs Keenan and T. Bennett (eds), *Discourse Across Time and Space*, Los Angeles, California, SCOPIL 5, University of Southern California.

Shore, B. (1977), *A Samoan Theory of Action: Social Control and Social Order in a Polynesian Paradox*, Ph.D. thesis, University of Chicago.

Shotter, J. (1978), 'The cultural context of communication studies: theoretical and methodological issues', in A. Lock (ed.), *Action, Gesture and Symbol: The Emergence of Language*, London, Academic Press.

Silverstein, M. (1976), 'Shifters, linguistic categories and cultural description', in K. Basso and H. Selby (eds), *Meaning in Anthropology*, Albuquerque, University of New Mexico Press.

Slobin, D. (1968), 'Imitation and grammatical development in children', in N. S. Endler et al. (eds), *Contemporary Issues in Developmental Psychology*, New York, Holt, Rinehart & Winston.

Slobin, D. (1973a), 'Cognitive prerequisites for the acquisition of grammar', in C. A. Ferguson and D. Slobin (eds.), *Studies of Child Language Development*, New York, Holt, Rinehart, & Winston.

Slobin, D. (1973b), *The Ontogenesis of Grammar*, Working Paper no. 33, Berkeley, University of California, Language Behavior Research Laboratory.

Snow, C. (1972), 'Mothers' speech to children learning language', *Child Development*, 43, pp. 549–65.

Snow, C. (1977), 'The development of conversation between mothers and babies', *Journal of Child Language*, 4, pp. 1–22.

Snow, C. (1979), 'Conversations with children', in P. Fletcher and M. Garman (eds), *Language Acquisition*, Cambridge University Press.

Spier, L., Hallowell, A. and Newman, S. (eds) (1941), *Language, Culture and Personality: Essays in Memory of Edward Sapir*, Menasha, Wisc., Banta.

Stern, D. (1971), 'A micro-analysis of mother–infant interaction',

Journal of the American Academy of Child Psychiatry, 10, pp. 501–17.

Stern, D. (1974), 'Mother and infant at play: the dyadic interaction involving facial, vocal and gaze behaviors', in M. Lewis and L. Rosenblum (eds), *The Effect of the Infant on its Caregiver*, New York, John Wiley.

Stern, D. (1977), *The First Relationship: Infant and Mother*, London, Fontana/Open Books.

Stern, D., Jaffee, J., Beebe, B. and Bennett, S. L. (1975), 'Vocalizing in unison and in alternation: the modes of communication within the mother–infant dyad', *Annals of the New York Academy of Sciences: Developmental Psycholinguistics and Communicative Disorders*, 263, pp. 89–100.

Strawson, P. F. (1971), 'Intention and convention in speech acts', in J. Searle (ed.), *The Philosophy of Language*, Oxford University Press, pp. 23–39.

Tannen, D. (1979), 'What's in a frame? Surface evidence for underlying expectations', in R. O. Freedle (ed.), *Advances in Discourse Processes*, vol. 2, Norwood, N.J., Ablex.

Trevarthen, C. (1979), 'Communication and co-operation in early infancy: a description of primary intersubjectivity', in M. Bullowa (ed.), *Before Speech*, Cambridge University Press, pp. 321–49.

Vennemann, T. (1975), 'Topics, sentence accent, ellipsis: a proposal for their formal treatment', in Edward L. Keenan (ed.), *Formal Semantics in Natural Language*, Cambridge University Press.

Vine, I. (1971), 'Judgement of direction of gaze: an interpretation of discrepant results', *British Journal of Social and Clinical Psychology*, 10, pp. 320–31.

Walcutt, J. (1977), 'The topology of narrative boundedness', in E. Ochs Keenan and T. Bennett (eds), *Discourse Across Time and Space*, Los Angeles, California, SCOPIL 5, University of Southern California.

Wallace, A. (1970), *Culture and Personality*, 2nd ed., New York, Random House.

Weiner, M., Devoe, S., Rubinow, S. and Geller, J. (1972), 'Nonverbal behavior and nonverbal communication', *Psychological Review*, 79, pp. 185–214.

Weir, R. (1962), *Language in the Crib*, The Hague, Mouton.

Weisner, T. S. and Gallimore, R. (1977), 'My brother's keeper: child and sibling caregiving', *Current Anthropology*, 18(2), pp. 169–90.

Author Index

Subject Index

ACQUIRING CONVERSATIONAL COMPETENCE

To communicate effectively, young children must know how to participate in conversation with others. Both grammatical structure and the social norms of conversation must be mastered if communication is to take place. This book, by two American researchers of international renown, examines how children and adults use language to perform a variety of informational, social and poetic functions — to introduce, sustain and elaborate topics, to provide relevant responses and to play (with sounds). The emphasis is on informal speech situations. Hypotheses are formulated to explain the dynamics of language variation and the acquisition of communicative competence through participation in conversational exchanges.

The authors show how the development of conversational skills enables the child to enter society. They describe the role of mothers and other care-givers in middle-class English-speaking households. They show how these care-givers support their children's efforts to communicate by helping them to express ideas, by guessing at their intended meaning and by filling in missing elements of their utterances. This does not happen universally, however, and revealing cross-cultural comparisons are provided.

Clear and readable in its presentation, the book will be of value and interest to teachers, other educators and speech therapists, who are professionally concerned with children's language, as well as to researchers in linguistics, psychology, sociology and anthropology.